THE TWO-CAREER COUPLE

FRANCINE S. HALL
DOUGLAS T. HALL

F

ADDISON-WESLEY
PUBLISHING COMPANY
Reading, Massachusetts
Menlo Park, California
London · Amsterdam
Don Mills, Ontario
Sydney

75118

F

Library of Congress Cataloging in Publication Data

Hall, Francine S
    The two-career couple.

    Bibliography: p.
    Includes index.
    1. Family--United States. 2. Married people--Em-
ployment--United States. I. Hall, Douglas T., 1940-
joint author. II. Title.
HQ536.H3   301.42'7   79-50799
ISBN 0-201-02733-X
ISBN 0-201-02734-8 pbk.

ISBN-0-201-02733-X
ISBN-0-201-02734-8
ABCDEFGHIJ-DL-79

For Elizabeth and Chip

PREFACE

This book is about what many people regard as the two most important things in their lives: loving and working. Can people have both? We lived with that issue in our own lives, talked to other couples, and observed our society change. Soon, it became apparent that there was a real need for a book about how couples can work and love and grow together, how they can combine career and family (or a serious love relationship).

The 1970s was a decade of narcissism. In contrast to the 1960s, a period of social concern, the 1970s focused on the individual. All around us people were gobbling up books on personal development, career success, power, assertiveness, and sexual performance. More women moved into the mainstream of the work world, even while ministers preached against "me-ism" and careerism. Accompanying this great emphasis on the individual was a doubling of the divorce rate over a ten-year period.

During these years many people attained the career success, power, assertiveness, and/or sexual mastery they sought. Now, however, they are finding that these achievements are not always enough to provide happiness. They are rediscovering that they are *social* beings.

People need love. We need commitments to other people to provide meaning in our lives. We are finding, as N.Y.U. Professor Abe Korman's research shows, that preoccupation with career success can lead to personal and family failure. We are finally realizing that our task is to attain both career success and family success.

Will couples survive? Survival, we know, involves more than managing two separate careers. To survive, couples need commitment. They need to move from an emphasis on "me" to a shared concern for "we," and they must learn to compromise in the process.

In writing this book, we have relied on personal experience, interviews with couples, and literature in the field. Invariably, our biases show through. Although our own careers have been very flexible (or *protean*, a term we will discuss in depth), our family life has been extremely traditional: we've been married for fourteen years, have two children, went through Scouts, Little League, seven houses in various moves, numerous dogs, cats, and gerbils, and never considered commuting or living in separate residences to increase career options. Although couples with nontraditional living arrangements (such as long-distance commuting) may be what the Sunday supplements and popular magazines always write about, our research suggests that the majority of two-career couples have fairly traditional life-styles, such as ours.

It is essential, however, that the effective two-career couple have some flexible or protean elements somewhere in their lives, either in their careers or in their relationship. Part of being flexible involves learning how to make trade-offs, how to compromise. And making trade-offs requires that you know your priorities in life. Until you can say with confidence and without conflict that A and B are what really count to both of you, and C and D are less important, you will be doomed to the impossible quest for A, B, C, and D. And in aspiring for all of these things, there is a good chance you will achieve none of them.

In our book we examine the two-career couple from three different perspectives. Part I considers the general issues or problems of dual careerism: the nature of the two-career couple, career and family stages, coping with multiple roles, and stress. Part II gets down to the nitty-gritty dual-career tasks: home management, children, sex and interpersonal relationships, work involvement, and job mobility. Part III looks to future trends and proposes alternatives for both couples and companies. Throughout the book we have attempted to assist couples in several ways—by clarifying the issues in a dual-career relationship through self-analysis, and by specific recommendations on methods of managing this relationship.

Our interest in studying and writing about two-career couples is both personal and professional. Over the years people would say to us, "How do you do it?" then add, "Your act seems so together." Our response was usually to say that the act is never completely together. The key is to have a plan for working on it. There is no doubt that two careers put stress on a relationship. As with physical exercise, however, this stress can lead to either strain or strength, depending upon the quality of the relationship and the way the couple responds. We hope this book will introduce new concepts and methods for converting these stresses into greater self-direction and mutual fulfillment.

F. S. H.
D. T. H.

IN THANKS

Many people deserve to be noted for the help they provided as we conceived and produced this book. Robert G. St. Clair will always be remembered for his interest, support, and advice. We would also like to thank Dominick Abel for stimulating us to prepare a prospectus; Donna Dreher and Keith Nave for introducing us to Addison-Wesley; Ann Dilworth, Martha Drumm, Cathy Redlich, and especially Doe Coover for their heroic efforts in developing the manuscript and producing this book; Andrea Woolard and Alison Martier for their research and interviewing assistance; and Thelma Soderling and Vonnie Lorber for typing our drafts. Thanks also go to all the people who agreed to be interviewed, especially Fran Gordon, Shelly Kleinman, and Peg and Wayne Woodard.

We would also like to thank Gail Lovig, Jane Staw, Nora Rado, and our parents for their support and insights. We especially appreciate Betty and Tom Edmunds for being such good friends and for sharing so much with us.

Research related to this book was supported by the Earl Dean Howard Chair, Graduate School of Management, Northwestern University. Special thanks go to Dean Jacobs for providing Tim with the autonomy to pursue his research.

Finally we would like to recognize our children, Elizabeth and Chip, to whom this book is dedicated. They have been our special partners in many endeavors, teaching us much about love and work, and they remain our most important collaboration.

CONTENTS

PART I

TAKING CHARGE

PROLOGUE

Used-car dealers are shady. Librarians are
quiet and a bit boring. Kindergarten teachers
are kindly. And two-career couples are glamorous.
Glamorous? That's the description that never
ceases to amaze us. Yet many people still think of two-career couples
as carefree, financially secure, and blissfully content people. After all,
with two incomes and the stimulation of two exciting jobs, they must
live well and rarely be bored. If a problem does crop up, they can
always afford to have someone else take care of it.

If this were true—and don't we wish it were—
we'd all live the way the Whitneys do. Who are the Whitneys? Let's
drop in on them for a few minutes to see.

The place: Their apartment, Regency Towers, uptown
The time: Friday, 6:00 P.M.
The people: Stevenson Whitney, trial lawyer
             Margaret Northridge Whitney, investment banker

As the scene opens, Stevenson is relaxing on the
sofa, a glass of white wine in one hand, the other languorously loosen-
ing his tie. The sun setting over the river bathes the room in a golden
glow that nicely complements Stevenson's Bermuda tan. A smile plays
on his lips as he remembers an amusing incident in court that day—
he'll have to tell Margaret about it over dinner.

3

The door chimes ring. Margaret, looking exuberant and lovely in her Calvin Klein suit and Ferragamo pumps, breezes in, hands her briefcase and a small package from Tiffany's to the maid, requests an aperitif, and strides gracefully into the living room to join her husband. They kiss briefly before Margaret sinks into a chair and happily kicks off her shoes.

Margaret: Lord, what a wonderful day! We wrapped up that Mexico City high-rise deal without a hitch. Of course the lawyers were tiresome. Picking nits off the nits! What do they teach you in law school anyway—Introductory Fine Print, Intermediate Fine Print, and Advanced Fine Print?

Stevenson: But what would you do without us, dear? After all, the only saving grace of your wicked investment shenanigans is that they provide lifetime security for every member of the legal profession.

Margaret: All right—truce, darling, truce. [*They pause as Jeanette brings in Margaret's drink.*] The flight from Mexico City was a disaster, though. The airport was an absolute zoo and getting on the plane was no relief. I swear my tablecloth hadn't been near a laundry in three flights. It's good to be home. [*She sips her drink appreciatively.*] Did Brooks Brothers deliver Richard's new blazer? That son of ours has outgrown his whole wardrobe.

Stevenson: Yes . . . and Jeanette said the decorator samples arrived. She has everything under control—as usual. I only wish certain of my colleagues in the firm had her capabilities. Our good friend Hettrick almost blew it in court today. Good thing I was there coaching him. I think my last-minute suggestion saved the day, but we'll have to wait until next week to be sure. God knows, I hope so—the fee from this thing could support a small army.

Margaret: So we both had victories today! How about celebrating with a nice candlelight dinner tonight, just the two of us? We can live dangerously with one of our bottles of 1962 Lafite, a nice sexy movie on the video recorder, and . . . who knows what?

Stevenson: That would be wonderful, darling, but the senator and his wife are stopping by to discuss the financing of his reelection campaign. He called from Washington this afternoon and I told him we were free this evening.

Margaret: Oh, she's such a bore . . . I'm really awfully glad you decided not to run for that seat, darling. I just don't think I'd ever want to live in Washington.

Stevenson: I agree. Let's send them home early. We can get up with the birds tomorrow and be on our way.

Margaret: How marvelous that country air will be. A nice work-out on the tennis court—you did tell Salisbury to have it ready for us?

Stevenson: Of course. And he should also have that new loam and organic fertilizer for my roses in by now. I'm determined to beat out Tom Mellon for the club prize this year. The best part, of course, is having Richard with us for a whole weekend. He's growing up so fast—it's hard to believe he's almost six.

Margaret: There's a small problem, darling. Richard has to attend a violin recital on Saturday morning. His teacher thinks it's wise to expose him to professional concerts early. And then his fencing lesson is in the afternoon. You know how he loves his fencing.

Stevenson: Well, we'll just have Abigail bring him out on Saturday afternoon then. He can bring one of his little friends, if he'd like.

At this point, Abigail, the *au pair* girl, brings Richard in for his daily half-hour visit with his parents. And another typical weekend for the Whitneys is underway.

A nice fantasy. Unfortunately, most two-career couples don't live like that. We have a few more pains and problems in our lives and we don't have a retinue of servants to head off every crisis. To set the record straight, let's look at a few minutes in the lives of a more realistic two-career couple, the Hacketts.

The place: Their home in the suburbs

The time: Friday, 6:00 P.M.

The people: Marge Hackett, college administrator
Pete Hackett, marketing manager

As the scene opens, Marge comes tearing into the house, arms filled with the two bags of groceries she managed to pick up on her way home from the office. Her blazer is crushed in the crook of her elbow, the bow on her white blouse has come undone, and her briefcase is slowly slipping from beneath her right arm. She looks around for Pete or one of the children to relieve her of her bundles. Thank God he didn't bring home another client. Lucky she picked up some chicken . . . she was right—Pete forgot to leave out the hamburger to defrost. God only knows what's in the refrigerator—or, more likely, *not* in the refrigerator.

Marge unloads the groceries, arranges some cheddar and crackers on a tray, and moves toward the living room, stopping en route to kick off her shoes. They've been killing her all day.

The scene is typical. Pete has already changed into corduroys and a cardigan and is just finishing a beer. Brad, their eight-year-old son, is spread out on the floor with his entire collection of one hundred baseball cards. From upstairs, Marge hears soft whimpering. Jenny, their ten-year-old, is quietly sobbing in her bedroom about something that happened at school that day.

Marge sets down the cheese and crackers and kisses her husband lightly on the head, pointing quizzically upstairs. Brad interrupts before Pete can answer.

Brad: Mom, did you remember about Chris's birthday party? We need a present. Did you get a present, Mom?

Marge: No, I forgot completely about it. We'll have to run out later. Did anything else happen? How was school today?

Brad: Okay. Nothing special, except that we have to bring in food for the charity drive and I volunteered to bring Hamburger Helper. Can you get that, too, Mom, when you go shopping?

Pete: Enough, Brad. Your mother just got home.

Marge: How was your day, honey?

Pete: I'm not sure . . . there's talk going around the office about a reorganization in the company. I don't know what that's going to mean for me. There may be some promotions and transfers in the offing. It's all up in the air right now, of course, but I think we really ought to talk about what we would do if . . .

Marge: Pete, can we talk about it some other time? I mean, I can't worry about some uncertain future right now. It's after six, dinner isn't even started, and I have a briefcase full of budget proposals to go over. Brad needs a present for Chris's party tomorrow, and . . .

Pete: Okay! We'll save it. Besides, I guess there are more immediate things to think about. Like the notice in the mail today about our checking account being over-drawn—again. Honestly, Marge, if we're both going to draw on the account we have to work out a better system of keeping track of things. Also, I called the service people about the washing machine. They can send some-one out tomorrow morning, but it will mean paying over-time for service on Saturday.

Marge: Well, we don't really have a choice, do we? If they get here in the morning, that should give us time to catch up on the laundry before the party tomorrow night.

Pete: The party?! I completely forgot. That dean of yours gives the worst parties. Why does he insist on trying so hard? This is the third one this semester, and I'm sure it will be as b-o-r-i-n-g as the first two. I suppose we have to go, though, huh?

Marge: Yes, I *suppose*. You *know* we have to go, Pete. We don't have to stay long, though. Or maybe Donna can come a little early and we can go out to dinner beforehand—I've always wanted to arrive at a party fashionably late.

At this point the phone rings and Marge goes to answer it. She returns grimacing.

Marge: That was Donna. She can't babysit tomorrow night at all, much less come early. Do you think we could leave the kids alone? It isn't as if we'll be that far away.

Pete glances at Brad, who is eagerly awaiting his parents' decision and doing a bad job of concealing his bias.

Pete: Oh, I don't think that's such a good idea. I'm sure you can work it out somehow.

Brad: Aw, Dad . . .

Marge: That's enough, Brad. What do you mean, Pete, that *I'll* work it out somehow? *We'll* work it out. I mean, really, Pete, it isn't all my responsibility. And what about Jenny? What's going on? I could hear her upstairs when I came in. I should go talk to her.

Jenny enters the living room, eyes red from crying, and regards her parents fiercely.

Jenny: All you guys ever do is talk to each other. What about me? Don't I count? I have a life, too, you know, and it isn't easy. I have problems, too.

Marge: Of course you do, Jenny. I'm sorry. Mother and father have just had a bad day, that's all. Why don't you and Brad take a walk down to Baskin-Robbins and buy some ice cream for dessert tonight, and you and I will have a private chat after dinner. Okay?

Jenny and Brad exit, arguing about the flavor of ice cream to buy. Marge smiles and turns again to her husband.

Pete: There was something else in the mail today that's bothering me. Someone sent a copy of the town rules about leaving trash cans by the street. It was unsigned. Who the hell would do that? The only time we left a trash can was when the leaf bag broke. One damn time and we get a poison-pen letter. I have enough to worry about at work without trash cans creating a crisis.

Marge: Let's ignore it. The old stuffs. It's after six and we should start supper. I'm surprised the kids didn't complain about being hungry.

Pete: They both had two peanut-butter sandwiches.

Marge: Swell. Well, let's hit the kitchen. We can talk about tomorrow. If you can stay here in the morning and wait for the service man, I can get Brad's present for the party and do the grocery shopping for the week. Then we can get to the laundry in the afternoon.

Pete: What about tonight? I mean some time to just relax and talk—just the two of us?

Marge: Well, if I can go over the budget proposals between nine and eleven, we could catch the late movie together.

Pete: Forget the budget proposals. They can wait. I can't.

Marge: But tonight's the only time. We're having your parents over for dinner on Sunday. It's your mother's birthday, remember?

Pete: Oh, damn! Er, Marge, while you're out buying a present for Brad's friend . . .

And another typical weekend for the Hacketts is underway.

CHAPTER ONE

THE TWO-CAREER COUPLE

She might be the mechanic who tunes up your car or the candidate running for city office. He might be your accountant, your child's teacher, or the man behind you in line at the supermarket. Together, they are part of what has been called the single most outstanding phenomenon of this century. To some, they represent a threat, perhaps to the very institution of the family. But they are no longer unique. Today their numbers are increasing by leaps and bounds. They are the two-career couple.

The traditional family model of husband as breadwinner and wife as homemaker may soon become a vestige of a past society. The rising young executive with 2.4 children and a compliant wife standing ready to pack the china and move the family to Houston, Atlanta, or Chicago is increasingly rare. Often *her* career determines what he will and won't do in pursuit of his career.

For many couples, two careers are an economic necessity. For others, the necessity is psychological—a need to avoid what Abraham Maslow once called "neurosis as a failure of personal growth."[1] For most couples, however, managing two careers is a serious business and a source of stress. Old values are questioned. New life-styles emerge. The relationship is challenged and there is an immediate need to cope. Most couples find themselves unprepared.

We are a society of women and men who have been raised to either pursue a career or manage a home—but rarely to do both. As couples, we are relearning. Some of us fail to find a way to juggle new roles and new demands. Others make the accommodation, emerging with a new sense of themselves and their relationships.

This is a book about that accommodation—about coping and compromise, about confronting conflicts, and, in the end, about creating relationships and life-styles in which both partners can win.

The Trend

According to the Bureau of Labor Statistics, 30.4 million U.S. families, or 53 percent of the total, have at least two earners. Of the 98 million people in the American work force in 1978, 46 million were married to employed spouses. If we put these statistics together, we find that there are between 23 and 30 million married two-career couples. The Labor Department doesn't keep tabs on people who couple other than at the altar, but live-together two-career couples would probably add several more million to that estimate.

Just a fad? We don't think so. Despite Talcott Parson's gloomy 1954 prediction that marriage between professionals was not a workable way of emancipating American women from domesticity, women have entered the labor force in increasing numbers and have continued to link up with working partners. Even the Bureau of Labor Statistics can't keep up with the trend. In 1976, they predicted that over 48 percent of all women over sixteen years of age would be in the work force. By September of 1977, the number had already exceeded that figure. Today, more than half of all wives are employed.

The two-career family is different from what has been called the "two-person career."[2] In the dual-career family, each partner has a distinct work role; in the two-person career, both partners focus their energies on one job. Thus, one partner (usually the female) derives vicarious achievement from helping her mate fulfill the requirements of his position. The wives of politicians and ministers, for example, are often contributors to a two-person career.

In addition to separate work roles, two-career couples are also defined by their life-style, a life-style designed to support, encourage, and facilitate—not just tolerate—the career pursuits of both members. Their relationship is grounded in and shaped by their two careers. They achieve status through the combined work roles of both partners. They do not have to be married—or even, for that matter, be a heterosexual couple.

The term *couple* is interpreted broadly. Our definition could apply to many types of coupling arrangements, the most
common of which is still the traditional marriage. But there are other
kinds as well. Stable cohabitation—commitment to a partner without
any permanent legal bonds—has become increasingly common. Other
people, married or not, choose to live together but are free to have
sexual relationships with others. Thus, it is life-style rather than sexual
fidelity or legal bonds that characterizes a couple.

Two people who share a life-style that includes
cohabitation, work roles for both partners, and a love relationship that
supports and facilitates both make up a two-career couple. Their relationship combines life's most important adult functions: working and
loving. To understand the phenomenon—and the problems it creates
for us—we need to look briefly at these two functions, how they've
evolved, and how they interact in our relationships.

The Work Ethic versus the Worth Ethic

The Protestant, or traditional, work ethic got its
start in the Garden of Eden. As punishment for disobeying God's orders
and yielding to temptation, Eve and Adam (the original working couple)
were banished from the Garden, stripped of their immortality, clothed
to conceal their shame, and condemned to a lifetime of work as a
means of regaining their lost state of Grace.

Of these outcomes, perhaps the most significant
was the requirement of lifelong toil. Work was important not only
because it produced useful goods and services, but because it kept
people too busy to succumb to temptation. According to the work ethic,
the main object is salvation, not satisfaction. Work is not meant to be
enjoyable, and even enjoyment itself is seen as sinful. Work is human-
kind's cross to bear, a way of demonstrating one's righteousness.

Exactly when the shift from this "work-as-calling"
philosophy occurred isn't certain, but by the time of our parents'
generation, the signs were definitely there. Opinon pollster Daniel
Yankelovich offers the following summary of the values held by workers in the quarter-century following World War II (up to approximately
1970):

- If women could afford to stay home and not work at a paid job,
  they did so.

- As long as a job provided a man with a decent living and some
  degree of economic security, he would put up with all its draw-

backs, because it meant that he could fulfill his economic obligations to his family and confirm his own self-esteem as breadwinner
and good provider.

- The incentive system—mainly money and status rewards—was
  successful in motivating most people.

- People were tied to their jobs not only by bonds of commitment to
  their family, but also by loyalty to their organizations.

- Most people defined their identity through their work role, subor-
  dinating and suppressing most conflicting personal desires.[3]

This post-World-War-II work ethic is certainly a
departure from the asceticism of the Protestant ethic. The postwar version views work as instrumental in providing a variety of extrinsic
rewards: pay, security, and status. Yankelovich's last statement—that
people were beginning to define their identities through their work
roles—is especially important, as it is one of the tenets of the new
work ethic of the seventies: the worth ethic.

The Protestant ethic told us to work for *salvation;*
the worth ethic encourages us to work for *satisfaction.* Where work
used to be a means to an end (survival, Grace, and the avoidance of
temptation), it is now sought as an end in itself (intrinsic satisfaction).
This is not to imply that all work *is* self-enhancing. It means simply that
people value and seek work that will add to their satisfaction and self-
esteem. This is the *worth ethic.*

A poll of the readers of *Psychology Today* (a sample more highly educated, professional, and better paid than the
national average) found that the five most important aspects of a job
for the 23,000 respondents are (in order of importance):

- The chance to do something that makes you feel good about yourself

- The chance to accomplish something worthwhile

- The chance to learn new things

- The chance to develop your skills and abilities

- The amount of freedom you have on your job.[4]

Patricia Renwick and Edward Lawler summarized
these and other findings in this description of today's working person:

> Like your parents, you are willing to work hard and even put in long
> hours. Although you value your leisure, . . . you still find much of your
> identity in work. But you want more control over the decisions in the work

place, especially those that affect your own jobs. And you want more freedom to set the pace of your own work, to control your own hours and schedules, to get in an hour of tennis before work or take a long skiing weekend. You have a whole hierarchy of needs, which you see as necessary for what Abraham Maslow called self-actualization.[5]

Self-fulfillment and autonomy seem to be both motivations and standards of judgment in the new psychology of work. It's a trend certainly in keeping with the values of the "Me Generation," a movement whose outward signs are the recent deluge of self-help books, the growing importance of leisure (often as a means to improve the self), and the desire of freedom *from* the job as well as freedom *on* the job. Daniel Yankelovich says that, of the two core values in the worth ethic, autonomy may be even more important than self-fulfillment.

> When we ask people in our surveys which aspects of their work are becoming more important to them, they stress, above all else, "being recognized as an individual person." They also stress "the opportunity to be with pleasant people with whom I like to work." Significantly, for the majority of people these demands come ahead of the desire that the work itself be interesting and nonroutine.[6]

The criterion for happiness has become personal satisfaction in a role *of one's choice*—a trend perhaps most emphatically demonstrated by the emergence of women in the job market. Of course there are other reasons why women have joined the labor force in such large numbers during the last decade. Often, it's a financial necessity. In addition, technological improvements in the kitchen and the bedroom have liberated homemakers. The pill as well as the crockpot have freed women to seek employment outside the home, if they so desire. Still, the search for personal freedom and fulfillment remains the best explanation why, in so many couples, both people choose to work. Although two jobs may be an economic necessity, they are also the key to new life choices.

The motivations of women are changing. In 1964, the Census Bureau found that two-thirds of working women with children were employed out of economic need; only one-sixth gave "personal satisfaction" as their rationale for working. A decade later, in a National Opinion Research Center Survey, 60 percent of married women and women with children gave "important and meaningful work" as their most preferred job characteristic, while 15 to 25 percent listed high income (the importance of income depended on the number of children they had—the more children, the greater the importance).[7] Today, in a national survey of women aged eighteen to thirty-

five, over 80 percent of the working women polled said they would
continue to work even if money were no problem. One women quoted in
the survey wryly expresses the contemporary view: "My life-style
wouldn't change if I stopped working, but my personality would."[8]

Myra Marx Ferree tells us that being a housewife
is not the source of many women's unhappiness. Rather, the *role* of
housewife has ceased to provide satisfaction, status, and social contact. Employment, regardless of the kind of work, provides a variety of
satisfactions not available to many housewives. In her research, Ferree
found that women who hold jobs by choice (even blue-collar, routine
jobs) are more satisfied with their lives than are full-time housewives.[9]
They have *chosen* to work; it provides them with social contact, clear
payoffs for their efforts, feedback on performance, a sense of accomplishment, and a sense of personal competence—things they were not
getting at home.

This concern for autonomy and self-fulfillment—
for both women and men—indicates that we are beginning to endorse a
new type of success: a psychological success based on the individual's
internal priorities, values, and standards of excellence as opposed to

"This is Henry. We live together, too. Only in our case, I'm afraid we're married."

Reprinted by permission of G.P. Putnam's Son's from *Terribly Nice People* by William
Hamilton, copyright © 1975 by William Hamilton.

more traditional, external measures of success. Salary, status, and position no longer get top billing. Our standards of success, like our criteria for valued work, are becoming more personal. In a reversal of the trend David Riesman observed a generation ago in *The Lonely Crowd*, we are becoming more inner-directed and less outer-directed.

Yankelovich sums up this shift from our postwar concern for external measures of success to our present internal standards very nicely: "If the key motif of the past was 'keeping up with the Joneses,' today it is, 'I have my own life to live, let Jones shift for himself.' "[10]

How do couples fit in?

How does the worth ethic apply to couples? Have the same two key desires—self-fulfillment and autonomy—changed marriage and other love relationships? Undeniably. The conditions under which relationships evolve are not what they used to be. The need to team up, to work together to ensure sheer physical survival, is no longer an issue for most people. Marriage by choice rather than marriage by expectation or necessity is now the norm.

This has brought about many changes, the most fundamental being that there are simply fewer unions. More than ever before, couples are opting for living together without marriage. Given that the average marriage lasts only eight years, many of these cohabitation relationships—even if they survive only a number of years—can be considered at least as permanent as marriage. When people do marry, they are doing it later, perhaps after living together first. At the least, each has experienced a few years of independent life out of the nest. They're postponing children, too, and having fewer of them. They're also organizing their time and money to improve their life-style and their leisure. Their expectations are higher. Thus, when people do marry, they seek a union that they expect (and perhaps falsely anticipate) will enable, if not guarantee, personal fulfillment.

Unfortunately, although personal expectations of marriage have changed, the structure, evolution, and relationships in many marriages have not kept pace. Whatever their prenuptial expectations, many couples still form a very traditional union. Their nontraditional hopes and expectations often remain unexpressed. Dr. Joseph Federico of The Divorce Adjustment Institute explains the problem as follows:

> It used to be that the goals of a couple required teamwork. Now the human potential movement is switching people to a predominantly "I"

orientation. When people say they can't adapt to changes in a relationship, it usually means that one or both partners are vigorously pursuing
their own fulfillment and they see the distance that creates as bad.[11]

What does this imply for couples? Simply that if
the "win/lose"marriage of the past is to be rendered obsolete, new
strategies for integrating coupling and careers must be created. Both
partners must benefit from the union, both partners must "win."

A New Style

The Greek god of the sea, Proteus, was able to
change his shape spontaneously—from savage animal to water to
rock—as frequently as he chose. Unless caught and restrained, he
would never limit himself to a single form. His adaptations guaranteed
his survival and his dominance.

Much like Proteus, people today are finding that
flexibility and adaptation are necessary first steps toward the self-fulfillment and autonomy so important to their personal and professional
selves. Emerging new values and an increased emphasis on psychological success have led to a new style of survival, a protean style in
which we take responsibility for our life paths and listen less to the
directives of organizations and society. The protean style is ongoing
and fluid; it creates alternatives rather than meets demands. It acts
rather than reacts. And it is always directed by the self.

The protean career

As people become less enchanted with formal
organizations and with advancement via the bureaucratic career
ladder, they are moving away from the notion that career success
equals upward mobility and toward the idea that a successful career
can be a lifelong sequence of fulfilling work experiences.

In the protean career, performance is judged ac-
cording to very personal criteria (psychological success), whereas in
the traditional career, the person accepts the organization's definition
of performance (salary, position). In the protean career, one's own
attitudes and preferences play a greater role in determining career
choices. Work satisfaction, achievement, and job involvement with low
organizational commitment are core values. Since the protean person
feels responsible for the long-run management of his or her life, he or
she is more likely to ask searching questions: "How do I feel about the
work I am doing? Now that I'm forty-five, what do I want to be when I

grow up? How can I maintain my flexibility and freedom in the coming years?"

In the traditional career, on the other hand, attitudes such as organizational commitment and loyalty are valued. Once the person becomes committed to a particular career ladder, he or she simply lets things take their course. It is a passive stance; there is little need to think about attitude, identity, or adaptability unless, of course, the career ladder begins to wobble.

In short, the person pursuing a protean career has opted for greater control and, accordingly, must accept the insecurity and fear of failure that greater personal freedom entails. He or she cannot take refuge in the corporate womb.

The protean couple

In a traditional couple relationship, two people will generally marry, raise a family, and make family moves dictated by career needs—his career needs, that is, not hers.

The protean couple is directed by the couple, not by any external force, be it an employer, community norms, stereotyped sex roles, or traditional definitions of "marriage" and "family." Because the protean form of relationship is self-invented and self-directed, it cannot be specifically characterized. Each couple's relationship will take a unique form. The core characteristics, however, are strong concern for the individuality, autonomy, and growth of each party and an active effort to monitor and shape the type of relationship that exists. The protean couple might decide to maintain two separate residences rather than commute long distances to work each day. They might decide to not marry, or to remain childless, or to live communally, perhaps "adopting" friends' children as a way of satisfying any parenting needs they feel. If their jobs are geographically separated, they might live together but switch residences periodically, to take turns living near each partner's job.

They will invent their own ways of sharing the roles and activities associated with living together. It might be an egalitarian relationship, with both sharing all activities. Or, they might assign separate tasks with the net effect being a fifty-fifty sharing. Perhaps they'll opt for a reversal of the traditional roles, with the male taking responsibility for more of the home activities and the woman spending more time on career activities. One couple has an intriguing way of striving for an equal sharing of home duties. They use what they call a "60-40 rule": "Each of us gives 60 percent to the relationship, expecting the other to give only 40 percent. Sometimes this means doing things for the other person you'd rather not do, but it's all part of the deal."

Currently, the most talked-about form of protean-couple relationship involves living apart during the workweek and commuting on weekends to be together. Shelly Kleinman and Fran Gordon spent their first year of marriage commuting between New Haven, Connecticut, where Shelly managed the Yale Repertory Theater, and Palo Alto, California, where his wife taught in the School of Business at Stanford. They had just been married and obviously would have preferred to live together, but each was in a specialized field and their jobs were among the best in their respective areas.

They tried to see each other once a month, if possible, which meant that high telephone bills and travel expenses became a part of their regular cost of living. However, contrary to what you might expect, when they look back to that year (now about seven years past), it has, as Shelly puts it, "a nice rosy glow about it."

As Fran says, "I think in many ways it was the nicest part of the marriage!" She laughs, and goes on to explain: "Because it was all romance. I mean, we were married, but because we weren't living together . . .

[Interviewer: "It was like having an affair!"]

"It really was. I would get letters three times, four times a week. . . . And I got flowers. When I was in Hawaii [at a convention] I was wired a dozen long-stemmed red roses. It was a very romantic year."

When they were apart, they both missed each other, but being so busy and involved in their work made the time pass quickly. Then, when they were together, work was left behind and they were *really together*. As Fran says, "It was like a Yale weekend. . . . There wasn't much real about it."

The reality

Obviously, not everyone can pursue the protean style all of the time. It is an ideal, just as is the organizational career or the traditional marriage. Usually, the protean style evolves out of a more traditional route, as in the example of a person who starts her career in a training program for, say, Procter and Gamble, becomes a product manager, and then decides to start her own small advertising agency and do some writing on the side. Or the small-town couple who marry young and start a family, as everyone expects, but then move to a big city, explore new roles, and take charge of their personal growth and the changes it brings.

One couple started their marriage in the midwestern town where they grew up, each working in a small business. Eventually, they realized they needed more freedom and variety in their lives. After some exploratory moving around, they evolved what for them is the perfect marriage: they are both army officers stationed in different parts of the country, each willing to accept any transfer or promotion that comes along. They see each other every two weeks and talk constantly on the telephone. As she puts it, "We are each other's best buddies; no one else has ever understood and accepted me the way he does. But neither of us likes to be tied down to the daily responsibilities of living with another person. We have the best of both worlds—two independent lives plus a beautiful relationship."

A common pitfall in evaluating just how protean our lives are is the *"pseudo-protean style,"* the traditional style in protean clothing. When looking back over actions we have taken, we all have a tendency to revise history for the sake of self-justification. It's hard to resist the natural impulse to make ourselves seem wiser, virtuous, or more in control. We all like to think that we had more control over events than, in fact, we did. It's satisfying to view our careers as the result of some grand strategy. We may say *now* that the choice to give up her job for the sake of his was a decision we both made with the full consequences in view when, in reality, the pressure of the moment—and the salary increase—had much more to do with the result than we care to admit. We tend to attribute the good things that happen to our own choices and actions; the bad things and problems are (obviously) due to other people or chance.

When assessing which style you have practiced to date, try to compensate for this tendency to "overproteanize" the good parts. The accompanying chart should help you to assess realistically the style you've adopted in both your career and your marriage.

Mixing styles

So far we have considered two types of careers and two types of couple relationships—traditional and protean. There are four combinations possible: traditional careers and a traditional relationship, protean careers and a traditional relationship, traditional careers and a protean relationship, and protean careers and a protean relationship. Of the four combinations, a couple with a traditional marriage and traditional career has the most difficult, stressful situation to

Issue	Protean Style	Traditional Career	Traditional Couple
Who's in charge?	Person or couple	Organization	Societal norms; man's career
Core values	Freedom; growth	Advancement; power level	Stability, marriage, acceptance, man's career success, woman's nurturance
Degree of mobility	High	Lower	High or low, depends on man's career mobility
Important performance dimensions	Psychological success; mutual satisfaction	Position level; salary	Staying together; successfully raising a family; success of man's career
Important identity dimensions	Do I respect myself? (self-esteem) Am I helping my partner grow? (mutual support)	Am I respected in this organization? (esteem from colleagues) What should I do? (organizational sensitivity)	Are we respected and accepted in this community? (esteem from community) Are we meeting social expectations here? (community involvement) Identification with husband's organization or profession.

manage. Two traditional jobs (nine to five, five days a week, perhaps with travel, little flexibility, high involvement), plus a close relationship with the spouse, plus children and all that entails equals three highly involving, time-consuming, and often conflicting roles. It can be done, but not without strong support and commitment from the two partners, excellent coping skills, and perhaps hired help.

The other combinations involve less stress, because either the career or the relationship is more flexible and can "give" a bit when necessary. One of us is a college professor, which we consider a protean career, with its high degree of autonomy and flexibility. Tim is also a tenured full professor, which further enhances his freedom in the job. In his last two jobs, his office has been situated very close to home, which adds to our flexibility. Our relationship, on the other hand, is very traditional. We've been married fourteen years, have two children, own a house, cocker spaniel, gerbil, hamster, and guppies—and have never seriously considered living apart to maximize career options.

When we lived in East Lansing, Michigan, Fran was a starting assistant professor at Western Michigan University, ninety miles away. Because she was a woman in a predominantly male department, because she was fresh out of graduate school and very junior in the department, and because she had a three-hour round-trip commute each day, she had far less flexibility and freedom in her job than did Tim.

One day our daughter, Elizabeth, was sick. Nothing serious or contagious, but she couldn't go to school. No sitters or neighbors were available that day. We both had two classes to teach, so neither of us could stay home.

What did we do? We got out our portable aluminum camping cot, our portable TV set, and some books, and Tim set Elizabeth up in his office for the day. She even sat in on a class lecture, since he was due to show a film that day. (She fell asleep.)

Although we were uneasy about bringing a child to the office, she did fine, Tim did fine (actually, his lecture performance was enhanced by having such a severe critic sitting in), and no one in the office was disturbed. Even if there had been some unfavorable reactions, this would present no serious difficulty for a senior professor. On the other hand, we both agreed that such a thing would have been very difficult for Fran to do.

The point of this example is that flexibility is necessary, either in one career or in the relationship, to meet the high demands of a two-career family. If both jobs are traditional and inflexible, a protean relationship (for example, living apart, no kids, role sharing) provides comparable relief. And, of course, if both the relationship and the career are protean, this provides the greatest flexibility and autonomy of all. Here, however, the lack of structure and stability (and perhaps security) may become a problem.

One unmarried couple we know was in this category for a few years. He had two university appointments, one in the Midwest and one in the Northwest, while she was a professor in California (both protean careers). Both traveled a fair amount and they lived together on weekends as often as possible. When one took a sabbatical, they spent half a year together.

Later they married and maintained four separate residences (hers in California, his in the Midwest and Northwest, plus his resort condominium). By their account, they were together at least once a month. Both were free to pursue their careers to the hilt and both were very successful. However, the strains of being apart and the ambiguity of the relationship before they were married presented some problems. Having a totally flexible life-style had advantages, but it was hard to maintain over the long term.

Our impression is that combinations of similar styles for career and relationship (traditional relationship/traditional careers; protean relationship/protean careers) are relatively unstable dual-career situations. They may be effective over a period of time, but they do involve certain stresses. On the other hand, mixed combinations (for example, traditional careers/protean relationship) provide security in one role and flexibility and autonomy in the other. A sense of security in one area often enables a person to take full advantage of freedom in the other part of his or her life. We would argue that a good two-career relationship needs the secure base of some traditional elements along with a good dose of the protean. The secret of effectiveness, then, lies in discovering ways to combine the two.

Effective Career Couples

Effective career couples are more than successful career couples. They are successful, but according to their own criteria for success. They are also highly satisfied with their relationship and life-style. Two people with successful careers are not necessarily an effective career couple. If their relationship does not provide satisfaction and support, they are successful career *people*, but are not effective as a couple.

Conversely, couples who are not setting the world on fire in their organizations may be highly effective career couples. Each may be achieving what he or she wants in career terms while enjoying the satisfaction of a supportive relationship. Of course, a couple, or one partner, may have a very successful career by external standards and still enjoy a satisfying home and family relationship. But the definition of *effective* hinges on personal satisfaction, not on career success alone. That is the essence of the protean style—self-fulfillment and autonomy.

How does a couple cope with two careers and a love relationship? The answer is to find ways of making your career(s) or your relationship more flexible—in effect, to "proteanize" whatever aspect of your life can best help you become both a good worker and a good lover.

Sometimes this process means sacrifices for one or both partners; always it is difficult. How much should you invest in work? How much in the relationship? Generally speaking, the more a person invests in and identifies with his or her career role, the less time and energy there is to invest in the roles of parent, partner, or keeper of the house. There is no single role structure for two-career families. There are, however, general types, each representing various degrees of involvement in career versus home, and therefore different degrees and types of conflict.

Accommodators

Couples who fit this type usually have one partner who is high in career involvement and low in home involvement. The second partner is just the opposite: high in home involvement but low in career involvement. Thus, each partner accommodates the other. One assumes primary (although not total) responsibility for home and family roles, while the second partner assumes primary responsibility for career roles.

This couple probably comes closest to the traditional family with a homemaker mother and breadwinner father. However, they differ from the traditional model in one important way: either partner may assume either role. The woman may be the one most devoted to career, while the man is content to devote himself to home and family.

If the partners are truly involved in their respective roles and value both work and family, then conflicts are minimized.

There may be some nitty-gritty housekeeping issues to work out, but neither partner experiences a great deal of psychological strain between work and nonwork roles or between their respective work roles. Accommodators are generally able to order priorities; they can achieve personal satisfaction without violating their partner's career or identity.

Adversaries

If both partners are highly involved in their careers and only minimally involved in home, family, or partner-support roles, they may be described as adversaries. The identity of each partner is primarily defined by career. Yet, having a well-ordered home and a family are important to both as well. They don't relinquish these aspects of their life-style; the home roles remain. The question is: Who will perform them?

This is probably the most stressful structure for couples, because they are competing over priorities. Each wants to put career before anything else, and neither is willing or able to assume responsibility for nonwork roles at home or in the family. Thus, not only is there competition over making career decisions and meeting career demands, but there is competition over who will provide the support structure for the other. Major decisions such as job relocation or having children are threatening to both partners. Neither may be willing or able to make career sacrifices to facilitate the career of the other or to fulfill home and family roles. Although both may want to have children, they would prefer to delegate child-rearing responsibilities to their mate.

Allies

In a third type of couple, the two partners are both highly involved in either their career or their home roles, with little identity tied up in the other area. As with the accommodators, their priorities are clearly defined. For allies who are high in home and family, being parents and partners is more important than career. Thus, neither values career above family, and both derive their primary identity and satisfaction from their family and their relationship. Again, the level of conflict is low. Not only are both partners willing to support the other at home, they also actively minimize the potentially stressful demands of their careers.

Likewise, allies who are highly involved in their careers and far less involved with home and family roles are also able to minimize conflict by minimizing the importance of domestic roles. They are not overly concerned with maintaining a well-ordered home, preparing gourmet dinners, or entertaining frequently. Often, they choose not to have children. Their support structure may be "purchased"—in dinners out, maids, and catering—or it simply may not exist. "If the house is a mess, so what? That's not where I *really* live," is their attitude.

Allies usually experience very little conflict over career or home issues. Neither resents the money spent to purchase a support structure—that's the price of independence. Since neither wants children, that conflict is eliminated. And, unlike adversaries, conflicting career demands can often be worked out by agreeing to alternative domestic arrangements, such as commuting long distance, living apart temporarily or permanently, or a home life that places "togetherness" low on the list of priorities. The major source of stress for career-involved allies is lack of time to devote to their relationship. Minimizing home and family roles does not remove them from the reality of being husband or wife.

Acrobats

If both partners are highly involved in all of their roles, they can be thought of as rather frantic acrobats. Their identities are not defined primarily by a single role—rather, they achieve fulfillment and satisfaction in all of them. These partners give equal weight to home and career roles. Like adversaries, acrobats are apt to experience a lot of conflict over career demands and decisions, but the conflict is internal rather than adversarial. In other words, both partners are equally concerned with performing home and family duties *themselves*. They are not looking to their partners to take over. In a sense, they both want to have *and* eat the cake. Thus, acrobats must constantly juggle a profusion of demands—they are unable to stop mid-juggle and toss a ball to their partner. They want to have a well-ordered home, provide real and emotional support for their spouse, pursue successful careers, be good parents, and still find time for the relationship. And they want to do it all themselves.

Transition

No relationship is static, not even the traditional marriage. People change, and it is more common than uncommon to find couples in transition—moving to or within the types described above.

As more women enter, reenter, and decide to stay in the work force, it becomes more likely that they will start to identify more strongly with their professional roles. Typically, many couples move first from the traditional family structure to being accommodators. The wife is generally less career involved than the husband, so his career comes first. If the wife's identification with her career continues, however, then the couple may move to being either adversaries, allies, or acrobats. Whatever the move, one of the major issues will be conflict—between their career roles or among multiple work and family roles.

In much of the rest of this book we will be looking at the conflicts dual-career couples face and at the coping skills needed to deal successfully with these problems.

Where We're Headed

The two-career couple is not an isolated phenomenon. It is intimately bound up in social changes toward greater freedom, equality, and self-fulfillment—in short, the protean style. The dilemma is how to combine individual fulfillment and freedom with responsibility to one's mate. How can you be your own person and still fulfill your commitments to your partner? How can you be together as a couple and still be "together" as a person?

We can't promise to provide you with any quick solutions in the chapters that follow, but we can promise to help you develop some solutions of your own. We start by identifying the basic tools you'll need to analyze and "proteanize" your two-career relationship: how to identify clashes between family stages and career stages, how to understand and control conflict between roles, and how to manage time and stress.

In Part II we turn to issues that can be especially troublesome in two-career relationships and offer some advice and insights to assist you in dealing with these issues. They include: managing a good home, deciding whether and when to have children, how to be a good parent, interpersonal issues (sex, jealousy, and competition), work involvement and workaholism, and (the number one problem) mobility and relocation. We also look at what organizations can and should be doing to help dual-career-couple employees.

In Part III we get down to the bottom line in your relationship: what determines whether or not you remain a two-career couple, whether or not you continue to pursue your careers, and whether you split up or stay together. We'll also cast an eye to the future of the two-career couple—what the next generation has in store for them.

We start by examining the predictable stages through which careers and families pass. More important, we consider how and when family and career stages mesh and when they clash.

CHAPTER TWO

CAREER AND FAMILY STAGES

There are certain predictable stages in our family life and our careers, just as in our personal development. These "life cycles" are all very much affected by one another. When people experience career problems or conflict with a partner, they often mistakenly assume that they are to blame. In fact, problems are generally the result of the particular stage of a person's career or a particular phase of family life.

If you can predict what career and family issues might arise in your future, you are, in a sense, forewarned and forearmed. Thus prepared, you are less likely to take these problems too personally and are better able to ride them out. Certain career stages and family stages may be more compatible than others. Similarly, certain combinations of individual career stages may mesh more smoothly than others. So, we need to look at how the life cycles of careers and families interact.

Career Stages

The growth and development of a person's career is similar to biological growth curves. For example, if you graphed the growth of a plant, say one of the nice giant zinnias now growing in our backyard, the first phase would be an initial natural selection: good seeds would get matched up with good growing conditions—sun, soil, and water. Some seeds would simply never germinate, while others would thrive.

Once germination occurs, a stage of rapid growth follows—growth in physical size and in the number of separate working parts, such as root hairs, stem, leaves, flowers, and so on. Then, as the plant approaches full size, it enters a relatively stable period in which it takes in various raw materials and produces oxygen, flowers, and visual pleasure for several months. Finally, when the season is over, a period of decline sets in and the flowers produce seeds for future years' growth.

Careers, like any other living system, follow this same growth curve. First, there is a period of exploration and trial, during which the person tries to find optimal growing conditions, a place to "put down roots." Once the person has found a place in the occupational world, the next stage involves becoming established and advancing in the chosen field. This is a period of rapid growth. After attaining a particular level of success (both psychological and external), the person reaches the midcareer period. Many options are possible here. This could be a long plateau, with continued good work but little movement into new areas. Or it could be a time of continuing exploration, experimentation, and growth. Or, sadly, with the security that being established provides, midcareer could be a time for letting up, becoming less involved, and entering a self-imposed and unproductive "early retirement." The final career stage, called "decline" by psychologists, is marked by a gradual drop in involvement in one's present job and increased involvement in other roles. Physical abilities and health may weaken or deteriorate.

The life cycle of a career can be summarized graphically as in the diagram on the next page. In the following sections, we consider each stage in turn and look more closely at the career graph.

Exploration and trial

Exploration and trial are two distinct phases. Exploration is a time for thinking about various occupations, jobs, and career possibilities. Much of it occurs before the person actually enters the world of work. Trial, on the other hand, refers to trying out actual work experiences and the trial-and-error process of finding a job and work environment that feels good.

Exploration is in many ways the most critical career stage, simply because it represents the very beginning of a career. Beginnings tend to be fragile, much like the first tender sprouts

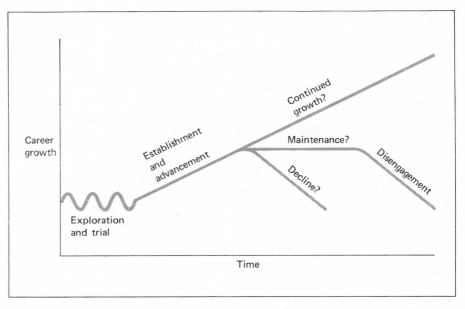

The career growth curve. (Adapted from D. T. Hall, *Careers in Organizations*. Santa Monica, CA: Goodyear, 1976, p. 57.)

of a young plant. The person is just beginning to seriously visualize possible career paths, interests and perceived capabilities are rather uncertain, and aspiration levels may be unrealistically high or low. Without encouragement, the person might settle for far less than he or she should. Or, without helpful feedback and direction, he or she could easily aspire toward an impossible position, unaware of the education, experience, and skills required for the job. The damage to self-esteem, when feedback comes in the form of repeated rejections and failures, could be crippling.

This exploratory phase is even more critical for people with interrupted work careers—for example, women who have spent the last fifteen years raising a family, managing a home, and serving in various community organizations. The danger of shooting too high or too low is especially evident here. On the one hand, the person (most likely a woman) may see no connection at all between the organizational skills she has developed and the skills required in a job.

An acquaintance of ours administered a two-million-dollar budget as president of a large volunteer association and supervised 200 subordinates, 195 of whom were volunteers—a group far more independent, marginally involved, and difficult to motivate than paid employees. In dealing with potential donors, she developed excellent sales and public-relations skills. Her planning and organizing abilities were finely honed through the variety of projects she organized and carried through.

Yet, ironically, her self-esteem as a potential manager in a corporate position was very low, far below her skill level. She was in critical need of assistance in the exploratory stage to help her translate her experiences into marketable skills. Many organizations, volunteer and for-profit, are springing up to help women make this transition from successful volunteer to successful employee.

In some cases, the problem is quite the reverse: a women may grossly overestimate her marketability. She may assume that, because she was president of a large Junior League chapter and dealt effectively with corporate executives as a peer, she should immediately qualify for an executive position herself. In calculating her abilities, she discounts the fact that she never finished college, unaware that most executives today have at least a B.A. and go through extensive formal and on-the-job training before they assume even their first low-level supervisory position.

In short, in the exploratory stage, people desperately need *realistic information* about their own interests and skills and about the occupational requirements in their chosen field. A variety of sources can help here: school placement offices, friends in business, counseling services, placement firms, even fellow job seekers. A good place to begin is Richard Bolles' book, *What Color Is Your Parachute? A Practical Manual for Job Hunters and Career Changers* (Berkeley, CA: Ten Speed Press, 1974).

Another way to arrive at the point of realistic exploration is to lead up to it very deliberately, step by step. Eli Ginzberg, an expert on human-resource development at Columbia University, has described career choice as a three-stage process. First, there is a *fantasy* stage, when the person imagines various kinds of work she or he would like to do. As a five-year-old, you might have fantasized about being a firefighter, doctor, police officer, or movie star. At the fantasy stage, the person is not really thinking very concretely about making a choice or even determining a preference. Rather, it's a lot of daydreaming, a lot of pie-in-the-sky thinking, a mental "trying on different jobs for size."

The second stage of exploration involves making *tentative choices*. The person begins to think through, in a more concrete fashion, his or her interests and how they would mesh with various types of work. Thought is also given to how one's capabilities or skills would direct or limit one to particular occupations. Later, as the person's values become more crystallized, these also begin to shape career preferences. These three characteristics (interests, capabilities, and values) are all important components of a person's identity. Considered together, they make it easier to envision oneself in particular career fields.

The third stage is one of *realistic choices*. The person makes real decisions and takes real actions to implement career plans: whether or not to go to school, whether to seek job training, what to major in, what trial jobs to try, and so forth.

To better understand how career exploration can match interests with career possibilities, consider the example of Peg Woodard. Peg and her husband Wayne run a thriving antique business, Wheat and Chaff, in Hopkinton, New Hampshire. Peg, although trained to be a special-education teacher, spent most of her time being a home-maker in the early years of her marriage. She and Wayne lived in several locations around the world (Calgary, Winnipeg, Halifax, Montreal, Hong Kong) and began collecting antiques both for enjoyment and for investment purposes. When in Hong Kong, they started collecting small oriental pieces (porcelain and glass) from mainland China. The pieces were very rare and also easily transportable.

After they had been transferred back to Peoria, Illinois, by Wayne's company, a career-exploration opportunity occurred, although Peg did not think of it in career terms at the time. Her experiences illustrate how important chance events can be in helping a person link up general interests (collecting antiques), values (autonomy and running your own show—very important for Peg), and skills (business and organizing abilities she wasn't even aware of). As Peg tells it:

> A friend of mine was chairman of a church antique show, and they had a last-minute cancellation. She'd seen all these *things* that I'd been stashing in cupboards, and she called me and said, "I just had a cancellation. Have you ever thought of doing an antique show?" I told her, "It never even entered my mind."

> She said, "Well, do it! We're desperate, and you have so much in those cupboards that you've been talking about." So I said, "Well, let me talk to Wayne." I called her back the next day and said, "Why not? It'd be fun."

> But for all the shows we had been to, we had never paid any attention to how anyone set up a show. So, we spent the next couple of weeks going to as many shows as we could, seeing the different arrangements . . . observing what people did to really set a booth off.

> And we did that show. We went out and bought whatever was necessary. And we had—besides being successful—a wonderful time! The bug bit me."

Getting established and advancing

After the person has hit on a congenial type of work and a good fit has been established, it's time for the next career stage: getting established and becoming successful. This is the fast-growth phase of a person's career—the tender sprout grows to a sturdy plant with large leaves and abundant flowers.

Growth at this stage occurs in what we call *success cycles*. A person accepts a challenge or reaches for a goal, works at it, achieves the goal, gets recognition from others and a lot of internal satisfaction, and enjoys a huge boost in ego. This increased sense of self-esteem and confidence generates increased job involvement. The person is getting "hooked on work." This leads to setting more challenging future goals, representing higher levels of aspiration. In short, "success breeds success." This success cycle is illustrated in the accompanying diagram.

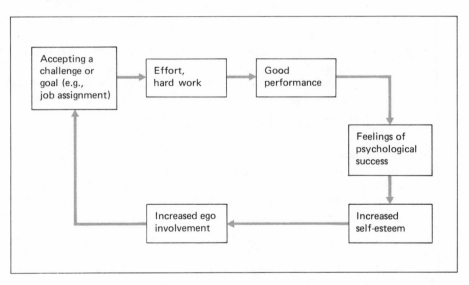

Let's follow Peg Woodard a little further into her career in antiques to see how the success cycle operates. She is still discussing her first booth in the church antique show:

Interviewer   When did you make the decision to actually go from the show, which was kind of fun and a favor, into the antique business?

Peg   Right then! After it was over, Wayne said, "How did you like it?" And I said, "I've never had so much fun. I absolutely loved it. . . . Did you enjoy it?'' He said, ''I really liked it.'' And so we decided, no matter what, whether it was frowned upon or not [there had been some feeling in the community that it might not be appropriate for an executive's wife to do antique shows], that if I really enjoyed it, the business would be under my name, but he would help me. He would help me set it up, he would help me do it. If the children's activities came into conflict, he would help me all he could.

Wayne   Well, to give you an example, she graduated from this little church show, and about five months later she was doing a show at McCormick Place in Chicago with 300 dealers.

A bit later, they made a move from Peoria to Hopkinton, where Wayne had accepted a job with a tractor dealership. They bought an old colonial house with a large barn, ideal for an antique shop. When we asked them if they'd had the shop in mind when they bought the house, their reply was immediate: ''Absolutely!''

Support from other people is also important in nurturing and developing a person's career in this fast-growth stage. In dual-career couples, the spouse or partner often is a major source of support. Peg describes Wayne's role in her career:

He always encouraged me, because I thought I was the type who would have been very happy just being a domestic person. But Wayne knew I wouldn't be happy. . . . When I think of the many women who want to do this type of thing, and their husbands absolutely keep them down, I really know how lucky I was.

Costs of success. The rapid growth stage of a career is highly rewarding, but it does present some unexpected costs. As the career growth cycle repeats itself over and over again, the person rockets to higher and higher levels of career kicks and involvement. After a while, he or she may realize that the career is becoming too consuming, has taken over too much of his or her life. At that point, the person is in imminent danger of becoming a ''workaholic'' (a problem we discuss in Chapter Eight). Success is extremely seductive. It is self-reinforcing and insatiable. In psychologist Abraham Maslow's classic model of human needs, self-actualization or growth is the only need that does not diminish as it is satisfied. For example, security or food may be extremely important if you are facing a lay-off or haven't eaten in two days, but if you are a tenured professor or have just consumed a Thanksgiving feast, these needs would probably matter little. Generally, the more you have of certain things, the less you care about them.

This is not so with success and growth. The more you get, the more you want. And you don't even realize how the other parts of your life are being cut back as you are drawn deeper and deeper into your work. The irony is, as with any effective seduction, as Duke University psychologist Roy Lewicki puts it, you do it to yourself— you're an active participant in the process.

A sobering way to view the upward, self-reinforc-ing spiral of success is to see it as an ever-deepening rut. As you sink deeper into one area of activity, it becomes harder and harder to glimpse what else is available outside that rut. And, as you put more and more time into your exciting work, your couple relationship may wither from lack of attention.

Wayne Woodard describes this dilemma in terms of both his job with a large corporation and his and Peg's antique busi-ness. Now that the antique shop is established and thriving, all is not perfect:

> I am going into a syndrome on the business such that I don't know how . . . how you slow down. [In the corporation I found] the higher you go, the busier you are, the more you travel, the more obligations, demands on your time, the more of a social list we are getting into, and I said, "How do I stop?"

> I think what's happening now is that the antique business is growing tremendously, which we're delighted about and feel blessed. But now I'm faced with the problem of getting some help. If we are going to grow any further, it is a necessity in the business. I've just modernized my shop in the refinishing area, so that it's more efficient. We have grown as far as we can possibly go and still maintain our sanity.

There is a paradox here which many couples share: we all want to be more and more successful, but we don't want to become so involved that we lose touch with the people we love. Peg goes on to describe some of the costs to the family of such high work involvement:

> My parents don't understand it, because they want us to come and visit. And I don't write as often as I used to. But they have absolutely no con-cept that from 6:00 in the morning until we go to bed at 11:00 at night Wayne and I basically are full out, every single day. And there's always something . . . something happens every day unexpectedly. We love it, we thrive on it, but we are definitely both to the point where we can't go any faster. We'll lose something in either our relationship or with. . . . Maybe we could go faster if we didn't have the children. . . .

Midcareer: growth, maintenance, or decline?

Peg and Wayne's comments express well the issues that must be faced as a person or couple makes the transition from the advancement stage to midcareer. At this point, as Peg and Wayne are painfully aware, there are three options: continued growth and exploration of new areas, a maintenance plateau, or decline.

More often than not, midcareer represents a plateau in a person's life. After the fierce strivings and achievements of earlier periods, it's time to ease off a bit from work involvement, spend more time with family and leisure activities, and work on "quality of life."

Often midcareer coincides with midlife, the forties and fifties. Douglas Hall has summarized the changes that a person experiences at this time:

- *Awareness of advancing age and death.* At forty, many people feel that "life is half over." There may be more time behind them than ahead. Time is suddenly a scarce commodity.

- *Awareness of physical aging.* Aches and pains become more frequent, physical conditioning becomes more important. There are numerous physiological changes associated with midlife, including a decline in metabolic rate, decreased energy, decreased muscle tone, a decrease in visual efficiency, hearing loss in the high-frequency range, hair loss, skin discoloration, and a weight shift downward, so the torso appears pear shaped.[1]

Depressing as these physical changes are, they are often not as troublesome as the emotional and occupational transitions the person goes through in midlife.

- *Recognition of probable success.* After fifteen or twenty years in a career, an individual has a pretty good idea of how successful he or she will be. If the level of success is not as high as originally hoped for, the person must adjust to that fact or think about changing fields. Ironically, the stress may be greatest for people who have met or exceeded their earlier goals. Great success often results in restlessness and a switch to a new area that can provide more challenging goals.

- *Reexamination of life goals.* Family and personal goals often change midlife as well. It is not unusual for people to make complete breaks with their old life-style and set off in totally new directions: a confirmed bachelor may marry and start a family or a couple married since high school may split up and vow never to be tied down again. A marriage counselor in one of our seminars shared a statement often heard among his colleagues: "Between the ages of forty and fifty, a man either changes jobs or changes wives." Of course, one result of the reexamination of life goals could well be a strengthened commitment to one's present goals and life-style.

- *Change in family relationships.* At this stage, one's children are probably teenagers, perhaps rebellious ones. The prince charming or sweet young thing pictured in the wedding album is now barely recognizable as one's spouse. People's needs and interests change as they grow, so it's not surprising that, over the course of twenty years, some partners simply grow in different directions. Women's attitudes about family and work have changed dramatically, as have sex roles, both male and female. All of these changes may lead to greater stress in the home.

- *Change in work relationships.* The person in midcareer is no longer the promising "up-and-comer." That close peer group of buddies who enjoyed poking fun at the boss dispersed long ago. Now, you are the boss! It's you that those younger people are

"I peaked too soon."

Reprinted by permission of G.P. Putnam's Sons from *Husbands, Wives and Live-Togethers* by William Hamilton, copyright © 1976 by William Hamilton.

criticizing and poking fun at. It's your job they're shooting for. Psychologist Harry Levinson describes this as the "King of the Hill Syndrome," the feeling that you have successfully made it to the heights and now have to fight off all the younger contenders for your position.[2] One morning on the NBC "Today" program, in an interview with the current Miss America, Jane Pauley asked the beauty queen what her career goals were. "I'd like your job," was the prompt response.

- *Growing sense of obsolescence.* With technological changes coming at such an accelerated rate, it is difficult to keep current in most technical fields. One oft-quoted statistic is that the half-life of an engineer (the time it takes for half of what she or he has learned to become obsolete) is about five years. To make matters worse, as people advance in their careers, they are often "rewarded" with administrative duties, which makes it even more difficult for them to maintain technical expertise.

- *Less mobility in the job market and increased fears over job security.* Most organizations prefer to hire younger people rather than older ones. Young people cost less (probably half or one-third of what a more experienced person's salary would be), they are more easily indoctrinated into the company's way of operating, and their future is ahead of them. At times, organizations will opt for more experienced, mature people, but often they prefer to "grow their own" executive and professional talent through a personnel policy of promotion from within. Therefore, for the first time, the person in midcareer may see evidence of decreased mobility: fewer "feelers" from other firms, comments about being too high priced or too senior for a particular job, and so on. This, in turn, breeds concern about the security of one's current position ("Where else could I go?").

In summary, then, midcareer is often a time for slowing down, leveling off, reconsidering one's direction, examining deeper "meaning-of-life" issues, and possibly setting off in a new direction. Research has shown that the differences between people (in abilities, attitudes, behaviors, etc.) tend to be greater in midlife than at any other point in the life cycle. As we noted earlier, there are three forks in the road at this point: continued growth, a maintenence plateau, or early decline.

Dr. Robert Morrison, of the Navy Personnel Research and Development Center in San Diego, has found that one of the main differences between people who continue to be adaptive and growing at midcareer and those who don't is the amount of career exploration they do.[3] This may seem surprising, since exploration is supposed to take place at an earlier career stage. However, growth requires constant exploration of new possibilities. If you become too established, too settled, and too satisfied with the way you're doing things now, the world might just pass you by.

Ray Kroc, the founder of McDonald's, is fond of saying, "As long as you're green, you're growing. As soon as you're ripe, you rot." If you're constantly exploring, you'll be trying things for the first time; you may feel a bit unsure of yourself and green, but you'll always be at the growing edge of your capabilities.

Many good books about midcareer and midlife processes are available. Some of the best are Peter Chew's *The Inner World of the Middle-Aged Man*, Daniel Levinson's *The Seasons of a Man's Life*, Roger Gould's *Transformations*, and Gail Sheehy's *Passages*. Many of these authors explore the transition and change involved in moving from early adulthood into midlife. However, we see midlife rather differently: for many people, midlife is a time of *getting back in touch* with important interests and needs that had to be put aside during early adulthood. Perhaps the person had always dreamed of being a writer, but ended up in public relations—that's where the jobs were and there were three kids to feed. Perhaps the person could never afford to finish college. Perhaps the couple couldn't live in the part of the country they loved, because the career opportunities just weren't there.

For various reasons, during the journey toward midlife and midcareer, one's activities and life-style can gradually drift away from the interests and loves of earlier years. At some point, the shift is likely to become distressing. If certain earlier constraints (such as financial worries) have been eliminated, the person can get reconnected with what Yale psychologist Daniel Levinson calls "the dream," one's youthful vision of the future.[4] So, in many ways, the midlife period may resemble a midcourse correction in flight, a change that appears to be a radical shift but is actually a getting back on track in pursuit of one's original target. Midlife exploration may be a way of linking up past dreams with future plans. T. S. Eliot expresses it well:

> We shall not cease from exploration,
> And the end of all our exploring,
> Will be to arrive where we started,
> And know the place for the first time.[5]

Late career: disengagement

The final stage of a career is disengagement. The most frequent end point is retirement, and the transition requires a shift in involvement from work concerns to postretirement activities: perhaps greater involvement with the family, leisure activities, or community organizations. Sometimes the person seeks a new job (often called a "second career," although it's actually just a new phase of the person's ongoing lifetime career).

Since work identity is such an essential aspect of one's overall identity, retirement can be a tremendously stressful step, a wrenching away of an integral part of one's self. Although we usually associate retirement with a life of leisure, the emotional effort expended in the transition can be staggering. Since activity is so important to keeping the body in shape, the sudden inactivity of retirement may lead to health problems, perhaps fatal ones.

Retirement can, of course, be a welcome transition, a time to leave job frustrations behind and devote attention to hobbies, travel, recreation, and family. An expert on vocational psychology explains:

> Retirement means different things to people. It may mean unwelcome inactivity, or freedom to do things one has not had time to do, or escape from pressures that are too great. Retirement requires changing the habits and daily routines of a lifetime, changing a self-concept which has been relatively stable over a long period of years, and changing a role which has been played for more than a generation.[6]

The inactivity and forced togetherness of husband and wife after retirement can present a problem for both. Unless they have carefully planned retirement activities, they may enter into a period of stagnation: they have no need to get up at a certain time, no place to go, and nothing in particular to do. This inactivity, after a lifetime of work, can be devastating and depressing.

To disengage from a work role successfully, a person needs to start engaging in more nonwork activities, gradually building involvement and interest in them. Some organizations help people adjust slowly to retirement by increasing their vacations, perhaps by one week per year when the person reaches a certain age, say fifty-five or sixty. Additionally, work assignments may be changed. Persons nearing retirement age may be given less stressful roles, preferably positions that make full use of their accumulated experience and wisdom. Retirement need not be the end of the line. With planning and forethought, it can be one of the most active and personally fulfilling times of life.

Family Stages

Adults have a harder time marking passages or transitions in their lives than do children. For a child, development is paced nicely by age and childhood stepping stones (such as the start of grade school; confirmation, bar mitzvah, or first communion; graduations; driving age; drinking age; voting age). Not as many of these nicely defined turning points exist for adults. Beyond marriage, the birth of the first child, and perhaps a divorce, there are very few "firsts" left in one's life until retirement.

So, how do adults pace the development of their lives? How do they mark time? Many of us use the development of our children. We rely on their age-linked signposts to gauge our own progress through adulthood. We measure our own life cycles in terms of the life cycles of our children and the family. Some sociologists have argued that a person's social behavior is probably related more to his stage in the family life cycle than to his age. As one observer noted: "To be the father of a teen-age daughter elicits certain behavior patterns, whether the father be thirty or seventy years of age."[7]

Sociologist Helena Lopata has developed a model for identifying family stages based on the ages and number of children.[8] They are as follows.

Stage 1: The couple. This stage begins at marriage and ends with the birth of the first child. Couples (married and unmarried) without children would remain in this stage throughout the course of the relationship. Conflicts and home-related pressures are low, since neither partner has a parent role to perform. Working couples probably have two major roles at this point: spouse (or partner) and career. Some other role, such as leisure, son or daughter, or friend, may also be important, but would rarely be as demanding or time consuming a role as that of parent. Perhaps as a result of this relatively low pressure and conflict, satisfaction and happiness are higher, on the average, during the couple stage than at any point later in the family life cycle.

Stage 2: Expanding circle. This stage starts when the first child is born and ends with the birth of a second child. Each partner now has an additional role: parent. In our experience, this transition into parenthood is one of the greatest adjustments a dual-career couple has to make; we discuss it in more detail in Chapter 6. In stage 1, both partners have a great deal of autonomy. They can be away from home as much as they please, either together or individually. At home, they can work, be together, or relax without interruption. With the birth of a child, the couple suddenly becomes much more interdependent. Simple matters like leaving the house, whether to go to work or to buy a newspaper, require advance planning and cooperation. Out-of-town travel together is very difficult once the child passes out of the sleepy newborn stage. Our four-hour weekend trips from Connecticut to New Hampshire with a year-old child crying nonstop (while our drive was anything but) seemed infinitely longer than a two-day drive from Chicago to New Hampshire with a ten-year-old and an eight-year-old. Our research shows that conflict and home pressures rise dramatically during this stage, while satisfaction and happiness drop correspondingly.

Stage 3: Peak stage. When there are two or more preschool children in the family, the family has reached the peak stage. As the name implies, pressures and responsibilities rise dramatically here, and the woman often bears the brunt of this. Rarely is she able to spare even a few minutes for herself. The only thing more demanding than a young child is two of them. Actually, the laws of mathematics are defied here, as one child plus one child equals three things to deal with: the first child, the second child, and the interaction between the two.

This is the point at which women tend to drop out of the work force. In one study, the percentages of married women who worked full time versus being full-time housewives looked like this:[9]

	Stage 1: Couple	Stage 2: Expanding	Stage 3: Peak	Stage 4: Full House	Stage 5: Shrinking
Full-time housewives (%)	17	53	68	41	27
Full-time employees (%)	76	25	2	21	27

Note that there is a huge drop in the proportion of women who work full time in stage 2, and an additional drop to near zero (2 percent) in the peak stage. (The percentage of full-time housewives is at a maximum here.) The great irony is that married women leave the work force precisely at the time they have acquired years of experience and are becoming most valuable to their employers. With more flexible employment policies, it may not be necessary for so many women to put aside their careers. Happiness seems to pick up a bit during this time.

Stage 4: Full house. This stage begins when the youngest child enters school and ends when the oldest child leaves home. Time pressures are great here, for while home demands are still considerable (children are beginning to participate in activities that call for parental involvement), many women make the decision to return to work. Satisfaction and happiness are at their lowest point. Conflicts begin to grow.

Stage 5: Shrinking circle. In this stage, the family begins to grow smaller. It begins when the first child leaves home and ends when the last one departs. This is an important transitional period, as both partners begin to define their identities less as parents and more as independent people or a couple. More women are employed during this time, and conflict is still rising. However, satisfaction almost returns to its higher stage 1 level. The children are almost adults, they are relatively self-sufficient, and they may be relating with their parents as friends rather than adversaries. Probably the most difficult aspect of this stage is simply the sadness of seeing the children leave the nest.

Stage 6: Empty nest. This is the final stage in the family cycle. All the children have left home and the parents return to the solitude of stage 1. They now have more leisure time together and may welcome the opportunity to plan a new phase of their lives. Stage 6 shares some of the psychological characteristics of stage 1; the cycle is thus complete. The two major issues at this time are health and the need to build a new relationship in which children and work are less central.

When we examined our data in terms of factors that caused satisfaction or dissatisfaction, we found certain patterns characteristic of different stages. Childless couples in stage 1 felt tension between home (spouse) and work. New parents, couples in stage 2, were not suffering from role conflict (either home or work) but rather from time pressure and role overload (too many roles, with the new parent role added). As the children grew older (stages 3 and up), work and time pressures were no longer sources of dissatisfaction, but home pressures were.

As we have seen, working couples have two specific cycles in their lives: the stages in their careers and the phases in the family cycle. However, neither of these cycles is independent of the other. How do career cycles and family cycles interact? How does the woman's career interact with the man's? Let's consider some of the most common combinations of career stages and family stages.

Matching Career and Family Stages[10]

In the beginning

Let's look first at one of the largest groups of two-career couples: young people starting off their careers and their relationships simultaneously. Generally, they share the following characteristics:

- *Similar career demands.* For both partners, the need to develop skills and contacts and gain broad work experience means travelling, relocations, long hours, and a high degree of job involvement. For each, the job is top priority. These responsibilities and demands often lead to conflict.

- *Conflicting career choices.* The best opportunity for each, in terms of advancing their respective careers, may mean moving in different directions geographically.

- *Intense commitment to career.* Both partners usually have a strong drive to succeed. Because of this, they understand and empathize with the other's commitment to career. This doesn't lessen the intensity of their own commitment, however.

- *Lack of preparedness.* Most couples have little information about managing two careers or about what lies ahead if they plan to have a family. Many have no plans or vague plans, and few have thought through what they will do if faced with a conflict, a crisis, or a baby.

- *No problem-solving skills.* For many couples, the conflict over a first job or relocation is their first experience in working on problems together. Their problem-solving skills may be limited and their outlooks rigid; often they perceive the situation in terms of "my career versus yours."

- *Fear of the organization.* Many couples are afraid to discuss their problems with a boss or superior in the firm for fear it will reflect negatively on their career commitment. They tend to see company policies as rigid (whether or not they actually are) and to accept corporate alternatives as "givens" without testing their assumptions.

- *Personal flexibility.* When pushed, most young couples seem willing to explore nontraditional alternatives for managing a family or marriage. Living apart, long-distance commuting, taking turns, and so on, are viewed as viable, if not always desirable, ways of taking care of both partners' needs over time.

Profile I. Anne and Mark never thought much about getting a job. The key to a successful career seemed to be getting an M.B.A. After a year into their program at Northwestern, they decided to get married—and promptly panicked! Alone, each knew he or she had tremendous potential on the job market and could pick the best offer from among many. As a couple, they wondered if they would be a liability to each other and to a company. They dreaded facing corporate recruiters and wondered if they would ever find jobs together. They also worried about how much competition they would feel.

Anne and Mark were not alone. When they realized that other couples in the program were equally concerned and unprepared, they organized a problem-solving session and brainstormed a number of practical ideas. Since Anne's major was more specialized and Mark's (accounting) gave him great mobility, their strategy was to go where her opportunities were the best, knowing that he would be able to locate almost anywhere. They eventually had several good options to choose from and are now off to a good start with major companies.

Profile II. Bob and Barbara brought us a different problem. After finishing their degrees, both landed jobs with firms headquartered in the Southwest—he in a management training program with an oil company, she in a staff position in the personnel department of a large national service organization. They have been in their jobs for a year. Today, Barbara is pregnant and Bob faces the prospect of a field assignment lasting at least a year. "Barb plans to continue her career," he told us. "Her career is very important to her. It's important to me. She shouldn't *have* to give it up."

Barb's chances to advance in her company are good if she stays in the city they live in now, but Bob knows his advancement is tied to moving through a variety of assignments in different locations. Yet he and Barb had not planned how they would handle this. He had not talked to anyone in his company about the problem, since he was worried that his concern about their two careers would be interpreted as a lack of personal ambition and an unwillingness to make sacrifices for his own career.

Midlife

What about the couple at midlife? Its crises are no less acute, just different. What are the typical traits of the midcareer couple? Our interviews with midcareer couples have helped us to pinpoint the following characteristics:

- *Career versus family conflicts.* In most cases, there are more than two people to think about. A spouse's career may be established beyond the point of mobility and relocation is viewed as traumatic.

- *Alternative career paths viewed as viable.* Midcareer couples are more likely to ignore the typical career-path alternatives where they conflict, and to view saying "no" or forgoing one's own needs as legitimate. The employer's expectations are not always central; the family's needs are.

- *Clear couple and family goals and priorities.* Couples seem to have developed a sense of what is important to them in life and what isn't. Their goals have crystallized, and factors such as geographical location may carry more weight than salary. Decisions and plans are made within the parameters of family/couple goals rather than in terms of individual opportunities.

- *Commitment to the unit.* Couples at this point seem to view themselves as a unit or a family. Their careers are no longer individual pursuits but are seen as a "package"—a collective, interactive arrangement. Commitment to career alone has been superseded by commitment to the family.

- *Better prepared to plan and cope.* Couples at midcareer have more experience in solving problems, planning together, and making decisions. They also possess more information about themselves, their values, their needs, their organizations, and their career options in general. They usually have fairly well-developed coping mechanisms and ways of handling conflicts.

- *Less fear of company or employer.* They are likely to share career concerns with their employers and are less hesitant to approach superiors at work to find a solution. They feel established in their jobs and do not see their personal or family career conflicts as a reflection on them as valuable employees.

- *Acceptance of family as "given," career as flexible.* Career constraints are now viewed as manageable (perhaps because the partners are more willing to compromise). Children and established-spouse career needs are often viewed as fixed. Thus, at midcareer, personal flexibility seems to decrease while career-decision flexibility increases. People are more willing to compromise themselves and their careers, less willing to compromise their family.

At midlife, more combinations of family and career stages are possible. This, in turn, creates more possibilities for conflict. For Jerry and Carmen, described below, there was a conflict between his established and her delayed career needs. There can also be a conflict when both spouses have established careers and a family to cope with, as we see in profile IV.

Profile III. Jerry and Carmen decided to follow his career opportunities, since his degree placed him in a visible, high-demand position. After a couple of moves, during which Carmen took jobs out of her field, they had a baby and settled into a city they both loved. He was a rising young star in his firm, but she was still taking on odd jobs. When the organization Jerry had left offered both of them jobs in their fields, his present employer panicked. Even though Jerry wanted to stay where he was, the job offer had a new twist: spouse bargaining. Turning down the offer would mean turning off his wife's chances to pursue at last a career in her field. According to Jerry, it was "Carmen's turn."

Unlike the couples described above, however, Jerry and Carmen went to his employer with the problem, a clear set of goals, and an acceptable solution: helping Carmen to find a position in the area. Jerry's employer, anxious to keep him in the firm, was relieved to be asked to help—and did. He contacted several local organizations and put Carmen in touch with employers who were able to use her skills on a part-time basis. In the end, Carmen had two local offers and the couple stayed. Interviewing them later, we found that Carmen felt an increased loyalty to Jerry's employer because of his efforts.

Profile IV. For Denise and John the problem was different. As assistant regional commissioner of a government bureau, she was comfortably settled with three children and a successful husband. But their career problems, according to her, went "way back." He had left a job in one location to join her and get married, then went back to school. Along the way, she had turned down offers in the auto industry as well as a commissioner's job because the location wouldn't offer John much opportunity in his field. As Denise put it, "If the place had no opportunities for him, I wouldn't even consider it." Meanwhile, he regularly turned down jobs in small towns that wouldn't be near the large cities that might offer her a government transfer. When he returned to school again to work on an M.B.A., he jokingly told her, "Now you're grounded for two years."

A year later she was approached about a commissionership in Washington, D.C. They agreed that she should pursue the opportunity and she eventually got the offer. John had told his wife that he would be willing to stay to finish his program and then join her later. When she got the offer, "He went into a tailspin. He thought it was the end of the marriage—that I'd get all caught up in my job in Washington and lose touch with the family." Denise turned down the Washington job. Now that John has finished his M.B.A., he is looking for a new position and Denise has again responded to opportunities elsewhere. She laughed at this point in the interview. "This time . . . whoever gets there first, wins."

Profile V. In midlife a couple must also sometimes consider the "careers" of their children. Ron's family problem was not two careers but several. When presented with the opportunity to move up and back to the Detroit headquarters of his auto firm, he turned the offer down. Not only was his wife happily settled, but his two remaining children at home were pursuing successful careers at local schools. One, a high-school student, was the local drama star at a school with one of the finest theatre programs in the country. Rather than sacrifice his family's careers, he compromised his own. Two years later, the company came back with the same offer. By this time, his son was graduating and going to college. Ron and his wife were ready to accept the move and, as she put it, "become corporate gypsies one more time."

For couples like these, midcareer also means midlife. It is a time when family concerns take priority over one's own career. Corporations find themselves on a collision course, running head on into the established needs of spouses and children.

In the midlife examples we have looked at thus far, all of the couples have had viable career options backed by a strong relationship. This is frequently not the case, however. Take Luis and Marge, for example, a couple faced with a conflict between his midcareer crisis and her early-career needs.

Profile VI. After many years in Washington, Luis found himself out of a job. Marge, on the other hand, had finally established herself as a successful photographer with a strong local following. For Luis, the options were elsewhere. He accepted a position in the South, planning for Marge and the children to follow if it worked out. The job didn't turn out to be what he had expected, and he realized as well that local living arrangements wouldn't be acceptable for his family. He quit.

When we met Luis, he was still unemployed and the couple was trying to figure out what he should do and where his many years of service in the government would be marketable. They had agreed that a large eastern city was what they wanted. For Luis, now in his forties, the options were not many. Marge, on the other hand, felt that if she was going to have a career, it was now or never.

Luis is typical of many men faced with the necessity or desire to change jobs, career fields, or companies. Often we find that the husband's midcareer crisis coincides with the wife's reentry into the labor market. Like the early-career couples, they must juggle competing career-path needs. In most cases, however, the couple is characterized by years of "giving" on the part of the wife. Marge, for example, had willingly moved all over the world in the early days of Luis's career.

Now liberated from caring for children and more fully aware of their own needs, many women are unwilling to compromise—one more time. Thus we find couples on the verge of a divorce after twenty years of marriage when faced with the prospect of managing two careers for the first time at midlife. Their old relationship, built around meeting the needs of the husband's career, cannot accommodate the wife's needs as well. She either gives up on the marriage, gives up on her needs, or bows out as "the little woman behind the successful man."

One wife we know sent printed announcements to the guests who would be attending an annual reception given by her husband. The purpose? To tell them that after years of standing at his side in the receiving line she would *not* be there this year. She was proud to announce that they were getting a divorce and that she didn't have to hostess one more reception for *his* business.

While this may seem extreme, it highlights just one of the changes working women have initiated: social entertaining is down, particularly at home, while pitching in to share home tasks is on the rise. Men who used to excuse themselves from a business meeting to race to a community fund-raising dinner are now leaving the office in time to cook dinner.

For some couples, the crisis arises because the husband cannot adapt to his wife's new work role. This was the case with Bill and Karen. As part of a blue-collar family, she found that her promotion to supervisor in a manufacturing plant was more than her husband could take. He didn't mind the fact that she could run and repair machines weighing several tons. It was when his wife had to go back to the plant at odd hours to deal with a problem or called to say she was going out for a beer with the other supervisors that their marriage faced a crisis—and, ultimately, a divorce. As some companies are finding, women are willing and eager to accept nontraditional roles; their husbands, however, are not equally pleased.

Another issue that can generate conflict in the relationship between a person in midcareer and one in early career arises from their different locations on the career trajectory: one is still in the take-off (advancement) stage while the other has begun to level off (maintenance) in terms of work effort and involvement. Most frequently to date, the man is at the leveling-off point and the woman is still taking off. She is likely to be experiencing the "highs" of the psychological success spiral and is becoming more and more involved in work as her successes mount. He, on the other hand, may have already experienced many successes and is ready to spend more time in leisure and recreational pursuits. In short, the conflict is between her need to be turned on by work and his need to have fun off the job. He wants her to play, but she is having her fun at work. He establishes boundaries between work and leisure—no work at home—and she loves to putter on work after hours.

An example of a couple experiencing this conflict is Shelly Kleinman and Fran Gordon, who now work together as executive producer and business manager, respectively, of the California Actors Theater in Los Gatos, California. We introduced Shelly and Fran to you in Chapter One. Shelly has been in the theater business for many years, is now well established, and works very long hours, but he leaves his work at the office at the end of the day. Fran has only been in the theater business for a few years, has been very successful, and is clearly turned on.

Fran	[Working hard] seems to be more of a problem now, because I bring a lot of work home, and he says "Why don't you leave it alone?" That just drives him nuts.
Shelly	I don't leave here very often, but when I do leave here, I don't take *anything* with me.
Fran	And I usually wind up taking the books.
Shelly	Right, I go home, and when I do go home, I want to putter in the yard, or I want to go sailing, or I want to watch television, or I want to go to a movie. I don't want to do anything [on work] at all. I mean, I don't want to come home and read a script. I don't want to do *any work*.

Interviewer	Is that an orientation you've had all your life . . . wanting to just leave work when you leave work, or is that something that sort of evolved?
Shelly	It's evolved. Because in my first years . . .
Fran	You used to be like me!

The problems for the established spouse with a highly involved early-career spouse can be mitigated by having a "turned-on" spouse. The energy from his or her excitement can spill over into other areas of life, making the person a turned-on parent and lover as well.

In Conclusion

Let's summarize this chapter with some hypotheses we have developed about different combinations of stages for dual-career couples.

• *Couples will be more likely to make family sacrifices in early career than in later stages. Family factors may take priority in midcareer.* This hypothesis is based on the idea that the partners are highly work involved early in their careers and may be more willing to delay family satisfactions at this point. However, after they have become more established, they are less willing to put off family gratifications and they have more time and career security to invest in family activities.

• *Conflict between career and family will be:*
a) Moderate (or latent) in early career. This is when work is granted primacy and family pressures are minimized.
b) Highest in midcareer. At this point, the career is established and the family sees no need for the person to continue to sacrifice family for work. Family role pressures increase at this stage, but the person may have become so highly involved in work that it's difficult to back off.
c) Lowest in late career. One way or another the severe conflicts of midcareer will have to be reduced; the relationship cannot stand them for too long. (If they are not resolved, the couple may split.) A clear priority ranking is established and a resolution is achieved.

• *Two careers are more likely to be compatible if one partner ranks career number one and the other ranks family number one (accommodators), or if both rank family number one (allies), than if both partners give career top priority.* It is generally difficult for both partners to be highly career involved. However, if there are no children (and therefore less of a family role), or if some of the qualities covered in the following hypotheses are present, this may present less of a problem.

• *Two careers are more likely to be compatible if both partners are in similar fields.* We get some arguments on this one. Some people feel that being in similar fields breeds competition. However, we have found that being in the same area or related areas increases each partner's understanding of the pressures and responsibilities the other is feeling. By knowing the partner's work, it is easy to provide support and show commitment to the other's career.

• *Two careers are more likely to be compatible if there are no children.* This is a critical factor in managing two careers. Two roles (career and spouse) can be fairly easily juggled. It is the introduction of the third role—parent—that reduces independence and flexibility and forces interdependence and role negotiation. Data comparing the couple stage and the expanding-circle stage support this idea.

• *Two careers are more likely to be compatible if they are in different stages than if they are in the same stage.* We have also had many arguments from friends and colleagues on this one. Some people point out that being at the same career stage makes one more understanding of a partner's needs and more supportive. Perhaps. But we believe that being at the same stage increases competition, especially for people in the exploration and establishment stages. Nothing seems more stressful than the plight of M.B.A.-candidate couples who are both interviewing for jobs at the same time. It is very difficult for one partner, especially the man, to be genuinely excited and supportive when he himself has had no offers and his partner has had five. Similarly, when both are in the highly involving and competitive establishment/advancement stage, it's difficult not to draw comparisons. One partner is bound to be more successful than the other, and this is very likely to cause some strained feelings.

On the other hand, an especially compatible combination would be a secure, well-established individual and a person just exploring or getting established. The more advanced partner can support the beginner and derive vicarious pleasure from his or her success without feeling threatened by it.

• *Two careers are likely to be compatible when the two jobs are protean and allow autonomy and flexibility.* The more freedom and flexibility partners have, the more they can adjust career demands to be compatible with family needs. If both jobs are nine-to-five, five days a week, with no options to shift one's hours, take work home, or perhaps take a child to work, conflicts between home and work are likely to arise.

• *Two careers are more likely to be compatible if the partners are mutually supportive, skilled at problem solving, and committed to each other's career.* Given the strains inherent in a two-career relationship, the more the partners can help each other solve problems, the more effective they will be. The more support they provide, the more problem-solving assistance they can give. And the more committed they are to each other's career, the more support they will give.

Support and commitment—these are two crucial factors in both loving and working, and in the conflicts between the two. In the next chapter we examine the nature of conflict for the two-career couple and suggest some skills they can use to minimize or resolve such clashes.

CHAPTER THREE

IN CONTROL
OF CONFLICT

The two-career couple is a fairly recent phenomenon that reflects shifting personal values
in our society and new ways of combining work
and relationships. In Chapters One and Two, we looked at the characteristics of two-career couples and their varying degrees of involvement
in work and other life roles. We tried to show how career and family
stages interact, often producing stress. A common theme throughout has
been the basic need for people to take control, to self-direct their
careers and personal relationships. Out of this need to control, conflict
is bound to arise.

What causes conflict for most couples? How can
they deal with it? To control conflict, we must first understand what
underlies it. To manage it, we need to identify its sources and symptoms. In this chapter, we begin by describing eight basic issues that
every couple must face, issues that often generate conflict. These
issues are similar to, and in fact parallel, growth stages for the individual. They are not isolated conflicts. Rather, they are confrontations
that are rarely resolved once and for all. They emerge, recur, and
often return again and again.

In the second part of the chapter we consider a
very basic problem for the two-career couple: role conflicts and how to
manage them. As our identities and roles expand in number, we inevit-
ably must deal with conflicting demands and questions of priority. How

can we manage the interaction between our multiple roles—spouse, worker, parent, and so on? And, how about the people—partners, co-workers, or children—who play integral or peripheral roles in these conflicts? To help you get started, we have provided a Role Inventory and some ways of assessing your techniques for dealing with role conflicts.

Finally, we turn to day-to-day problems of conflict resolution through decision making and problem solving. Here we offer some suggestions for changing your decision style from win/lose to win/win.

Confronting Ourselves

The capacity to engage in work as well as relationships is the ultimate accomplishment of the mature adult. To achieve this capability is the quest of the individual. To achieve it *together* is the quest of the two-career couple.

Achieving anything in tandem is not easy. Not only must each partner resolve his or her own developmental issues, but together they must resolve theirs as a couple. Thus, there are three quests going on, and they interact in important ways to force, facilitate, and sometimes hinder growth. Ultimately, our capacity to love and work and remain together depends on our capacity to confront ourselves.

One of the greatest contributions to our understanding of human development has been Erik Erikson's book, *Childhood and Society*. In his chapter "The Eight Ages of Man," Erikson describes eight stages through which a person progresses. Each stage is characterized by certain conflicts, and each must be resolved in order for the person to progress to and through the next developmental stage.

Whether people ever fully resolve these developmental conflicts is questionable. What seems more likely (or "normal") is that people resolve them sufficiently to be able to move on and cope with new, emerging conflicts. The growing body of literature and research on midlife crises among men seems to support this notion. Often, midlife conflicts are a return to former issues that were never totally resolved.

In our studies we have been struck with the fact that many of the issues that couples work through parallel certain of Erikson's stages. The process of becoming a mature, two-career couple seems to force people to recycle their conflicts, to "[re-solve them] in order to remain psychologically alive."[1] Working through *couple* issues means first going back to resolve *individual* issues, of either one or both partners. To better understand this, let's look at the eight couple issues in detail to see how the partners' earlier experiences play into their resolution.

Trust

Trust is one of the most basic elements in human development. It is also the essential foundation for an effective two-career marriage. People who do not learn to trust others can never fully trust themselves; partners who do not trust and have the trust of each other are no different.

Basic trust develops from the support of others. In a couple, the most significant other is our partner. Thus, confidence in the viability and strength of a relationship is built through mutual support. Both partners must share the basic assumption that each will pursue a career within the context of the marriage or relationship.

Women have been valuing and supporting men as both husband and provider for centuries; it's nothing new for them. But, for many men, supporting one's wife in the dual role of wife and career person is something that has to be learned.

Women are especially in need of support from their partners when combining career and family roles. Although they have learned to trust themselves as women, mothers, or spouses, they often have not developed this confidence in the area of career. And, unless they have had very good role models, they are likely to doubt their ability to juggle multiple roles. Increasing evidence suggests that girls do not develop the same feelings of success through work roles that boys do. Girls are reinforced for traditional female roles—caring for, nurturing, and looking after others. They develop their identities through relationships rather than through objective accomplishments. Even the woman who believes herself capable of being a successful career person may wonder what effect her success will have on her marriage and her spouse.

Trust implies that your spouse will love and continue to love you even if you change roles. A husband needs the security of his wife's trust, for example, if he decides to quit his job and pour all his efforts into a fledgling business. But again, it is most often the wife who is in need of this support.

For partners, but perhaps especially for women, having the love of the other builds the basic sense of trust necessary to develop a mature partnership. The ability to provide this kind of love is, to some degree, a measure of one's own sense of trust and security. If you don't feel good about yourself, it's extremely difficult to support and encourage another person's search for identity and inner strength.

Many of the conflicts we find in two-career couples are simply reflections of this lack of basic security. Women who feel threatened by their husbands' careers are often insecure about the relationship; the career, in effect, becomes "the other woman," a dangerous rival. They fear that, eventually, their marriage must give way to the husband's marriage to his organization or profession.

Men who are threatened by a wife's career are also usually insecure about their own. The relationship between husband and wife here is analogous to many other types of relationships that demand mutual support and reciprocity. Within organizations, for example, we find that those middle-level managers who are most threatened by "young turks" are those who feel least secure and successful themselves. People who have succeeded (relatively speaking) and feel secure are most likely to be willing and able to help other people on the way up.

Success alone, however, does not guarantee security. If a person does not have a sense of personal worth, if he or she grew up feeling that self-esteem was contingent only on accomplishments, then the person will probably never feel secure, regardless of objective success.

Control

Just as each person must develop a sense of individual autonomy, couples, too, must wrestle with the question of control. Not only does each partner need some degree of autonomy, but the couple must deal with the issue of its autonomy in the larger social environment. This encompasses relationships with families, friends, and employers.

As Erikson states, learning to be your own person (or your own couple) is accompanied by feelings of shame and doubt. And it is these feelings, perhaps, that present the most difficulty. Working wives are different from traditional, homemaker wives. And role-sharing husbands are a departure from traditional male models as well. In both cases, socially acceptable norms are being flaunted. Who wouldn't experience some degree of shame or doubt in a society where partners who share work, home, and parent roles have been labeled "deviant" or "odd"?

For women, the issue again revolves around socialization as a female. In our society, most women have grown up identifying with traditional female roles rather than nontraditional work roles or work *and* family roles. Resolving the issue of control and autonomy as an adult female means encountering again and reevaluating the validity of all the things one has been taught to do or told one "ought" to be doing. Before a couple can achieve autonomy, the woman first must come to terms with her own psychological feelings of role conflict or ambivalence, the residue of earlier development. She must recognize that she can exercise discretion and control in her life, her work, and her family relationships.

To resolve the conflict, many women either achieve through family and social relationships only (the traditional route) or try to do everything (the "supermom" phenomenon). Neither solution is really satisfactory. Giving up the desire to pursue a career is self-denial of satisfaction and growth; it is opting for ambivalence. Trying to do everything well is virtually impossible and, ultimately, physically exhausting.

The only satisfactory solution is for both men and women to reform their notions of control, assertion, and autonomy—with respect to each other and to their outside environment. For a woman, the basic issue is asserting her right to pursue a career, to achieve outside the home, and to share control within the home rather than playing a passive or dependent role. For a man, the issue is learning that being in control, maintaining a "macho" image, and having the superior position in a relationship are not valid measures of maleness.

But it doesn't end here. The next step is to consider the relationship of the couple to the outside world. Together, they often experience the conflict between what a traditional marriage should be like and what they are trying to make theirs become.

Women are socialized to be; men, to do. In a mature two-career-couple relationship, both partners have equal access to being and doing at home and at work. In fact, it is essential that both share in the being and the doing tasks associated with a marriage. Accomplishing this sometimes involves communicating to the outside world that you have opted for a "different" arrangement.

Sometimes it is the neighbors, or the in-laws, who need convincing that, even though *she* makes more money and *he* does the laundry, a stable marriage is not an impossibility. Frequently it is the employer who is in for a surprise: the assumption that a man or woman will unquestioningly pick up and leave one city for another, or take a promotion with longer hours or more responsibility, is no longer necessarily a valid one.

In encounters with skeptical or critical observers, the couple is often made to feel that being different, being autonomous, and doing their "own thing" may be less good, less right, or less successful than the traditional alternative. Thus, it is not surprising that working women, especially working wives and mothers, seek out others in the same situation for support and reassurance. And working couples, rather than flocking to the haven of suburbia, are buying homes and condominiums in neighborhoods populated by other career couples. They wisely seek out others who share their problems and can reinforce, rather than undermine, their attempts to pursue a self-styled, nontraditional life together.

Parting with tradition: desocializing

Choosing to combine work and family roles and to grow away from the traditional marital roles involves shedding old values and adopting new ones. This is easier to talk about than to do. Just as children experiment with roles during their stage of "initiative," when they learn to take risks and "stick their necks out," adults in two-career couples have to be rather bold and adventurous. Often, they experience the sense of guilt that accompanies childhood role experimentation. In trying on some of the role attributes traditionally reserved for the opposite sex, many men and women experience a sense of "selling out" or "copping out."

The problem is often exacerbated by the fact that our only reference group may be people who strongly uphold the old values. Or, we may look to those who instilled those values—the people (usually parents) with whom we shared and revered them—only to experience disapproval and more guilt. Women who combine the female, career, and family roles are often extremely threatening to those who combine only female and family or female and work roles. And, when you threaten a person, he or she will often strike out. Guilt is a strong and effective weapon.

The experience for men is often no different. The man who chooses a life-style that incorporates traditional female roles and who refuses to put in an eighty-hour week is telling his colleagues that he has found something better and more satisfying. And they may suspect, if not know, that he is right. But to say so is admitting to being a damn fool. Consciously or unconsciously, they build up the value of their chosen roles, even if it means eighty hours a week, and denigrate any departures from the norm.

To whom do people turn for reinforcement in their efforts to shed their old socialization and values while developing new ones? To others like themselves? Unfortunately, many couples may be too isolated to do so.

Susan A. Darley describes the problem of reference groups among women, but her point is equally applicable to men.[2] People who combine both work and family roles are caught between two reference groups that have conflicting values and standards for self-appraisal: the traditional worker reference group and the traditional family reference group. Success according to one implies failure according to the other. Thus, if a woman compares herself with wives and mothers, she is less than perfect—too much of her life is directed toward work. But, if she compares herself with women who pursue careers only, she again falls short—she has set aside time and priorities for her family and her spouse, so she can't *really* be serious about her career.

The same holds true for men. If a man compares himself to his successful male counterparts at work, he is failing— failing to give the job 100 percent of his time and energy. And if he compares himself to those spouses and fathers who stay at home (or even just devote a lot of time to their families), he sees men who, by the standards of his work place, are viewed as failures or "low achievers."

Thus ambivalence is really not limited to females. Lower values attached to female roles and role attributes create as much, if not more, ambivalence for men. If they, too, wish to partake of traditional "female" activities or satisfactions, then they also have to come to terms with a society that tells them that these are less important, less valuable, and less successful things to be doing.

Creating new roles and values: resocializing

The transition from one role to another is neither quick nor smooth. The process is further complicated by the fact that people rarely give up old roles or values in their entirety.

Men don't stop being men and become women any more than women stop being women and become men. The ideal is to find a comfortable hybrid of male and female roles that meets one's individual needs. Thus, to talk about "new roles" for couples is really to talk about the self-creation of roles rather than the exchange or mastery of existing ones. More often than not, self-designed roles simply incorporate what is best for the particular people.

For men, the desire to establish a new role in society and in the family may, in part, reflect a recognition that they, too, have been exploited. The emphasis on career success for men in our society is sometimes an intolerable burden to bear. It isn't without reason that the life expectancy for men is several years lower than for women.

A spouse's second income can make it possible for a man to try on new behaviors. Increasingly, especially in two-career couples, men are cutting back on working hours, putting in less travel and overtime, and focusing on the quality of their lives rather than on the quantity of their earnings or success. They are also measuring success in new ways. They are doing more role sharing at home, in some cases, and they are getting more involved in their role as parents. This does not mean they are turning into women. They are simply claiming roles that they have had a right to all along. Both sexes, then, are not really branching out into new roles as much as they are exploring *all of their own roles* for the first time.

Many studies report that nontraditional life-styles are most prevalent among the young people who have come out of college and married or entered careers during this decade. They have grown up in an era in which relationships and self-fullfillment have been important values. And, as Erikson tells us, it is the ideology of a society that speaks to the adolescent. Thus, younger men and women seem more comfortable with egalitarian roles, less obsessed with being feminine or masculine. They are more concerned with their relationships and the quality of their lives. They apparently decided at an early age that the relationship and the self should take precedence over the job.

Middle-aged people, on the other hand, are having the toughest time coping with role changes. Even those who want to create new roles have lived too long and too intensely with a value system that told them the male identity is found in work—his "doing"—and the female identity at home—her "being."

Now the carpet is being pulled from under them. The workaholic is out. So is the little brown hen. The self-fulfilled person is *in*. The trouble for many middle-aged people is that they feel they are running out of time. Their children have a lifetime ahead of them in which to learn new roles, attach themselves to new tools, and redefine or stabilize their identities. But the middle-aged person doesn't have the luxury of time. It is not surprising that so many people at midlife, especially people in their forties, abruptly make major life shifts. If they act quickly, they still have time to do with their lives what they want, and they are determined to use it.

Identity

How does one integrate multiple roles and values and still maintain an identity as a person and as a pair? What makes it so difficult is that the two-career couple doesn't have an ideal model to pattern itself after. In fact, our research leads us to strongly believe that there isn't one—and probably shouldn't be. The task, really, is to figure out what will work for you—what will meet your needs at a particular time.

So, just as each partner in a dual-career couple has to search out an independent identity, the couple has to somehow meld those identities to function as a unit. Sometimes the process provides more humor than pain.

Mike McGrady, author of *The Kitchen Sink Papers: My Life as a Househusband,* recalls the night he and his wife eloped—and drew up their first marriage contract.

> All in all there were two dozen clauses covering such things as the guaranteed care and feeding of her old alley cat. One other stipulation provided that we wouldn't let a day pass by without making love. In time the alley cat died and so would I have, if we had followed the contract to the letter.[3]

Most couples, like the McGrady's, seem to agree that contracts specifying everything to the letter simply don't work. The McGrady's simple solution? Their contract is to have two breadwinners and two housewives, a sum total of two people, each with the capability of being a husband and each with the experience of being a wife.

We have never tried to write a marriage contract, but we have spent fourteen years integrating our roles. Looking at us today, you could see either a very traditional marriage or a very liberated one. But what you do see probably depends on what time of day it is, or *what* day it is, for that matter. Where we are now, of necessity, is a very different place from where we were several years ago.

When we started our life together, Tim was a graduate student and Fran was a newly graduated B.A. in philosophy with no sense of what she wanted to do with her life. But she did have a strong conviction that she wanted to find that something and, when she did, it would also include baking chocolate-chip cookies for our kids to eat after school.

In the first year of our marriage, we tried the first and only kind of contract we've ever had. Fran would iron Tim's shirts (rather than send them to the laundry) if he would keep her supplied

"I tried all May, June, July, and August. Then I said to hell with it and slipped back into my stereotype."

with Chanel No. 5. It lasted about two weeks—just long enough for Fran to realize that she could keep herself supplied with Chanel No. 5 and for him to realize that the laundry did a better job on the shirts.

Then there was the time when Fran worked as Tim's research assistant, and appeared one day to tell him that she would not be finishing some work. She had been accepted into graduate school and given a fellowship. So, she became a footnote instead of a co-author. Later that year, while finishing up her master's degree, she became pregnant. How would Tim feel if she worked after the baby was born? He didn't care one way or the other—whatever made her happy.

Fran felt disappointed that it was such a nonissue for Tim. She did go to work and she played supermom, and he began to see that Fran was not only different, but happier and more enjoyable on the days she worked. So, he began to realize that her working was an issue for him, too. Working was good for her and the baby and therefore for *our relationship.*

Our first experience with role sharing was probably that year. Fran remembers groping under the covers in the middle of the night. "It's your turn!" "No, it's your turn—I rocked her last night!" In retrospect, we weren't really role sharing so much as competing for the right to sleep. But, in the end, we both came to realize that one can't have rights without the cooperation of the other—so the sharing evolved.

Later, our second baby was born and we faced a crisis that year that made us realize it was "us against the world." We moved and Fran went back to school to work on her Ph.D. Tim was promoted and got tenure. The roles and the attitudes shifted again. While Fran tackled reading and writing papers, he took over more with the kids. And, when another promotion that meant moving again came along for him, he said he wouldn't take it if Fran couldn't finish her degree.

It was important to both of us, so we worked it out. Fran commuted and Tim took over the kids and the laundry. And soon Fran realized that she was not indispensable. There was no need for a freezer full of ready-to-bake casseroles and drawers full of clean clothes when she left. Not only could Tim cook, he even enjoyed it. And Fran admitted that Tim really did get the kids calmed down more when he put them to bed. But Fran still did the cooking and shopping, when she was home. And Tim did lawn work, the monthly bills, repairs and took care of the cars. But we did it because we enjoyed doing those things.

When Fran took her first university job ninety miles away from home, Tim took turns getting the kids to the day-care center and picking them up, and going to parent conferences. And when a child was sick, he took over, because he was closer and his job was secure.

Several years and another move later, when Fran took on a more responsible job with long hours and much stress, we both admitted that things had to be worked out anew. Tim has taken over the laundry as a regular task and Fran does the cooking and shopping, because she likes cooking and hates doing laundry. Tim hates shopping, but doesn't mind laundry. We share the dishes at night and whoever is last out of bed in the morning makes up the covers, as it has always been. When the cleaning woman doesn't show up, everyone pitches in. Now Elizabeth is baking the chocolate-chip cookies and mowing the lawn, and Chip is learning to cook as well as play baseball.

Today we see ourselves as partners. When we were married in 1965, it was as husband and wife. During our marriage, we have both come to realize that our professional lives are as important as our personal life together is, and it takes a partnership to have both.

It has been almost fourteen years. During that time we have managed to acquire two Ph.D.'s, make four geographic moves, renovate several houses, publish five books between us, raise two children, and start our own corporation.

We doubt that we could have done it and become the partners we are if we hadn't made ample room for us to be the *people* we are. But then we wouldn't be the people we are today, either, if we hadn't both wanted something besides the chocolate-chip cookies, or realized that work fulfillment *is* an important issue, or respected each other's autonomy, or said "to hell with the shirts!"

We have evolved. The only place where we have a fifty-fifty split on paper is in our corporation stock. And that, we both know, is only worth the value of our ability to work together.

Intimacy

It is doubtful whether a couple can achieve true intimacy—be able to give love *and* receive it—unless each has resolved his or her own identity issues and integrated this identity into family and work roles. It is also doubtful that couples can go on forever "getting their heads together." There comes a point when they want and need to enjoy the relationship and to be interdependent. They are past the point of negotiating or contracting; they want their love to be an unspoken act of giving.

To be able to love, as we said earlier, a person needs to have worked through any personal identity issues. In couples, this also means feeling secure enough about one's maleness or femaleness to enjoy it and rejoice in it, without feeling ashamed or in need of proving anything. A woman who is still trying to work through her liberation in life will probably carry her ambivalence into the bedroom, as will any man who still feels in need of proving himself. True intimacy means recognizing your interdependence as a couple, both sexually and in relation to your roles as parents, homemakers, or whatever. It means being free from hang-ups about who I am or who you are or who we are. It is *knowing* who you are and really loving yourself enough to be able to let someone else love you back.

Nadelson and Eisenberg, both two-career husbands and psychiatrists, suggest that "the challenge to narcissism is far greater when co-equal sacrifice is demanded at the beginning of a marriage."[4] Co-equal sacrifice means giving up one's self-absorption and making sacrifices for the other person. As they point out, it is a challenge early in a marriage. At the stage of true intimacy, it is *not* a challenge; it shouldn't even be an issue. If giving in to and sacrificing for another person (one's partner) is an issue, then the relationship may be sexual, but not truly intimate. Intimate partners recognize that sex and selfless affection are integral and complementary components of loving.

It is not surprising that many two-career couples speak of each other as best friends. For, in addition to being able to share sex and affection, they enjoy one another's companionship. Does this mean that these partners meet all of each other's needs? Hardly. More likely, they don't even try to. And, in taking that attitude, they are more able to enjoy the needs they do meet.

Productivity versus procreation

We once interviewed a woman—a dual-career wife and mother—who was working on a graduate degree while holding down a full-time job. She and her husband had three children. Theirs was a hectic but happy household. During the interview, she spoke worriedly about some of her female colleagues and friends, women who often dropped by to visit. Some were choosing not to marry and others not to have children. They said it was because their careers were important to them. They insisted that they were happy with their lives as they were—childless or partnerless. As we talked, we began to speculate on what would happen to these women and how they would feel when they reached menopause, being neither a partner nor a parent.

Could a career *alone* be so satisfying as to sustain a person for a lifetime? We decided that our biases were showing. We had chosen the spouse and children route, so naturally our opinion reflected our values. Finally she announced: "No, it's more than our biases. If these women are so damn happy with their careers, why are they always hanging around our house every weekend? My husband and I don't need *them!*"

The incident raises an important issue for many couples today. What are their sources of satisfaction? Will they be happy—be able to achieve fulfillment—if they only invest themselves in their careers?

Erikson would have us believe that procreation is an important part of our life cycle. To him, it is not only biological fulfillment; it is the ultimate expression of our ability to work (produce) and to love. Many childless couples would disagree with him, however.

Erikson observed that an adult reaches a point in life where he or she either is able to engage in *generative* endeavors or stagnates. Generativity is not the same as procreation. There are many ways to produce and create—to invest, as it were, in the future. The way one does it is not so important as the ability to do it. Those unable to plan ahead, to look forward creatively, are locked into the self or, at best, into a relationship with a partner.

The real issue is coming to terms with how to invest energies and time. Careers have a way of taking over, as we all know. But the reason they take over is because we let them. A career can be an ego trip. Sacrificing career satisfactions for the sake of the family—or to have a family—is another major challenge to narcissism.

Many couples realize this themselves. Others don't need to. They reach a point where the career, although satisfying, is not all they want out of life. And they feel secure about themselves and their relationship. Now where to go? They don't need extrinsic strokes; they are seeking intrinsic satisfaction.

Children are but one choice. Many couples have found satisfactions and outlets in other productive and creative pursuits. Many childless couples, for example, focus their energies on their environments. Creating an environment, whether decorating an apartment or renovating an old brownstone, is one way to produce something that is an expression of themselves. Others invest their energies in hobbies. Here, too, the hobbies are a way of gaining intrinsic satisfaction out of creative acts. Why has photography, for instance, enjoyed such a resurgence? Not everyone is gifted enough to be a good painter, but almost anyone can create with a camera. Then there are the plant stores. We once thought this was simply a reflection of the "back-to-earth" movement of a few years ago. But the plant stores are proliferating, perhaps because they provide an easy way for people to feel they are doing the same thing.

Erikson also describes generativity as a time when one takes on leadership roles and becomes a model for others, guiding the next generation. This, too, can be a generative pursuit. Thus, for some people, acting as a mentor for younger people at work or elsewhere can be a way of investing oneself in the future.

Success

Success as a couple is no less important than individual success; couples also need to experience a sense of satisfaction with how they have lived their lives together. This doesn't necessarily accompany the stage of imminent death, but certainly it should be there by then. Ideally, most couples will achieve a sense of success before the onset of old age.

In Chapter One, we defined psychological success as the person's *feelings* of success as opposed to traditional external measures of success. We believe couples achieve this when both partners are able to fully integrate and balance their love and work: the selves that derive satisfaction from careers come together with the selves that derive satisfaction from the family. There is no longer struggle and continuous strain, for both partners value the identity they have as a couple as much as, and perhaps even more than, the identity each has a working person.

Anne and Frank Smerka, a two-career couple for almost forty-two years, reflected with us on their definitions of success.

Anne	Success has different facets. Success in marriage means living a congenial life . . . meeting each other's needs. In togetherness you meet each other's needs. Each has strengths and weaknesses. You have to blend these things. If people would only realize this. They don't realize this. They think there has to be sameness, but there have to be differences.
Frank	What is most important for success is to live a happy life, a married life, to produce a family, raise a family, and then, as you attain a ripe old age, success can be that you are still healthy to enjoy life—that you can still attain goals that give you personal satisfaction.
	But, when you do leave this earth, success can mean that you are a person who maintained a degree of integrity—you've personified it.
Interviewer	You feel together?
Frank	Yes, integrity is a very important thing in your life. In other words, it's your quest.

For some couples, differences in perceptions of success or feelings of integrity produce conflict. We see it most often when one partner has suppressed or put off career aspirations for the sake of the other or the family. The husband may be feeling great: he has achieved success in his career and is now ready to turn inward toward the relationship, to seek satisfaction in their togetherness. But the timing is all wrong. Now that the children have been raised, his wife feels that it's her turn. She is now freer to work on achievement drives, to invest more of herself in career and less in family. What he has defined all along as a successful relationship and family does not coincide with her perceptions of success. She is looking outward while he is ready to turn inward. Thus, for many people, the conflict emerges when their career and family cycling are on different time tables.

Confronting Our Roles

As we have seen, the eight "development" issues are often a source of conflict for couples, both within and between themselves. Sometimes the conflicts are covert. Mistrust, guilt, or jealousy can simmer without ever boiling over into a fight. Often, however, they are manifested more overtly.

One of the most basic types of overt conflicts is the clash of roles. Without clear role definitions and a shared sense of priorities, couples may experience crossed signals, different motivations, a lack of support, and, more often than not, sheer overload. For the two-career couple managing multiple life roles, this is one of the most frequent sources of stress.

In the traditional single-career family, the wife's role as homemaker overlaps considerably with her roles as spouse and as parent. By identifying with the role of homemaker, she is able to achieve a high degree of role adjustment—she views herself as others do; thus she is able to meet their needs and expectations. The husband, in turn, takes his identity more and more from his career, so, as the only breadwinner, he also achieves a degree of overall role adjustment. Doing well as a career person usually also means being a good provider—his major task as a parent and spouse.

Adding a second career role to a family does not necessarily eliminate the other roles; it merely puts them in a different perspective. The woman's career role no longer overlaps with her parent and spouse roles as in the homemaker example. But those roles may still be there. And, because the husband is no longer the only breadwinner, he can no longer meet parent and spouse obligations simply by having a successful career. A working wife changes the picture entirely. Thus, when both partners pursue careers, the roles of parent, partner, and homemaker are up for grabs—they have to be eliminated, redefined, or redistributed. In the two-career family, there is no longer a full-time parent, spouse, and homemaker at home. Both partners are engaged outside the home.

The problem of housework may be the most common kind of role conflict (and for that reason, we discuss it extensively in Chapter Five), but there are other, less obvious problems for the two-career couple.

When Ned had a sabbatical and wanted to spend the year in Europe, his wife's position at the bank precluded going together. It also forced them to reconsider what would be best for their careers.

Barb and Jeff's conflicts revolved around money. With two incomes, she felt that they should be investing in real estate. He had different priorities—a sports car and travel.

Dan and Maria's conflicts surfaced over the use of leisure time and their respective involvement in community activities. He found coaching hockey to be an important source of personal satisfaction. For her it meant that his time on Saturdays and Sundays was devoted to other people instead of to her or their home.

All of these problems reflect a clash of priorities, a conflict of roles. Coping with any of them demands that the partners recognize the importance of problem solving and are willing to work at it. This willingness depends on the person's priorities—in other words, the value he or she attaches to self and career versus the relationship and family.

As we saw in Chapter One, being highly involved (or uninvolved) in a career does not alone determine either your lifestyle or your effectiveness as a career couple. What determines both of these is the way you *manage* your career involvement vis-à-vis the other roles in your life, especially your partner role. This involves identifying the roles you want in your life, what you want out of them, and what you are willing to give or give up to have them.

To help you assess yourself and analyze your own priorities, fill out the Role-Orientation Inventory that follows.

Role-Orientation Inventory

I. **Identifying your roles**

One way to begin to understand yourself is to ask the question: Who am I? On the answer sheet provided, list all of the roles that together form your identity. It may help you to think of roles in terms of three major areas of activity: career or work roles; home and family roles; and personal roles. For example, a list might include roles like these:

partner	sister
parent	friend
manager	community member
author	self (a person)
neighbor	church member
daughter	grandparent

Answer Sheet

I. Life Roles	II.	A Importance to Identity	B Amount of Attention Devoted To	C Ratings of Success	D (B – A)	E (C – A)	F (C – B)
Career							
Home and family							
Personal							

II.   Analyzing your roles

A. Now think about how important these different roles are for your identity. Which roles make an important contribution to who you are and which roles are a minor part of you? In column A next to your list of roles, rate the importance of each in terms of your identity. Use the following scale:

5 = extremely important to my identity
4 = very important to my identity
3 = fairly important to my identity
2 = not very important to my identity
1 = not important to my identity

Remember, we acquire certain roles—like being a neighbor—by chance, not choice. These roles may be very important or very unimportant, but they are still there.

B. Now think about the attention you devote to roles. How much time, effort, or emotional involvement do you invest in that role? Use the following scale:

5 = an extreme amount of attention
4 = a great deal of attention
3 = a fair amount of attention
2 = a small amount of attention
1 = not much or none

Rate each role that you have listed. Enter your rating in column B.

C. Now think about how successful you feel in each role. To what extent do you experience feelings of personal satisfaction from your efforts? Use the following scale:

5 = extremely successful
4 = very successful
3 = fairly successful
2 = not very successful
1 = not successful

D. Look at the difference between importance you attach to a role (the rating in column A) and the attention you devote to that role (the rating in column B). Subtract the value in A from the value in B. Enter the difference as either a plus or a minus number in column D.

   Are you devoting time and attention to roles in your life that are important to you? A *negative score* suggests that you are neglecting a role in your life that is personally important. Time and attention devoted to other roles may be preventing you from following your true inclinations. A *positive score* suggests that you are devoting time and attention to a role that is relatively unimportant in your life.

E. Now look at the difference between the importance you attach to a role (column A rating) and the success you experience in that role (column C rating). Subtract the value in A from the value in C. Enter the difference in column E as either a plus or a minus number.

A *negative score* in column E suggests that you are failing to succeed in an important life role. The results leave something to be desired. A *high positive score* in column E suggests that your success experiences may be hollow. You are succeeding, but in a role that is relatively unimportant to you.

F. Look at the difference between the attention you are devoting to a role (column B) and the success you experience in that role (column C). Subtract the value in B from the value in C. Enter the difference as either a plus or a minus number in column F.

A *negative score* suggests that you are getting little success out of a lot of effort. A *positive score* suggests that you are getting a lot of success for little effort.

III. Summarizing your analysis

The purpose of this analysis has been to help you understand your life roles. Which ones are important to you? Are you devoting sufficient attention to these? Are you succeeding in the important ones? To develop a profile of your own role orientation, respond to the following questions.

A. What roles are *most* important to your identity?

B. How would you rank the importance of the three types of life roles? (1 = most important; 3 = least important)

Career roles   ____

Home and family roles ____

Personal roles   ____

C. What roles would you like to devote more time and attention to? (List those roles for which you had a negative score in column E and a negative score in column D. In other words, what important life roles are being set aside because of a lack of time, attention, or emotional involvement?)

Career roles

Family/home roles

Personal roles

D. What roles would you like to devote less time and attention to? (List those roles for which you had a positive score in column D and a positive score in column E. In other words, identify those unimportant roles to which you are devoting time, while perhaps achieving only a hollow success.)

Career roles

Family/home roles

Personal roles

What does your inventory (and your partner's) tell you about your own role orientations and the appropriateness of your life-style? How do your role orientations relate to each other?

- What roles are important to each of you?
- Which do you want to devote more and less attention to?
- How does your present life-style and role structure fit with what is really important to each of you?
- Is there another life-style that would provide a better fit for both of you?

Coping with Role Conflict

"If we need time off, we just take it. We play hooky."

"I dream, fantasize, and plan for what I will do on my own. I keep saying to myself, 'It won't always be like this.' I dream of the day I will be able to screw my employer. It's the only way I can face the work years ahead of me."

"I play sports aggressively—work off my frustrations. It's a release mechanism."

"I work longer and harder at all of my roles."

"We just don't socialize much."

"I focus on my current goal and take things one at a time."

"We share responsibilities, compromise on issues. You can't be a stubborn person."

Each of these people is describing what he or she does to deal with the major problem confronting career couples: coping with role conflicts. If you completed the Role-Orientation Inventory, you probably have a better idea of what your personal priorities are. Fine. But having this knowledge doesn't magically diminish the very real demands that others place on you.

One way to understand the coping process (and thus get a handle on how to cope more effectively) is first to understand how our role behavior is shaped. In other words, why do we behave as we do, giving too much attention to some demands, not enough to others, or exhausting ourselves trying to be everything to everyone?

A role consists of three parts: the demands, expectations, responsibilities, and pressures that *other people* impose on us in any given role; our own perceptions of what we think we ought to be doing in that role; and our behavior—how we act, consciously or unconsciously. Our behavior is really shaped by the first two role components. We respond to two different sets of expectations, our own and those of others.

Coping with role conflict involves managing these competing sets of expectations as well as our own behavior. Thus, there are really three ways to cope: we can attempt to change the expectations that other people hold for us (redefine our roles); we can change our own attitudes or expectations about what we "ought" to be doing (change our own orientation); or we can accept the various demands placed on us and find a way to meet all of them. The first two ways of coping involve redefining one's role. They are *proactive*, in the sense that we are *reshaping* the demands placed on us by others or by ourselves. The third way is really *reactive*—trying to do everything.

How do you cope? How could you cope more effectively? The following Role-Coping Inventory can help you and your partner to evaluate your current coping strategies.

Role-Coping Inventory

I. Think about the major roles in your life. What conflicts or strains, if any, have you experienced between your various roles in life? For example:

____ parent vs. partner	____ career vs. other career
____ parent vs. career	____ community vs. career
____ partner vs. career	____ insufficient time

II. How do you deal with these conflicts or issues? How often do you do each of the following?

	Nearly All the Time 5	Often 4	Some- times 3	Rarely 2	Never 1
1. Decide not to do certain activities that conflict with other activities.	_____	_____	_____	_____	_____
2. Get help from someone outside the family (e.g., home mainte- nance help or child care).	_____	_____	_____	_____	_____
3. Get help from a member of the family.	_____	_____	_____	_____	_____
4. Get help from someone at work.	_____	_____	_____	_____	_____
5. Engage in problem solving with family members to resolve conflicts.	_____	_____	_____	_____	_____
6. Engage in problem solving with someone at work.	_____	_____	_____	_____	_____
7. Get moral support from a member of the family.	_____	_____	_____	_____	_____
8. Get moral support from someone at work.	_____	_____	_____	_____	_____
9. Integrate or combine roles (for example, involve family mem- bers in work activity or combine work and family in some way).	_____	_____	_____	_____	_____
10. Attempt to change societal definition of sex roles, work roles, or family roles.	_____	_____	_____	_____	_____
11. Negotiate or plan with someone at work, so their expectations of you are more in line with your own needs or requirements.	_____	_____	_____	_____	_____

	Nearly All the Time 5	Often 4	Some- times 3	Rarely 2	Never 1
12. Negotiate or plan with members of your family, so their expectations of you are more in line with your own needs or requirements.	____	____	____	____	____
13. Establish priorities among your different roles, so that you are sure the most important activities are done.	____	____	____	____	____
14. Partition and separate your roles. Devote full attention to each role when you are in it.	____	____	____	____	____
15. Overlook or relax certain standards for how you do certain activities. (Let less important things slide a bit sometimes, such as dusting or lawn care.)	____	____	____	____	____
16. Modify your attitudes toward certain roles or activities (e.g., coming to the conclusion that the *quality* of time spent with spouse or children is more important than the *quantity* of time spent).	____	____	____	____	____
17. Eliminate certain roles (e.g., deciding to stop working).	____	____	____	____	____
18. Rotate attention from one role to another. Handle each role in turn as it comes up.	____	____	____	____	____
19. Develop self and own interests (e.g., spend time on leisure or self-development).	____	____	____	____	____
20. Plan, schedule, and organize carefully.	____	____	____	____	____

	Nearly All the Time 5	*Often* 4	*Some-times* 3	*Rarely* 2	*Never* 1
21. Work hard to meet all role demands. Devote more time and energy, so you can do everything that is expected of you.	_____	_____	_____	_____	_____
22. Do not attempt to cope with role demands and conflicts. Let role conflicts take care of themselves.	_____	_____	_____	_____	_____

III. Scoring

- Add up the values you entered for 1–12. Divide by 12. This is your *role-redefinition score:* ____
- Add up the values you entered for 13–17. Divide by 5. This is your *personal-reorientation score:* ____
- Add up the values you entered for 18–22. Divide by 5. This is your *reactive-role-behavior score:* ____

IV. Interpreting your scores

The three scores give you some indication of the extent to which you use each of the three coping strategies. The scores can range from a high of 5 to a low of 1. A high score indicates a frequent use of a coping strategy; a low score indicates infrequent use of the coping strategy.

If your role-redefinition score is low, you too often let others place demands on you, often unrealistic demands. You need to negotiate with these people, your role senders, to make certain that the roles they impose on you are compatible with other responsibilities and interests. Some ways of doing this include:

- Simply agree with role senders that you will not be able to engage in certain activities. (For example, in our community, a hotbed of volunteerism, we are both known as "spot-jobbers." We will accept specific, one-shot volunteer jobs, but we will not accept continuing positions.)
- Enlist assistance in role activities from other family members or from people outside the family (for example, cleaning or baby-sitting help).
- Sit down with role senders (boss, spouse, children) and discuss the problem. Together, work out an acceptable solution.
- Integrate conflicting careers by working with your spouse or working in related fields (so that the two careers become more like one). This method of coping has been described as "linking up."

If you can successfully reduce role conflicts by practicing some of these proactive negotiations, you will be stopping them at the source, and chances are you'll be very happy with the results.

If your personal-reorientation score is low, your problem is that you don't distinguish between the roles assigned to you: you lack a clear vision of what roles are truly important. You need to reevaluate your attitudes about various roles and take on only those heading the list. Some hints to help you achieve this are:

- Establish priorities. ("A child with a high fever takes precedence over school obligations. A child with sniffles does not. A very important social engagement—especially one that is business related—precedes tennis.")
- Divide and separate roles. Devote full attention to a given role when in it and don't think about other roles ("I leave mý work at the office. Home is for the family and their needs.")
- Try to ignore or overlook less important role expectations ("The dusting can wait.")
- Rotate attention from one role to another as demands arise. Let one role slide a bit if another needs more attention at the time. ("Susan needs help now. I'll pay those bills later.")
- Remember that self-fulfillment and personal interests are a valid source of role demands. ("Piano and organ playing are a release for me while the children are small and need me at home.")

This style of coping means changing yourself rather than the family or work environment, although personal reorientation may be a necessary step to take before you can accomplish real role redefinition. Before you can change other people's expectations of you, you have to be clear about what you expect of yourself. Personal reorientation alone is not significantly related to satisfaction and happiness.

If your reactive-role-behavior score is high, it means you try to take on every role that happens your way. You cope with conflict by working harder and sleeping less. Your style of coping includes:

- Planning, scheduling, and organizing better.
- Working harder to meet all role demands. (As one expert on women's roles and role conflict said in frustration, "After years of research, I've concluded that the only answer to a career and a family is to learn to get by on less sleep!")
- Using no conscious strategy. Let problems take care of themselves. This reactive behavior, in contrast to role redefinition, is a passive response to role conflict. Not surprisingly, people who use this style report very low levels of satisfaction and happiness.

Reactive behavior is not a very effective way of coping with your roles. Rather than managing *them*, you are letting them manage *you*. If your goal is to eliminate conflict, then you need to reorient your own perceptions as a first step toward negotiating with others to restructure the roles in your life.

Confronting Problems

Not all conflicts couples encounter involve competing role demands. Often conflicts arise when a crucial decision must be made. How partners approach a decision generally determines their success in finding a satisfactory resolution.

The process people use to arrive at decisions depends on whether they agree about the goal they are trying to accomplish; whether they agree about how to achieve the goal; and whether they assume a cooperative or a competitive attitude toward working on problems.

There are two dimensions to making decisions and each can be the basis for disagreement. First, there is the issue of goals or outcomes—what each partner is trying to accomplish. Second, there is the issue of solutions—how to achieve a goal.

Borrowing from the work of James Thompson, we can see four possible decision situations, determined by how the partners feel about goals and solutions.[5]

Agreement on goals/agreement on solutions. This is an ideal decision situation. Both partners are after the same thing and feel clear about the best way to accomplish it. Decision making is fairly routine, unhindered by conflict.

For example, a couple may have to decide how to clean the house each week. Let's assume that the goals of each are (a) to have the house cleaned weekly and (b) to free up their time. Let's also assume that both believe that the best way to do it is to hire a cleaning service. The solution is obvious and no disagreement exists— the couple hires a cleaning service and both partners get what they want.

Agreement on goals/disagreement on solutions. In this situation, the partners again agree about what they want, but they disagree about how to achieve it.

Let's assume again that both partner's want the house cleaned weekly and both want free time. One partner, however, believes that the other partner should take over cleaning responsibilities. The second partner believes that hired help is the answer.

In this example, the immediate solution is not obvious. Furthermore, there may be constraints associated with both alternatives. The couple may lack the money to hire help, there may not be time for one partner to do everything, and so forth.

What now? A creative process to find the best alternative or solution for getting the house cleaned is called for. The couple needs to engage in problem solving. Whether they can effectively solve the problem, however, depends, as we shall see, on whether they approach the conflict with a cooperative or a competitive attitude.

Disagreement on goals/agreement on solutions. In this situation, the partners agree on how best to accomplish certain goals, but they disagree about the goals themselves.

For example, both partners may agree that hiring a cleaning service is the only way to have a clean house. But one partner may feel that saving money should be their primary goal, while the other partner may feel that having a clean house is more important. It's impossible to accomplish both.

In this situation, the couple needs to work not on alternative solutions, but on their goals. The goal of each partner cannot be fully accomplished, but, if the couple is willing to bargain, to negotiate a compromise, then it may be possible to arrive at a solution that will be satisfactory (if not ideal) to both partners. One obvious compromise would be to clean the house every other week and save the money on alternative weeks. Thus, one partner lowers cleanliness goals while the other lowers savings goals.

Again, whether couples are able to negotiate such compromises depends on the extent to which they are willing to cooperate, to discuss their goals, and to view them as at least partially compatible.

Disagreement on goals/disagreement on solutions. The fourth situation is one in which total conflict reigns. Neither partner can agree with the other on either what should be accomplished or how. When this is the case, there is little basis for trying to work together on solutions—both partners are inflexible and there may be a total deadlock. In such situations, couples may or may not turn to outside help or counseling in an attempt to resolve their differences.

The second and third situations both require a spirit of cooperation. Both parties have to be willing to collaborate to solve the problem. Whether we are able to collaborate or not depends on how we have worked together before; how we perceive the situation; and how we feel toward our partner.

If we have a history of unresolved conflicts or if one partner is always "the winner," the probable outcome is less promising than if we have successfully collaborated to find solutions in the past. If one partner consistently wins at the expense of the other, then we develop competitive feelings. We approach problem solving

with a "me against you" or "win/lose" attitude. On the other hand, if
we have a history of working things out, then we approach the situation with a positive attitude—the belief that a "win/win" is possible.

Both our perceptions (seeing things as win/lose
or win/win) and our feelings (suspicion versus trust) affect how we
behave. In problem solving and decision making, our behavior is mostly
our communication. Thus, whether we are able to find solutions or
make compromises ultimately depends on the extent to which we can
communicate.

Let's look at the difference between two types of
relationships and how the partners approach making decisions and
solving problems. The first is the *me* relationship, in which partners
compete with each other for self-interests. The second is the *we* relationship, in which partners cooperate for the sake of their mutual
interests.

The basic difference between the two revolves
around whether a couple can agree on *mutual* goals that support the
needs of both partners over time. Problem solving is based on the prem-
ise that there is a shared objective. This objective may simply be to
work things out, to stay together. Without this basic consensus, the
prospects for a couple remaining together are slim. The accompanying
chart outlines the differences between a "we" relationship and a "me"
relationship.

From win/lose to win/win

How do couples avoid competition and learn to
cooperate? How do they move from a win/lose to a win/win strategy?
Based on the people we have interviewed and on our own experience,
we think there are five essential ingredients for creating win/win situations or arriving at satisfactory compromises.

Talk about problems regularly

When we were first married, our time to talk together was at dinner—
evenings were reserved for writing. When the children arrived, talking at
dinner was impossible, so we started having a drink together—tea, a mar-
tini, V-8 juice—it didn't matter what. What counted was time to share. As
the kids got bigger, the time before dinner and at meals was increasingly
taken up with them—their homework, their projects, and listening to their
problems. That's when we switched to the nightcap and watching the late
news together. It was the end of the day and a good time to relax without
anyone bugging us.

Approach to Decisions and Problems	Me Relationship	We Relationship
Orientation	Self-interest comes first.	Concern for finding mutual interests and compatible goals.
	Objective is to accomplish own goals even at the expense of other. Unwilling to compromise.	Objective is to find way to accomplish goals of both if possible. If not, both willing to compromise.
Perception	Conflict is assumed to be inevitable.	Conflict is assumed to be manageable.
	Goals and solutions perceived as incompatible.	Compatible goals and solutions can be worked out.
	See the interests of the partner as threat to self.	Interests of both more important than interest of either one.
	If you win, I lose.	Win/win possible, at least sometimes.
Attitude	Negative—pessimistic.	Positive—optimistic.
	Suspicious—low trust.	High trust.
	Unwilling to respond to partner's needs and ideas.	Willing to respond to partner's needs and ideas.
Communication and behavior	Little sharing of information and feelings.	Open sharing of information and feelings.
	Discourage, intimidate, threaten, or coerce the other.	Encourage, pursuade the other.
Possible outcomes	Avoid resolution.	Find best alternative.
	Force partner to give in to self.	Compromise.
	Suppress conflict.	
Consequences	Reduced willingness to solve problems together.	More positive attitude about ability to solve problems together.
	Lower trust level.	Higher trust in each other and in relationship.
	Increased "me versus you" attitude.	Increased sense of "us."
	Reduced communication.	Increased communication.

The biggest barrier to collaborating is lack of communication. If people don't at least discuss issues, they will never be able to resolve them—and usually problems *don't* go away. Several suggestions are:

- Set aside a time each day just to talk to each other about anything. This keeps the channels of communication open.
- Set aside a time to talk specifically about problems. Try to make it a time when you feel relaxed and free from distractions. If the phone is ringing, the kids are "at you," or you are exhausted, you probably won't be very effective at listening to each other or expressing your own feelings.
- Be willing to adjust the time, but don't give it up.

Be willing to listen to your partner
as well as express your own feelings

When we talk, we each get air time. That's important. I can concentrate on what he's saying if I know he will listen to me. Then, when we've both had a chance to tell how we see things, we can discuss our differences of opinion. Getting things off your chest helps you open up to the other person.

Another barrier to collaboration is that partners don't listen to one another—or don't listen very effectively. To communicate more effectively, try the following:

- Sympathize with your partner—try to understand what he or she is feeling or experiencing.
- Ask questions that are open-ended and help you and your partner probe what the real problem is.
- Don't argue mentally with what your partner is saying.
- Avoid making premature assumptions.
- When giving your partner feedback, try to be specific. Describe what happened, but don't evaluate it or attribute motives.
- Ask for what you want. Let your partner know exactly what it is you desire. Complaining isn't constructive, but specific requests are.
- Try to focus on the *present* problem. Dragging out ancient history won't solve today's issues.

Discuss goals and explore expectations

The biggest problem we had to face was finding time to do fun things together. Both of us were on crazy schedules and usually brought work home at night and on weekends. When we finally talked about it, we realized that we both wanted the same thing—just more time having fun together. I thought his work was more important to him and he thought that mine was to me, but we found we had a common enemy—work. We both decided to readjust our work goals. We would bring work home at night, but not on weekends. Sometimes that meant working harder during the week, but at least we were able to salvage some regular time off.

The biggest barrier to finding satisfactory solutions is the assumption that one's own goals and expectations are incompatible with a partner's. This is what sets people up for a win/lose situation in the first place. Try the following:

- List what each of you wants out of a particular decision or solution.
- Now see whether your objectives are really incompatible.
- Make a list of goals that require compromise—where one or both of you would have to give or give up something. Call this your negotiation list.
- Make a separate list of goals that are *not* mutually exclusive. This is your problem-solving list. You will need to explore alternative ways to accomplish what each of you desires.

Practice problem solving

When we first started talking about Pete's job offer, I was dead opposed to going. I felt sure I would have to give up my degree—and I was so close to finishing. Then we stopped arguing—thank goodness—and looked at what was bugging us. I realized that finishing up just one semester of course work was what I needed. He needed to leave in the fall to take the new job. The more we thought about it, the more we realized that his new job and my degree might both be possible—if we could work out a way to cope for about six months.

We decided to explore the alternatives. Again, we *assumed* we'd have to live apart. That seemed like the only solution. Then a friend suggested that I might be able to take courses where Pete's new job was going to be and transfer them back. I checked into it and sure enough—it was possible. Not only did we both get what we wanted, but we moved *together*.

The secret to effective problem solving is exploring and generating alternatives. Take a problem you are working on and try the following:

- Agree first on what you each want to accomplish and then decide to find (and use) a solution that will allow both of you to accomplish that goal or set of goals.
- List all the alternatives you can think of to accomplish your goals, no matter how crazy they sound. Don't criticize or evaluate them yet, just brainstorm.
- Ask other people for ideas. They can be helpful in creating alternatives you've overlooked.
- Now examine the alternatives. Evaluate each in terms of costs and benefits.
- What is the *best* alternative? It may not be the perfect one, but if it allows each of you to have what you want, it may be the most preferred.
- Try the preferred solution, but be open to revising things. A solution may work for a while, but if circumstances change, you may have to find a new one.
- Remember that regular monitoring—talking about how it's working—is important to making it work.

Practice negotiating compromises

We compromise now for the simple reason that neither of us can do it alone and neither of us is willing to do it all. Once we got through *that* understanding, things became easier.

A compromise means giving in or giving up something to get something. It's really a bargaining process—trading off. Most of us are willing to do that when we can't accomplish our goals alone. By pooling resources, partners are able to achieve what each wants rather than remaining in an unproductive "locked-horns" position. When faced with a need to compromise, try the following:

- Make a list of what you want from your partner.
- Now make a list of what you are willing to give your partner in return.
- Compare lists. Start with one thing that each partner wants. What can you trade to each other in return?

- Try listing your trade-offs in the form of a contract: "John will do _____ if Kris will do _____," or "I will do more (or less) _____ if you will do more (or less) _____."
- Remember, bargains and negotiations between partners are only good if both partners are willing to uphold them. Good faith is essential. They are also only good when each partner recognizes and admits that he or she *needs* the other.

In this chapter we have explored many of the basic issues couples face, the conflicts these produce, and possible ways of managing these clashes. We have tried to help you develop a basic understanding of your role priorities and how you can cope with role conflicts and interpersonal decision making.

Later in the book we get more specific and tackle some of the nitty-gritty issues couples encounter, such as managing a home, raising children, workaholism, sex, and other involvements. To manage the broader conflicts as well as the day-to-day issues, we need to understand how time and stress affect our lives. In the next chapter, we examine stress as a phenomenon: what it is, what causes it, and how to manage it. We also consider the problem of time and ways in which we can change our behavior to be managers of time rather than slaves of time.

CHAPTER FOUR

MANAGING STRESS AND TIME

Two-career couples must constantly be on the alert, scouting the terrain for potential problems—from bosses and secretaries, baby-sitters and in-laws, husbands and wives, friends and enemies. To meet these problems head-on, we need experience and practice, and in Part II, we talk about the most common of these problems and share some specific strategies for dealing with them. Two basic skills that can help us cope, however, are time and stress management.

Stress

The problem with managing stress, as one dual-career partner observed, is that it can become a way of life. In choosing a two-career life-style, couples voluntarily put themselves into an inherently stressful situation. Thus, it is not surprising to find that many couples come to accept stress as inevitable—just another one of the costs attached to having two careers.

Many people, however, don't anticipate stress as a component of a two-career life-style. They learn the hard way that managing two careers, a family, role conflicts, and life-style changes is a tough, demanding job. Only then do they recognize the need to *manage* their lives in a way that will minimize stress and moderate their reactions to it.

Stress is what we feel when our body reacts biochemically to demands made on it. These demands require us to adapt, to absorb change, and to cope with disruptions and imbalance in our lives. When this happens, we experience physiological changes. Our body releases chemicals and adrenalines and musters its defenses. It puts us on alert to fight or flee. It readies us for action. Our heart rate increases, we breathe faster, our blood pressure goes up, our muscles tense, and we may perspire or experience changes in body temperature.

Whether or not we experience this stress reaction depends on how we (and hence our bodies) respond to the demands of our environment. Thus, stress is the result of the interaction between an individual and the environment. Not all events produce stress for everyone. But those that do are called *stressors*. For each person, different situations can be more or less stress producing. Similarly, we differ in terms of our ability to tolerate stress. Each time we do experience stress, however, our body needs time to adapt and to restore its equilibrium.

If we continue to be exposed to stress-inducing stimuli or situations, our bodies may not be able to restore equilibrium and we will exceed our threshold or tolerance level. At this point, we may suffer from a serious physical or emotional breakdown. Our resources for fighting the stressors have been depleted and our body is signaling that it just can't take any more.

If managed properly, stress can be an energizing force. Professor of management Robert Kreitner reports that whether stress is energizing or destructive depends on two dimensions of how we experience it.[1] The first is frequency—how often we encounter stress-producing situations or events. The second is the magnitude of the stress—the intensity of our responses to potentially stressful events. When we either experience stress frequently or respond to it too intensely, we are entering a danger zone. Stress becomes potentially destructive. The person who responds violently to infrequent stress or the "slow burner," the person who continually absorbs stress but does not respond to it until the accumulation becomes too great, are examples of individuals who have not learned to manage stress. Perhaps the most self-destructive type of person is the one who not only experiences frequent stress but responds intensely to it each time. This is the individual who continues to push beyond reasonable limits in a dizzying downward spiral toward collapse.

One way to think about stress as energizing or debilitating is to consider how it affects performance. If we had no demands placed on us, no stimulation to act, we would accomplish nothing. Up to a point, then, stress enhances performance by activating us. Beyond this point, our performance decreases because of too much stress. This point of tolerance is different for everyone, and to understand how we reach it, we need to understand the causes of stress.

What Causes Stress?

Stress is our body's nonspecific reaction to demands placed on it.[2] But demands alone do not cause the stress. It is what the demand represents to us—the effect it creates in us—that causes us to experience stress.

Change, conflict, and pressure or overload commonly produce stress. Often the three are interrelated—for example, major life changes may lead to conflict or increased pressure. Thus, the effects are not always experienced in isolation. All of them, however, put us in a state of imbalance or disequilibrium. The extent to which this happens is unique to each individual, a part of his or her overall makeup. In addition, it is a function of the circumstances associated with the change, conflict, or pressure. Three factors seem to moderate the amount of stress any demand or event causes for a person: uncertainty or unpredictability; lack of control; and the value or feelings associated with the event.

When we are able to predict what will happen to us, we can take steps to prepare for it. This doesn't mean that it will not be stressful. It just means we can minimize the amount of stress we experience. If we are totally unprepared, we may experience complete shock rather than stress.

Some people experience stress just because they live with perpetual uncertainty. This often happens at work, but can occur at home as well. People whose jobs lack clear definitions or expectations frequently report stress. Working for a boss who changes plans abruptly or springs last-minute rush assignments on employees can be extremely stressful. For working parents, uncertainty may be associated with the reliability of the baby-sitter or with the health of the children. In each instance, the person lives with the constant fear that at anytime something may happen to upset the status quo.

Related to uncertainty is lack of control. Part of the stress-inducing quality of uncertain or unpredictable events is that we have no control. At other times, although we do know what is going to happen, we can't do what is necessary to meet the demand. We may know what the logical or adequate solution would be, but we are powerless to control the people or events necessary to bring about this outcome.

Consider your reaction to changing jobs. If you know there are several openings and you will have a choice among them, your reaction is probably quite different than if you know you are going to be transferred but you don't know where. In the first example, you have both predictability and control. In the second, usually the more stressful, you are stripped of all control. Control enables us to make some conscious choices about how we are going to adapt. Without it, we can only absorb the stress, not really manage it.

A third factor affecting our stress response is how we feel about an event. Are there compensating factors? If the stressful event is associated with satisfactions, with accomplishing valued goals, or with enjoyable activities, we may experience the pressure but will not perceive it as being overwhelming. We value and desire the outcome.

Consider the difference between meeting a deadline on a "hot" project that is important to your career and may result in a bonus and meeting a deadline on a project that you know will never get off the ground. Although the real pressures of each project may be the same and may cause just as many disruptions in your work or home life, you are likely to experience them in very different ways. The first project has more riding on it, but the pressure is a turn-on—it is as exciting as it is stressful. The second project, because it lacks excitement and value, is more purely stress producing.

Let's now consider in more depth specifically how the three sources of stress affect the two-career couple.

Change

Much of the research on the effects of change on a person comes from the work of Thomas H. Holmes, M.D., of the University of Washington. He found that various life changes produce differing degrees of stress and that the magnitude of accumulated stress is related to the probability of illness. A person's yearly stress accumulation can be scored to estimate the likelihood of that person becoming physically or emotionally ill during the following two-year period. The Holmes scale is reproduced on the next page.

Go through the list of life changes and total the ratings that apply to you. If you have a score of less than 150 within a

Holmes Stress Scale

Life Change	Rating	Life Change	Rating
1. Death of spouse	100	22. Son or daughter leaving home	29
2. Divorce	73	23. Trouble with in-laws	29
3. Marital separation	65	24. Outstanding personal achievement	28
4. Jail term	63	25. Spouse begins or starts work	26
5. Death of close family member	63	26. Starting or finishing school	26
6. Personal injury or illness	53	27. Change in living conditions	25
7. Marriage	50	28. Revision of personal habits	24
8. Fired from work	47	29. Trouble with boss	23
9. Marital reconciliation	45	30. Change in work hours, condition	20
10. Retirement	45	31. Change in residence	20
11. Change in family member's health	44	32. Change in schools	20
12. Pregnancy	40	33. Change in recreational habits	19
13. Sex difficulties	39	34. Change in church activities	19
14. Addition to family	39	35. Change in social activities	18
15. Business readjustment	39	36. Mortgage or loan under $10,000	18
16. Change in financial status	38	37. Change in sleeping habits	16
17. Death of close friend	37	38. Change in number of family gatherings	15
18. Change in number of marital arguments	35	39. Change in eating habits	15
19. Mortgage or loan over $10,000	31	40. Vacation	13
20. Foreclosure of mortgage or loan	30	41. Christmas season	12
21. Change in work responsibilities	29	42. Minor violation of the law	11

Social Readjustment Rating Scale, by Thomas H. Holmes, M.D., Dept. of Psychiatry and Behavioral Science, School of Medicine, University of Washington, Seattle, WA. Reprinted by permission.

period of a year, you have only a 37 percent chance of getting sick within the next two years. Should your score be between 150 and 300, your chances of an illness increase to 51 percent. But, if you score over 300, there is serious danger—the odds are 80 percent that you will get sick within the next two years.

Interestingly, not all of the stressors are negative experiences. Positive life events such as personal achievements or even a vacation can be stress producing (i.e., require adaptation on our part). Most people fail to think of these experiences as stressful and, ironically, often react to positive events by taking on even more stress-producing activities. Thus, the person who receives a promotion or raise may unwittingly compound the stress of this event by buying a more expensive home.

Change is not inherent in the two-career life-style but becomes a problem when couples have to manage simultaneously what Rhona and Robert Rapoport refer to as "multiple role cycling."[3] What this means is that partners may have to adapt not only to transi-

"It seems like only yesterday I was OK, you were OK."

Reprinted by permission of G.P. Putnam's Son's from *Terribly Nice People* by William Hamilton, copyright © 1974 *The New Yorker*.

tions in either or both partners' çareers but to transitions occurring in their personal or family life as well. In other words, the possibilities for change multiply.

If the transition involves either a change in the number of role responsibilities or in the responsibilities themselves, both partners will need to adapt to the altered status quo. Major transitions in careers are frequently occasions for stress. A partner who is promoted often takes on additional responsibilities at work: longer work hours, more frequent travel, additional social obligations. All of these may require a shift in role responsibilities at home or a change in the existing support network.

When Fran went back to work on her Ph.D., we had to adapt in several ways. She now brought more work home, changed her sleeping habits (usually a 2:00 A.M. bedtime), and needed extra help with household tasks. We employed a full-time live-in housekeeper, naively believing that this would reduce the stress of managing the home and children. What we were unprepared for was the change that having another person in the house would mean. Not only were we coping with the change in status, hours, pressure, and activities that accompanied Fran's school work, but we also lost much of our privacy and were faced with another set of responsibilities—managing the maid.

Many couples are able to manage their careers quite successfully, but are totally unprepared for the turmoil a new baby can bring. Like a career, children are always in transition. Their needs change and the support structure that enables you to work and raise them is continually changing. Nothing stays the same or in place for very long. The family has to adapt as the kids grow up, which means each year brings a shift in responsibilities and in the way we meet them. Small children require physical caring. Outside help or day care may be the answer. But as the children grow older, their lives become more complex and their activities more diversified. Parental role responsibilities seem to multiply endlessly.

Couples also often experience role change in their relationship with parents. Frequently, parents experience debilitating illnesses or other problems associated with aging at the same point in life when one's own career and family responsibilities are increasing. Often the change is unexpected and calls for immediate action or difficult decisions.

Conflict

A second common source of stress among couples is conflict—our inability to reconcile demands or to meet our ideals and goals. In the dual-career couple, each partner is bound to experience conflict between roles. Sooner or later, they learn it's just not possible to be in two places at once. If an out-of-town client wants to set up an appointment for the evening you've planned to go to the theatre —and it's your spouse's birthday—you face several conflicts simultaneously. Work is conflicting with partner demands as well as with your own need for a night out. The conflict, though reconcilable, is stressful. The more roles one has going in life, the more likely that conflicting demands will arise.

Another type of conflict is between the role demands of the two partners. For example, both may need to be out of town at the same time. Once one of our children became ill on a day when we both had to teach. We had no one to turn to. The only solution was to leave our six-year-old daughter at home taking care of her four-year-old brother. We each called home every hour to check in. It was probably one of the most stressful days of our lives. It was unexpected, we were unprepared, and we had no control over the situation.

Children are not always the problem. The career mobility of working partners probably causes as much conflict for professional people as anything else. And even seemingly simple things can be a source of conflict. Some couples are never able to schedule vacations together. Others find that their work hours keep them apart substantial amounts of time. Still others report that a difference in priorities causes conflict and, hence, stress. One young woman who was becoming established as a college administrator described the stress she and her husband experienced:

> He is pulling back, putting more energy into relaxing. He wants me to play racquet ball with him, but I come home late, have evening meetings, travel. I'm just getting my career launched and he is cutting back on his. This has created a real problem for us—we're just coming from different directions. It's causing real strain in our relationship.

A less obvious type of conflict involves unmet expectations: the conflict between what we think we ought to be and what we are. For many of us, stress is caused by the feeling that we are not living up to the standards we have set for ourselves, as parents, partners, or professionals. Guilt and a sense of failure often accompany the stress.

One woman, who held a high-ranking administrative position with frequent travel obligations, described the stress she felt when her son began to experience serious problems at school. As successful as she knew her career was, she was plagued with doubts about how she was fulfilling her mother role. She interpreted his failure as her own and, as a consequence, experienced intense stress.

Couples who seem to be able to avoid conflicts and stress from unmet expectations are those who recognize their limits and set realistic standards. As one woman told us: "There are enough sources of stress without creating your own. If you expect too much of yourself, you become your own worst enemy."

Pressure

The most common source of stress for couples is sheer pressure caused by work or role overload. Even people who do not go through change or experience frequent conflict often are subject to intense or recurring pressure. They live, in short, in a high-demand environment at work and/or at home. The pressures never cease. New demands flood in to take the place of those already met. The problem seems to be particularly acute among couples with children. In most cases, the number of demands on the partners exceeds the time and energy needed to meet them. Anxiety and stress are the inescapable consequences.

Overload can result from having to juggle too many roles simultaneously, or it can result from having too many demands at one time from fewer roles. One working mother suggested to us that working partners should take their vacation in September. "When the kids go back to school it's sheer hell. Everyone needs to buy clothes. There are fees to submit, forms to fill out, sports start, music lessons start, dancing lessons start, Scouts start, and I go crazy!" What this women is describing is the overload that just one role presents each year.

Consider another couple. Bea and Don get up at 6:30 A.M. each morning, shower, dress, and start breakfast by 7:00, when their two children awake. By 7:30 they are all at the breakfast table, checking schedules for the day. At 8:00 the kids make lunches and leave for school. Bea begins her drive into the city. Traffic is heavy and she usually doesn't arrive at her desk until 9:00. Don takes the train to his job. If it's a normal, uneventful day, Bea and Don leave at 5:00 P.M. and are home by 6:00. More often than not, unexpected problems delay their arrival until 7:00 or later.

A part-time housekeeper arrives at 3:30 to be with the children and begin dinner. Whoever arrives first drives her home. When Bea and Don are both home, the family eats together. If not, the kids eat first and the parents "survive on lukewarm leftovers." Not having regular meals together is one source of stress they report. The family does dishes together. At this point, Bea and Don shift into their parent roles. Helping the children with homework, going to school meetings, shopping for Scout uniforms or Halloween costume materials, or listening to one of them practice a band instrument takes up the evening, often until 10:00. "Sometimes I don't even get to check the mail," Bea reports. At this point she gets ready for the next day, listing instructions for the housekeeper, checking the children's after-school schedule, and so forth. If either of them has work to do, it gets done after 10:00. They try to be in bed by midnight, although both admit it doesn't always happen.

On weekends, the shopping and errands take up most of Saturday, with their son's sports sandwiched in between. The family goes to church on Sunday and, adds Bea, "That is the only after-noon you could even call 'free'." Her major complaint? "No break in it all. I'm always working, doing something. If I'm not going, going at the office, then I'm coping with something that's come up at home. I almost went nuts when our son became a Cub Scout. There was no way he was ever going to pass his achievements without scheduling that into our evenings. The problem is that there's always something. If it isn't Scouts, it's a broken clarinet, or discovering at 8:00 A.M. that there's nothing in the house for the kids' lunches."

Bea and Don seem to have their roles well bal-anced, although they have little leisure time to relax—a common prob-lem for most couples. Balancing home, work, and family demands not only produces stress, it also creates a situation that prevents people from doing the very thing that would help them manage stress—taking time to rest and play.

Another common source of overload is what we call simultaneous career demands. When both partners are engaged in demanding jobs or when both jobs "peak"—i.e., become unusually demanding—stress escalates precipitously. Typically, one partner can support the other if he or she is in a lower-demand situation or work is going along routinely. But when both partners are responding to dead-lines, crises, increased pressure, or heavy travel commitments simul-taneously, there is virtually no slack in the system. One couple described it as follows:

> When we're both under the gun at work, there's just no energy left for anything else. The apartment can go for a while, but what hurts is that neither of us has anything left at the end of the day for each other. At times like that there just isn't any support for anything or anyone. I don't know how people with kids handle it.

One problem for many two-career couples, espe-cially professional couples, is that they are often both in stressful jobs or are responding to their careers in stress-producing ways. It's not uncommon to find achievement-oriented people married to each other. Both partners work intensely and competitively. They may sense greater urgency in accomplishing job tasks, invest more of themselves in their careers, and take on more pressures. If both partners are bringing home job stresses, the entire relationship may consist simply of coping with work pressures. This is typical among young couples just launching careers. Thus, stress overload can result from the interaction of two people intensely involved in their own career pursuits. That alone may be sufficient to stretch the relationship beyond its tolerance limit.

Analyzing and Managing the Stress in Your Life

Stress appears to be inevitable for dual-career couples. Given that fact, how can they manage it? Many techniques have been extolled for dealing with stress, but not all are related to managing stress. As Robert Kreitner points out, there is a difference between coping and adaptation.[4] Coping techniques help us put up with the problem, while adaptation solves the problem by either modifying the sources of stress or our reactions to them. Thus, to manage stress, we have to find ways to eliminate, minimize, or modify both the demand situations that cause stress as well as our way of responding.

Coping techniques generally involve things that seem to help us get through a stressful time. Two common ones are alcohol and drugs. Neither, however, relieves the stress. They may temporarily mask the feelings we experience, but they do not change the stress-producing event or our feelings about it. In many cases, the use of drugs or alcohol only compounds a person's problems, leading to dependence, addiction, poorer performance, and physical deterioration.

Two other popular techniques have more positive effects, but again do not change the stress. These are exercise and various forms of recreation.

There is good evidence that regular exercise has two benefits. First, it can provide a release for pent-up energy and aggression. People who respond to stress by storing up anger or other emotions find this sheer physical release helpful. (Many would argue that punching a pillow can have the same effect.) Second, regular exercise helps to improve and maintain one's physical well-being. Thus, by staying in good shape, we are better prepared to deal with stress when it occurs.

Recreation is simply a way of getting away from it all, escaping from the situations that bring about stress. We take vacations, go to the movies, or engage in hobbies to relax and rejuvenate ourselves. But we don't eliminate the source of our stress. We simply try to relax enough to muster the energy to return to our normal, and often stresssful, routine.

Adaptation, or managing stress, requires us to modify either our stressors or our responses. To do this, we must:

- develop an awareness of the stress-producing events or situations in our life or work;
- develop a sensitivity to our own style of responding to these stressors.

What produces the stress in your life? To do something about stress, you first have to identify its source. Consider your own life in terms of the stress factors we presented earlier. Is overload and pressure your problem? Change? Conflicts? Are you subject to uncertainty or the inability to predict demands? Is a lack of control or dissatisfaction with the demand situation itself adding to your feelings of stress? What aspect or aspects of your life involve conflict, change, or overload? The accompanying Stress Inventory should help you identify your major areas of stress.

Stress Inventory

I. What kinds of stress are you experiencing?

Conflicts? _____

Changes? _____

Pressure or overload? _____

II. Consider each kind of stress you checked. Now think about why the stress exists. What is producing it?

- Describe the major conflicts in your life:

- Describe the major changes you are adapting to:

- Describe the major pressures or overload you are absorbing:

III. The following list should help you pinpoint stress producers. Remember, several aspects of your life may be interacting to create stress. Thus, check all situations, events, or demands that are possible sources of stress for you.

Work components
- the nature of your job
- relationships at work
- dissatisfaction with job
- change in job duties or responsibilities
- professional organization responsibilities
- career development and concerns about your future
- commuting or travel
- other

Family components
- effects of your partner's career on you
- your responsibilities as spouse or partner
- parent responsibilities and concerns
- kinship and family responsibilities or concerns
- home-maintenance responsibilities
- financial obligations
- support for home and child care
- other

Self components
- leisure needs, desires
- personal-development goals
- education or training obligations, demands
- recreation needs, desires
- own attitudes
- other

Social and community
- relationship building or maintenance
- entertaining, meeting social obligations
- community organizations
  schools
  religious
  political
  charity
- other

IV. Now pick *one* of the types of stress you have described. Ask yourself the following questions:

- What aspects of the situation are under your control? What can you do to change or modify the situation?
- What aspects of the situation are under the control of other people?
- Who do you need to influence to get others to help you change or modify the situation?
- What can you do to change or modify the situation? What are some specific steps you can take to relieve the stress?
- What can you ask others to do to change or modify the situation? What could others do differently to help you relieve the stress?

V. Finally, ask yourself the following questions:

- What would help increase your control over the stresses in your life?
- What would help you to predict events in your life or decrease the uncertainty associated with stresses for you?
- What would help decrease or eliminate negatively valued demands that produce stress for you?

Action steps

What a person can do to modify stress-producing events or situations will vary depending on the circumstances, but we can suggest several general action steps.

- Limit the number of obligations you take on at any one time. If work obligations are demanding, avoid trying to do anything you don't absolutely have to do in other areas of your life. If other words, reduce the number of role demands you have going at any one time.
- Learn to say "no!" This is absolutely essential if you are ever going to accomplish the step above.
- Schedule your life, when you can, so that conflicting demands can be avoided.
- Ask others, like spouse, boss, and/or family members, to do the same for you. In other words, share your need to avoid conflicts with other people who help create them for you.
- Take a good, hard look at your own goals and expectations as well as those other people hold for you. Try to reduce or eliminate any unrealistic or overly demanding ones.
- Analyze the demands on you at work and home. Delegate responsibilities wherever you can. Keep asking yourself: "Do I really have to do this? Can someone else do it?"

- Try to reduce uncertainty as much as possible by establishing a regular routine for those things within your control.
- Plan your life and career with your partner to avoid or eliminate mutual sources of stress. Don't just assume things will work out. See what decisions you both can consciously make to avoid stressors.
- Manage and plan for the changes in your lives. If you have experienced or anticipate a major life change, avoid others that are within your control. Even small changes like going on a diet or using a new birth-control method can significantly affect your stress level. Minimize the amount of change you induce in your life.

Modifying responses to stress

Some of the steps mentioned above, along with your own inventory, may help you to eliminate or modify stress-producing situations or events. But what about the stress you can't change or control? Can you reduce its destructive effects on you? Most experts feel that by learning to control our reactions to stress, we can.

One psychologist has suggested that people fall into one of three categories in terms of their response to stress.[5] The first type of person represses the stress experience. Rather than react to what is producing the stress, he or she internalizes any feelings of anger, impatience, hostility, or even exhaustion.

The second type reacts to stress emotionally and acts out his or her stress response. Sometimes the acting out may take the form of visible, physical symptoms—allergies, fatigue, moodiness, depression, loss of appetite, insomnia, and so on. It can also take the form of verbal or behavioral demonstrations—shouting, blowing up, or other expressions of feelings.

The third type of person is able to moderate his or her responses to stress. By effectively controlling any emotional as well as psychological reactions to potentially stress-inducing events, the person simply does not experience the event as stressful.

How do people learn to moderate their stress responses? Two techniques are growing in popularity. The first is meditation and learning to relax (rather than react) when exposed to stress. The second is biofeedback, learning to actually control our physiological response.

Transcendental meditation (TM), one popular form of meditation, involves a regular twice-a-day routine. Proponents of TM claim that it alleviates fatigue, stress, anxiety, and lowers blood pressure. Many books are available on TM and seminars abound to train people in specific TM techniques.

A more general form of meditation involves developing what Harvard professor Herbert Benson calls the "relaxation response."[6] This is the opposite of the stress response. By learning to relax when subjected to potentially stressful stimuli, one can actually counter the stress.

Four factors are essential to elicit the relaxation response:

- *Select a quiet environment.* In order to learn to relax, you have to set aside some time each day for contemplation in a setting removed from all stimuli and distraction.

- *Find something to dwell on.* What it is doesn't seem to matter. People use words, phrases, short prayers. The important thing is to develop a mental mechanism for keeping your mind from wandering. Repeat the word or phrase over and over to help you block all thoughts out.

- *Develop a passive attitude.* This is considered essential. In order to relax, you have to give in to total mental and physical passivity. By learning to breathe slowly and deeply and by mentally letting go of your body, you can achieve complete relaxation.

- *Assume a comfortable position.* Find a position that reduces your awareness of external stimuli. For some people this can be sitting on the floor or lying down. The important element is to eliminate all physical sources of tension—anything that might press, rub, or otherwise distract or anger you.

The second technique, which also requires special training, is biofeedback. Through operant conditioning and the use of machines, the individual is trained to control voluntarily his or her physiological reactions to stress, such as pulse rate, skin temperature, muscle tension, and so forth.

One thing is clear about the management of stress. While we do not have complete control over all of the stress-producing events in our lives, we do have some choices. We can choose to eliminate those sources of stress under our control and we can choose to respond in different ways to stress we can't control. Learning to relax, rather than tense, is a first step. But adopting an attitude that allows us to relax also seems to be critical.

In our interviews with couples, we have noted a difference between couples who seem to be managing the stress in their lives and those who are simply coping. The basic difference is their attitude toward themselves, their careers, and their lives. The managers seem to have come to terms with what is realistic or possible. They don't expect themselves, their jobs, or their spouses to meet unreal criteria. One man described his philosophy as follows:

> You have to accept the fact that you aren't perfect and you can't be the perfect father. You can't do everything, can't finish everything. You feel a lot less stress when you learn to accept your own and others' limitations as a human being.

Time Management

Closely related to stress for couples and one of the most commonly heard complaints is lack of sufficient time to get things done in their lives. Again, overload and multiple-role demands are usually to blame.

While people can't manufacture more time, they can make better use of the time they have. As is often said, managing time does not mean working harder, it just means working smarter—using the time available to accomplish what is truly important.

One of the most useful approaches to effective time management is described by Alan Lakein in his excellent book, *How to Get Control of Your Time and Your Life.*[7] Basic to his system is learning how to *plan* what you want to do and then organizing your use of time to get it done. As two other authors observe: "Time is a constant that cannot be altered. . . . We cannot manage time itself. We can only manage our activities with respect to it."[8] In other words, managing time, like managing stress, involves learning to manage our own behavior.

The first step in planning is to identify goals and objectives. What is it you want to accomplish? It helps to think in terms of time frames. We have long-term objectives as well as short-term, day-to-day objectives. Without conscious planning, important or long-term objectives may be lost in the rush to carry out day-to-day activities. Or, we may fail to accomplish meaningful short-term objectives because we are allotting too much time to unimportant tasks—perhaps things we could forget altogether.

Whether you are planning for today or for next year, the key to getting things done is learning how to establish priorities. You have to identify and concentrate on those tasks and activities that are of highest priority and eliminate those that are low priority. Lakein suggests using a simple ABC system.

The ABC system works like this: First, list all the goals you want to accomplish. Now ask yourself which ones are really important (will result in the rewards you value) and which are less important. The most important goals are labeled as "A"—top priority. Less important ones are designated as "B," and lower priority goals as "C." Now that you have some sense of what your A goals are, you can begin to plan your time to accomplish these. If you've listed a lot of C goals, you may want to reconsider whether they are worth having as goals at all. Some, however, may be tasks you have to do and cannot ignore forever.

Once you have identified your goals and established priorities, the next step is to think about activities that will help you accomplish them. What will you have to do to achieve your priority goals? Are you building those activities into your schedule or ignoring them? Planning, the key to time management, revolves around consciously allocating and using time for those activities that will help us accomplish our important goals. This doesn't mean that we devote all of our time to them, but only that we ensure that as much time as possible is being used for top-priority items.

Get into the habit of scheduling your day in order to use time efficiently. One of the basic techniques is to make up a daily list of things to do, along with the priorities for those activities. Try the following exercise:

- List all the things you have to do tomorrow.
- Now prioritize your list using the ABC system. Which activities are really important for accomplishing priority goals and which are not?
- Once you have the activities labeled as A, B, or C, look at the B activities. Which of these could qualify as A's and which are really C's?
- Now think about scheduling your day to ensure adequate time to get your A activities accomplished.

Lakein offers several important tips for scheduling time and using it more efficiently.

- Keep a daily TO DO list and review it each morning.
- Block out time for priority activities—either save a time slot in each day or set a day aside each week.
- Don't let anything interfere with this time.

- Use your time efficiently. Handle paper only once, don't keep reshuffling it. Don't procrastinate—if something has to be done, do it immediately. Minimize the steps involved in what you do. Delegate as much as possible to others. Unless you absolutely have to do something, assign it to someone else.

- Learn to know your "prime time." When do you work best? Save it for priority projects.

- Try to be flexible. Always leave time in your schedule for emergencies or catching up.

- Plan time to relax. If you are exhausted, you won't be able to work effectively or efficiently.

- Learn to use transition time to get things done. For example, can you read, catch the news on the radio, or discuss matters with your partner or family while you dress, do your nails, or eat breakfast? How do you use time spent in commuting, coffee breaks, lunch hour, or waiting in offices? Do you carry your list with you so you can use time to plan? Do you carry paper and pencil for writing or have something along to read?

- Finally, can you turn C activities into things that can be put off indefinitely? How many C activities do you do that, in the end, don't have to be done, or can be done later if they turn out to be important? Learn to discriminate and put them aside.

If you take a close, hard look at how you are presently using your time, you may surprise yourself. Three important questions to ask are: What am I doing that doesn't need to be done? What am I doing that could be done more efficiently? What am I doing that someone else could be doing?

What do couples report as the best time-management techniques for them? Not surprisingly, many have stumbled on the very techniques that Lakein and others propose. At the top of their lists is learning to set priorities. Some couples have also learned the art of "doubling up"—doing two or more things at once. Lunch hours are more often than not used for errands or shopping. Extra minutes at the office may be used to squeeze in phone calls.

Another technique is to segment time—that is, set aside a specific time for a specific task and then concentrate fully on that activity. Most couples report that this technique requires carefully planning given times well in advance. A spur-of-the-moment decision to spend the next two hours cleaning the garage may not be the most efficient allocation of time.

Other couples simply try to build in extra time. Getting up early in the morning and saving that time for oneself is a common strategy, an example of creating a "pocket" of time that might otherwise be wasted. Related to this is planning ahead. As commitments emerge, many people try to schedule them into a long-term agenda of activities, eliminating unimportant time demands and making space for priority items.

Unwinding

A final issue closely tied in to both stress and time management is making the difficult transition from work to home or personal life. One partner explained the problem as follows:

> My spouse-versus-career conflict concerns the ability to be able to wind down after a pressuring day at work. This is hard to do at times. It calls for me gathering my self-control together and forcing myself to be divorced from the work problems.

This is a problem shared by many. As Jane G. Bensahel suggests, "It is not so much the physical exertion or the long hours of his job that drains the executive. It is the tension and the nagging doubts which accompany the cut and thrust of the job that leave the executive exhausted and unable to 'switch off' when it is finally time to leave for home and family."[9] Bensahel describes five factors that make it difficult for a person to separate from work and suggests helpful ways to deal with them.

The first is *preoccupation with undone tasks.* If you leave for home worrying about what didn't get done or resolved, personal or family matters will take a back seat to leftover work concerns. Bensahel suggests the following ways of putting tasks out of your mind at the end of each workday:

- Organize a list of specific things that you didn't get done today and plan time for these tomorrow or later in the week. In other words, don't let them linger on as part of today. Move them up and organize them (in your list and in your head) as part of a future schedule.

- Spot check yourself during the day to make sure you are tending to important tasks. This will help minimize what is left undone at the end of the day.

- Accept the arrival of the end of the day. Try to make this a transition time. Begin to ease off a bit before your departure.

The second problem is *having second thoughts.* People often go home with nagging doubts about decisions made or actions taken during the day. Usually, you can't go back and undo them, so it helps to find ways to accept the day's events and the part you played. Try the following:

- Recognize afterthoughts as simply that. Don't dwell on them. Identify them quickly and move on to something else.
- If you really feel you made a bad decision or move, don't brood. Think instead about what you have learned from it, the positive insights you have gained.

A third factor is *stopping work suddenly.* Many people find the transition from office to home difficult simply because it always happens so abruptly. They are intensely involved at work and suddenly realize it's time to go home. Try to develop a slowing-down approach at the end of the day.

- Plan something stimulating to do at home. In other words, don't go from high excitement at work to a slump routine at home. Make sure your home life includes some activities you enjoy and look forward to.
- Set up a transition period at the end of the day to slow down your pace. The last hour should be devoted to less frantic activities, like organizing your desk, planning the next day's schedule, or tying up loose ends.

A fourth problem is *worrying about the past or the future.* People who concentrate too much on other than the here and now often have trouble clearing their head for home activities and relationships. Don't think about past or future problems unless doing so helps you solve current problems.

The last factor is *preoccupation with tasks half completed.* Living with loose ends is mentally and emotionally exhausting. It is important to create a sense of completion for yourself if this is not built into your job. Two ways to do this are:

- When you start a job, plan on specific segments that will constitute completion points. In other words, divide the task into parts that can be used to chart your progress.
- Reward yourself for things you have completed. Treat yourself to something that feels good. Dwell on what you have done, not on what remains undone.

The Bottom Line

No one chapter in a book can change your life or tell you how to get rid of stress entirely. There does, however, seem to be a basic principle underlying much of what we know about managing both stress and time. And that principle is that the demands associated with valued and rewarding activities seem to be consistently less stressful and more energizing than the demands associated with activities that are not personally meaningful.

The bottom line, then, appears to be not how much you are doing, but what you are doing and why. People who take on unwanted demands at work or at home may be creating more stress for themselves than people who lead incredibly hectic lives but derive satisfaction and pleasure from the things they choose to do.

Be selective about how you use your time and your energies. For the two-career couple, this ultimately means managing goals and priorities. If the goal of the couple is to manage both careers simultaneously, then stress may be viewed quite differently than it would be under other circumstances. The real issue for couples is not how to avoid stress, for it seems inevitable, but how to recognize the sources of stress and their reactions to it. If they can keep stress within optimal limits, they can actually use it to energize their efforts toward valued goals rather than letting it sap their resources in the pursuit of unwanted or unnecessary obligations.

PART II

CREATING YOUR OWN LIFE-STYLE

CHAPTER FIVE

MAKING THE HOUSE WORK

Most fights over women's rights take place in the kitchen, not the state capital. As more and more couples choose the dual-career path, the issue of housework has become an increasingly explosive topic. And, despite Betty Friedan's assurances that the women's movement is meant to liberate both men and women, it is still the female, even the corporate executive or bank vice-president, who most often winds up with responsibility for household chores.

Thus it is not surprising that when Erma Freid, a New York woman, started her company, The Surrogate Wife, she found that many of the people who called for her services were women! The average fulltime homemaker spends fifty-five hours a week doing household chores. The employed woman spends less than half that time trying to accomplish the same thing. Clearly, the working woman can no longer match her homemaker counterpart. It's no wonder that so many working wives have cried out in desperation, "I need a wife!"

Keeping a home has traditionally been defined as the woman's responsibility. When she no longer accepts sole responsibility or is simply unable to do everything, it's necessary to rearrange the division of labor. Along with this redistribution there is usually a change in housekeeping standards. Tasks that were once considered essential may begin to seem dispensable.

113

How does the two-career couple manage a home and two careers? First, they must change their expectations about what will get done, as well as their attitudes about who will do what. This involves learning to share or exchange home roles and tasks. They must also accept as permanent the changes in living and spending patterns that evolve when two partners are employed outside the home.

How couples come to terms with each of these factors varies, depending on their income, time demands, and the availability of outside help. But, in most cases, there are adjustments to be made—in attitudes, roles, and living patterns.

Changing Expectations At Home

Most couples have two different sets of expectations about keeping a home: expectations about responsibility for housework and expectations about what constitutes a well-run home. Let's look at each and see why they are the way they are. Can these expectations be changed to the satisfaction of each partner?

Most people agree that, even when a woman works, she usually bears primary responsibility for housekeeping functions. Is this purely because she can't escape traditional sex-linked associations? The answer in most cases is no. The real reason many women continue to carry the primary burden is that *they* believe they should, or have to. In other words, most women don't expect their partners to be willing to take on home chores. Women who work by choice rather than necessity often view their jobs as primarily of benefit to themselves. Thus, they may not perceive that an exchange *is* taking place, and they feel bound to keep up with all the home duties of the nonworking woman.

As Gabrielle Burton tells it, many women (and men) have "bought in" to the traditional division of labor on the rationale that the man is contributing more to the household via his larger paycheck.[1] (On the average, the woman earns 60 percent as much as her partner.) Thus, he is excused from housework—he's made his contribution. Many men, of course, enjoy their work and get off the hook just because they also happen to earn a paycheck. If a woman accepts this argument, then her paycheck, too, should justify less obligation at home. Frequently it doesn't.

It's also frequently argued, according to Burton, that the man is doing "important" work in his job. Housework is beneath his dignity and takes time away from "more valuable" tasks.

Ridiculous? Of course. Working women hold responsible positions as well. Why should the status of a man's job give him any advantage?

Another rationale is that men put up with so much unpleasant stress on the job that they need to be relieved of any extra burdens at home. Again, many women face the same pressures at work. Yet no one seems to feel that they should be relieved of the unpleasant chores at home.

Each of these rationales crumbles rather easily on close inspection. None seems to justify why working men, but not working women, should be relieved of responsibility for running the house.

Power in the home

A basic difference between traditional homes and two-career homes is the distribution of power. In two-career homes the balance shifts from favoring the male to a more equal distribution or, in some cases, imbalance in favor of the woman. As women increasingly come to acquire and contribute resources equal to the contributions of their partners, their bargaining power in the relationship increases proportionately. *Both* partners are now in a position to bargain for what they will and won't do or can and can't do. Housekeeping is no longer arbitrarily assigned to the nonworking partner, a commodity provided in exchange for support from a working partner. A well-run home is something they both need, but now can have only at some cost.

Couples who recognize and acknowledge the redistribution of power are more readily able to change their expectations about responsibility for home chores. For both partners this seems to be important. People need to *justify* their actions and those of their partner. If one has to give up something, then it helps if some clear compensation accompanies the sacrifice. If the husband recognizes that he is *gaining* something when his wife works, rather than just losing a housekeeper, he is more ready to compromise. Clearly, additional income seems to be a big factor in helping many men shift their own expectations. But men are also experiencing other forms of liberation in addition to financial ones.

Warren Farrell, in his book *The Liberated Man*, suggests several compensating factors or gains that men derive from working partners.[2] Some of these are:

- A woman with her own life will be less controlling of her husband.

- Men are no longer burdened with being a "security object" for their wives.

- Sharing the breadwinner role lessens the man's pressure to succeed in a particular job or company, thus decreasing an organization's "leverage" over the man.
- Men are freed economically to seek self-satisfaction at home and work rather than make life choices for economic reasons alone.
- Men have options of doing and enjoying home roles rather than being closed out of them by rigid role definitions.
- Men are relieved of being the sole source of meaning or happiness for a partner.
- Partners who have autonomy outside the home appreciate and understand the other's needs in this area.
- Sharing roles reduces a man's need to prove himself only by male sex-linked standards.
- Men can sometimes shed some of the "male" chores they have been forced to perform in exchange for support from a partner or outside help.
- Men can enjoy a relationship based on mutual support or genuine sharing rather than an artificial dependency relationship.

Thus, the male partner needs to view the exchange as a benefit to him rather than an encroachment on his masculinity. For a woman, the knowledge that her partner appreciates the benefits he stands to gain helps to alleviate her own guilt about not being the sole homemaker.

Generating change

Different circumstances seem to precipitate a couple's ability to confront the issue of division of labor. First, one or both partners openly acknowledge their relative contributions to the relationship and the home. The woman might say, "Damn it, because of my income you were able to buy that new stereo you've been wanting for the last two years, and what do I get? No help!" Or, the man might acknowledge the benefits he has accrued. He now feels indebted. As one husband put it:

> Before my wife went back to work she was a real drain on me. I would come home at night and she looked to me for all of her stimulation, conversation, and contacts with people. We were trying to get by on one income and were always going into debt. When she suggested getting herself a job it felt like a big burden off me. She was afraid of trying to manage her job and everything else. But I told her I would help. I'd rather do

dishes and wash out a toilet than sit there every night feeling like I had to carry both of us forever.

A second type of precipitating event is when things start to disintegrate and a crisis forces the partners to take stock.

It got to a point in our house where there was never enough food in the refrigerator or no one could find any clean socks. My husband was getting angry with me, but I finally threw up my hands, sat down, and cried. Only then did we talk about it. I started laying out my schedule and for the first time he understood that I just couldn't do everything. There just wasn't enough sheer physical time. I didn't even ask him to help. I just told him he had to if he wanted things to be different. I think he understood and he's really been very supportive, sharing the burden. But I am not sure he would have been willing to if things hadn't broken down.

Most people agree that any change in division of home labor causes serious strain—at first. Some men feel threatened; some women feel guilty. But couples who do not confront the issue face a far more serious problem: the pent-up hostility or anger that one partner feels (and the other probably suspects) when a relationship is not equitable.

It is one thing to believe intellectually that it is only "fair" for both partners to share the burden of managing a home. It is quite another thing to enjoy doing it. Most of us experience feelings of ambivalence, guilt, jealousy, or resentment when asked to switch roles. Being able to express these is essential, for they are a normal part of the change process and should be talked through.

Probably the most difficult part of role sharing is giving up some of the ego needs that we satisfy by keeping a role all to ourselves. Most people think that only men have problems sharing traditionally female roles, but many women experience a loss of ego identity, too. It's difficult to admit that one's husband can bake a terrific loaf of bread or finish the laundry in record time. We all want to feel indispensable, so when a spouse proves just as capable of sewing or cleaning or juggling the kids' schedules, it's only natural to feel threatened. Similarly, it's difficult for a man to accept that his wife is a successful businesswoman and a family provider.

Thus, the biggest hurdle most couples have to scale is giving up their territory. Role sharing means sharing the turf that may have been previously reserved for just one partner. It also means "going public," letting others know that things are different at home.

Men have to adjust to the threats imposed by their wives' independence. Many women, recognizing that they are capable

of earning a living, no longer are willing to let their partners make all
the big decisions. Thus, decision making becomes as much a shared
responsibility as housekeeping and breadwinning.

Part of the process of learning to share roles is
learning to *trust* the other partner. When we exchange roles, we are
trusting someone else to do things we would normally do. And part of
learning to trust our role to a partner is allowing him or her to make
mistakes or do things differently.

Effective role sharing gets back again to dealing
with our own expectations. If we expect a partner—or a child—to do
things exactly as we would do them, we may be setting ourselves up
for disappointment. We also are likely to be very critical. This decreases the partner's willingness to share or help.

One woman described to us the process she and
her husband went through when he took over the laundry and occasional cooking.

> I could not get used to the feeling that Dave didn't do things right. His
> idea of a spaghetti supper was to open a jar of sauce from the store. I had
> always made sauce from scratch. I kept telling him that that stuff was
> horrible. FInally he just said, "The kids and I like it." I had to accept the
> fact that if I was going to have him cook, I'd have to get used to his way
> of cooking. It was that or do it myself.
>
> Then there was the laundry. He would fold things loosely and pile clothes
> up for everyone to put away. I had always put the clothes away for every-
> one. I got angry that he was "cutting corners." But when I thought about
> it, I realized that a lot of my anger was at myself for having done so many
> things that I really didn't have to do. Dave recognized the efficient way
> immediately and I think it threatened me to see that he was really better
> at organizing around a home and a job than I had been.

Role sharing eventually brings about increased
empathy for one's partner. By actually taking over a job, you see just
how tough it is. But before the empathy is established, couples often go
through the strain of experiencing for the first time the same feelings
their partners suffered through when they occupied a particular role.

> The days I would come home and Jack would be responsible for dinner, I'd
> go through all the same behaviors that he used to lay on me. I'd drop
> exhausted into a chair, grab the paper, want to be left alone, and *expect*
> the dinner to be ready when I was. He would get furious with me. Usually
> he would be struggling with setting the table and want me to help—and I
> didn't. Just like he didn't when I was the one making dinner. It took a
> while for us to recognize that we not only shared responsibility for dinner
> on different nights, but we shared the responsibility for understanding
> what the other person was going through.

Most two-career couples, regardless of the specific role-sharing arrangements they work out, agree that they no longer take each other for granted and now feel much closer emotionally. Several men who have taken over the total running of a home express disbelief at what their partners had been doing single-handedly. Their new perspective has increased their willingness to provide at least some household help, if not continue to take over forever.

How clean is "clean"?

Interestingly, both men and women who try to share career and household tasks agree that lowering their standards of home care is essential. Many men, however, only come to this conclusion after they have spent some time actively participating in home chores. Only then do they realize the pleasure of a "perfect home" is not worth the time and energy it takes to keep it that way, especially when it is their time and energy.

Most couples we have interviewed reported that they quickly pared down their lives (especially homemaking) to the essentials when they took on two careers. They are also much less

"Hi, darling—everything is in the crock pot, including yours truly."

Reprinted by permission of G.P. Putnam's Sons from *Husbands, Wives and Live-Togethers* by William Hamilton, copyright © 1976 by William Hamilton.

inclined to measure their worth in terms of the cleanliness of their home or their domestic accomplishments. Even people who strongly identify with home roles are able to partition their expectations. Workdays may have different standards than weekends. Cold cereal for breakfast (self-prepared) is acceptable during the week, but waffles are a Sunday brunch ritual. Likewise, a bit of dust on the furniture is a reasonable exchange for an evening of relaxation together.

One of the major barriers to lower standards for most people is the fear of social disapproval. But, as many couples have learned, people who judge them only on the basis of how they keep house are dispensable friends. Often, the standards couples are trying to keep up with are not their own, but are unrealistic demands inherited or internalized from mothers, relatives, or neighbors whose only contribution to the family was the maintenance of a spotless house. A good question to ask yourself is: "Whose approval am I seeking?"

In lowering their standards, most couples first have to accept that their home will be a little less clean and a little less tidy. They learn to ignore or to live with some degree of dust, disorder, or disorganization. Barbara Harrison offers the following advice for people who feel guilty about lowering their standards of cleanliness.

> Standards of house cleaning really separate people. Maybe people who are unreasonably oppressed by other people's judgments can't afford to become intimate with people who use housework to justify their existence. What bothers you most? Your overflowing ashtrays, or what your aunts would say about them? Make friends with other slobs![3]

Secondly, couples must set *realistic* expectations about what tasks should be included on their list of essentials. Ask yourself, "How can I reduce what I am now doing?" Most people find that they continue (at first) to expect that cooking, entertaining, decorating, correspondence, holidays, children's clothes, and so forth will receive the same amount of attention that they do in a traditional home with a full-time homemaker. This is not only unrealistic, it is impossible. Something has to give—preferably housekeeping perfection rather than your sanity.

One way to deal with the problem of home management is to first analyze what is being done now. This helps you to get a handle on what *has* to be done, what you can let slip, and who can do it. The first step is to break down your life by functions. For example, list all the functions that are performed in your home and the tasks that are part of each function. The following list may suggest some ideas:

- *Food chores*
  shopping
  cooking
  cleaning up/dishes
  garbage
  packing lunches
- *Clothes chores*
  shopping
  washing
  folding
  putting away
  dry cleaning
  mending
  ironing
  weeding out old clothes
- *Money chores*
  budget planning
  bill paying
  bank accounts
- *House or apartment maintenance*
  cleaning
  appliance maintenance
  lawn or yard
  furnace
  storms, screens, etc.
  house repairs
  dealing with service people
- *Social obligations*
  gift buying
  entertaining
  holiday and birthday obligations
  coordinating the family's social schedules
- *Children*
  meetings at school
  driving
  support for activities (Scouts, etc.)
  volunteer work on children's activities (e.g., Little League umpire)

help with projects, homework, etc.
other care
getting baby-sitters, etc.

- *Pets*

  daily care
  regular maintenance (the vet, etc.)
  boarding for vacations, trips

- *Leisure*

  planning social activities
  vacation arrangements
  weekend activities

The list will differ, of course, for each couple. When you make your list, you will probably feel overwhelmed at first by the magnitude of things that have to be done. Just relax and read on.

The second step is to see if you can eliminate any of the chores you have listed. This is probably one of the most helpful steps a couple can take. Eliminating tasks not only reduces the sheer number of things that have to be done, it relieves both partners from having to share or cope with the task. As you consider each task, ask yourselves, "Is this essential to maintaining our home life?" Many people continue to do things simply because they always have done them.

Sally and Marshall found that they were able to eliminate a number of nonessential chores without drastically altering the quality of their life together. They found, for example, that they could reduce the amount of cleaning in their home simply by scheduling it every other week rather than weekly. With no one home during the day, weekly cleaning wasn't really required. Further, they eliminated ironing entirely by using wash-and-wear fabrics and relying on the dry cleaners for everything else. They also gave up having pets. Although your children may object, you do have a choice over pets. You don't have to have them.

A third step is to see if you can simplify the remaining tasks. This is often easier than eliminating things entirely. There are a number of ways people can simplify home chores. Consider the following:

- Shop once a week.
- Have groceries delivered.
- Shop for clothes and gifts from catalogues wherever possible.

- Cook simple meals on workdays.
- Get a microwave oven.
- If you don't have a dishwasher, get one.
- Do laundry once a week.
- Throw things out immediately to reduce clutter and eliminate the need to sort them later. For example, don't save nonessential mail, old clothes, kids' clutter, etc.—it just piles up and creates another task.
- Have the dry cleaning picked up and dropped off, if possible.
- Pay bills once a month.
- Use low-maintenance decorating or home products (triple-track storms and screens, etc.).
- Entertain once a year (a big brunch is good) to get rid of obligations; then do your socializing by going out with friends.
- Get a regular baby-sitter lined up for Saturday nights—even if you don't go out you can guarantee to pay the person. This may be easier in the long run than those desperate last-minute phone calls.

Once you have pared down and simplified your list, write in the name of the person usually responsible for the chore. Is one person carrying more than her or his share? Can jobs be reallocated to distribute the burden more equitably? There are several alternatives open to you. Who else is available to do the chores? This may simply be you and your partner, or you may have children who can help. Another possibility is to hire help. This will reduce the tasks that you and your partner or children have to share.

Families allocate tasks in many different ways. One way is to set up a regular schedule based on daily, weekly, or occasional tasks and then assign jobs. Sometimes the first round of decisions is based on who wants to do what. This is the easiest and most agreeable way to allocate tasks. Or, expertise may be the deciding factor. Sometimes it is easier to do things we do well (and therefore can do quickly) than to share difficult tasks just to get a fifty-fifty distribution. The goal is two-fold: to get things done and to leave partners and family members feeling satisfied with the system.

Usually there are some tasks that no one wants. A system of alternating may be the answer here. Or, a lottery can be fun. All the tasks that are left after people choose their regular chores are thrown into a grab bag. Once a week everyone has to fish for his or her task of the week. While the job may be awful, it only lasts a week and then someone else takes over.

Living with any new system takes a while to get used to, especially if one or the other partner is clinging to old standards of perfection. It is also hard to ignore the temptation to do things that aren't getting done. One woman came to terms with the mess in her husband's study only after forcing herself to accept that it was his responsibility, not hers. But she admits that it still bothers her to look in and see the desk covered with papers, books, ashtrays, and other paraphernalia. On the other hand, making the cleaning of each person's special room a personal chore has reduced her cleaning load by a significant number of rooms.

An important factor to consider in the reallocation of tasks is whether you are striving for equality or fairness. Most people find that the "tit-for-tat" strategy or the perfect fifty-fifty split just doesn't work. What is more important is that each partner be flexible enough to share in the maintenance of a support structure that allows both partners to pursue their careers. This may mean alternating or sharing roles, rather than a firm or constant division of labor. Both partners may pitch in to help or just one may take over, depending on the schedule that works best on a given day.

Most of the couples we have interviewed do not have rigid fifty-fifty relationships. What they value most is the mutual recognition that home care is not just the woman's responsibility. This perceived sense of equity is essential, even if, as in most cases, women still do more homemaking tasks than men. What leaves them feeling fairly treated is the attitude of their spouses toward sharing the responsibility. This seems to be where most couples are today, at stage one, both changing their expectations about who will do what and both willing to settle for less than perfection.

Accepting New Living Patterns

Perhaps the most important step in solving the problems of home management is learning to accept and adapt to new patterns of living. This is, in a sense, the incorporation stage of changing our expectations. For many couples, the recognition that their lives are different (from their parents' lives or from their old way of operating) doesn't come until after they have established different roles and different living or spending patterns. Only then do they acknowledge that all this isn't temporary—it is their way of life.

Among couples we have interviewed, there seems to be a marked difference between those who start out together consciously choosing (and designing) a two-career life-style and those who start with only one partner employed. Couples who evolve into a two-career life-style experience more drastic change than do couples who have no previous "traditions" to cast off—the sharing of work and home *is* their tradition from the start. For those who have to adjust their life-style, the need to accommodate and accept change is an important and sometimes difficult experience. Many men and women initially think that the changes imposed by two careers are temporary, merely a period of adjustment. But gradually, over time, partners come to recognize that the ad hoc changes they have made are becoming permanent. One woman describes her realization as follows:

> At first I thought that my inability to keep up with everything would go away. I couldn't seem to get around to certain things, like making cookies or gifts for Christmas or sorting out the summer and winter clothes before the next season was in full swing. We would talk about how things would be different—more organized—next year. But when the next year came it was just like the one before. Out lives changed slowly because we weren't fully aware at the time about how little things were slipping away. We were so busy coping with each week that it would be months before we realized we weren't entertaining or that the basement *still* hadn't been cleaned. I can't say it felt very good to wake up and realize that things we used to do were not going to suddenly just pop back into our lives. As long as we both worked, we were going to have to settle for less time to do certain things and that was a reality we had been postponing.

CHAPTER SIX

BUT WHAT ABOUT CHILDREN?

The first accusation nonworking mothers (or fathers) usually hurl at two-career couples is that their children suffer for want of full-time parental care. A mother and father who both work long and exhausting hours, they point out, can't possibly provide proper parenting. Children of two-career couples grow up unloved, undisciplined, and insecure, and any mother who would forsake her child to go back to work only months or even weeks after giving birth is clearly an unfit mother.

Before we go any further, let's dispel a few of these myths. If you are now a working mother or father, you already know that holding a job and being a parent are not mutually exclusive; men have been doing it for years. In fact, it's likely your own parents did it—thus you may be excellent evidence for the defense.

Most experts agree that it is not the quantity of time spent on parenting but the quality of it that counts. Most career couples, well aware of their time constraints, more carefully plan how to spend the time they do have with their children. They also consciously encourage their children to assume responsibility and to take part in family decision making, therefore helping them to become more independent and self-sufficient than they might otherwise be. This seems to be the comment most often made by people after they encounter children who have been raised from birth by working parents. The children seem to be far more able to cope with problem situations, rely less on parents and more on their own resources for solving problems, and, if they have had experience in day-care centers, appear to be comfortable moving in and out of social situations and interacting with both adults and children.

Thus, children of two-career parents are not necessarily a neglected group of kids doomed to failure and developmental difficulties. If anything, our interviews indicate that two-career couples are very concerned about what's happening to their children. Their constant self-questioning about the effects of two careers on kids may be causing them to both seek and provide more quality in the relationships they have with their children and in the outside care they provide for them when they aren't there.

So much for myths. There are still a multitude of problems connected with being parents, whether you are a traditional family or a two-career family. In this chapter, we focus on some of these problems, beginning with perhaps the most difficult one: whether or not to have a baby.

A Complex Choice

It used to be a lot simpler. Having a baby was the natural sequel to getting married. But this, of course, is no longer true, especially for the two-career couple. In deciding to have children, a couple is also making two other important decisions: to accept the role of parent and to make the transition from being a couple to being a family. They are commiting themselves to new roles and a new style of life. It is a radical shift, one that will have repercussions in every area of their lives.

Several trends are clearly emerging as more women enter the labor force and two-career couples become commonplace. First, more couples are consciously choosing *not* to have children. Second, couples who choose to have children are choosing to have fewer of them. And finally, the timing of when to have children has shifted—people are delaying until after their relationship and, often, their careers are well established.

All of these trends are reflected in the fact that 47 percent of all families in the United States have no children under eighteen years of age and the average birthrate among women of childbearing age has dropped from 3.7 in 1955–1959 to 2.6 in 1965–1969 to an estimated 1.8 in the last part of this decade.

Perhaps the most significant reason many couples offer for why they choose not to have children is that they do not perceive children as necessary for their satisfaction or happiness. In the May 1975 issue of *Psychology Today*, a survey by Angus Campbell revealed some interesting findings about perceived happiness among married couples. All of the married people surveyed, male and female, under thirty and over, with or without children, were more satisfied with their lives than were all of the unmarried individuals. Campbell also found, however, that married couples with small children, while happier than single people, still experienced the greatest amount of stress of those surveyed. The most satisfied group in the study was the young, newly married, and childless couples. Parenthood, however, changes the picture.

> Almost as soon as a couple has kids, their happy bubble bursts. For both men and women, reports of happiness and satisfaction drop to average, not to rise again significantly until their children are grown and about to leave the nest.[1]

The birth of a child puts a lot of strain on a marriage and changes the basic relationship. Many couples realize this and simply don't want to subject themselves to that. Furthermore, couples without children no longer have to feel pitied, unfulfilled, embarrassed, or apologetic. In the Campbell survey, husbands over thirty without children reported the highest levels of satisfaction with life, and wives over thirty without children, although not as happy as their husbands, were no less satisfied with their lives then were women of comparable age with children.

Children are also extremely expensive. As *Newsweek* reported: "The sheer cost of raising a child is enough to make any potential parent pause—and current parents shudder."[2] They estimated that, at 1977 prices, a family of four earning between $16,500 and $20,000 a year could expect to spend at least $54,297 to support a child to the age of eighteen. This does not include any expenses for college or other forms of higher education.

For the two-career couple, however, money may not be the real issue. The real issue may be whether either or both partners want to deal or feel capable of dealing with the added responsibility of parenthood. Children not only add to the already complex logistics of running one's life, they present a more intangible burden—the responsibility of determining another person's fate. Increasingly, people seem to be looking beyond the idealized version of parenthood and into the realities. While previous generations pondered the question of whether a person, especially a woman, could really be fulfilled without having a child, people today are asking themselves how *they* can fulfill the developmental needs of children. As one couple observed: "It isn't having the child. It's thinking about what he or she is going to become—or not—and maybe because of you." Not surprisingly, another important issue in decisions about children is their effect on career plans. While not making an active choice *not* to have children, many couples postpone the decision indefinitely because of career concerns. Many women see having a baby as something that will either require them to drop their careers at a critical point or prevent them from putting in the energy needed to get ahead. Although they may want to have children, the timing never seems to be right.

Finally, many working couples are coming face to face with the fact that having a baby is no longer just a matter of motherhood. For many people the question really is: "Are we truly willing to assume and share the role of parent? What will happen after the baby is born?" One woman expressed her feelings as follows:

> Whether motherhood is for me really depends on what fatherhood will ultimately mean to my husband. I'd like to have a family, but I don't feel obligated to have one and I don't think I need to have one to be happy, successful, or fulfilled. What that means to me is that having a baby would not be just *my* accomplishment or my responsibility. If we have children it will only be because my husband feels the same way. A baby will have to be just as much his responsibility as mine. Until I know he feels this way, I'm not ready.

To better understand what lies behind the indecision and anxiety many couples experience, let's look at the impact that having a child can have on a couple. Are their fears valid or exaggerated? What are the realities behind becoming a parent?

Having a Child

Many couples describe the birth of their first child in euphoric terms. It is a "high," an intense emotional experience accompanied by feelings of elation, fulfillment, and togetherness. But what happens when the immediate thrill subsides, when the parents are finally alone with their newborn child and, perhaps for the first time, realize they are now a family?

A study by Philip and Carolyn Cowan and Lynne and John Coie gives us some insight into the impact of a newborn on a previously childless couple.[3] They studied a sample of couples from midpregnancy to six months following the birth of their child. Their findings, some rather startling, are nonetheless realistic for many new parents.

- Partners experienced radical changes in their self-esteem. Both partners tended to develop more negative self-images after the baby's arrival.
- The initial elation was short-lived. Women found themselves taking longer than they had anticipated to regain former physical strength and "snap back." Men experienced unexpected conflicts about their jobs and the balance of professional and domestic commitments.
- Communication between partners changed, with more conflicts surfacing in some cases.
- Career concerns emerged among the males, either about their jobs or the adequacy of salaries.
- Patterns of initiating sexual activity also changed. Where it had been shared equally, it increasingly became a male task.
- Even where couples had realistically anticipated changes in the time schedules, all were unhappy with the reduction in leisure time they experienced as individuals and as a couple.

In short, how they felt, saw themselves, and related to each other changed with the introduction of a child in their lives.

Few people really stop to consider how parent roles will change their lives. It is not by accident that we use the plural here, for each partner now has to assume multiple parent roles. He or she is not just a parent in relation to the child, but also in relation to the other partner and to the myriad of other people whose lives overlap the child's—grandparents, baby-sitters, teachers, playmates, other parents, and so forth. In other words, most people regard becoming a parent as simply adding one new relationship to their lives. But it is not that simple. Becoming a parent involves one in a new and complex network of role relationships, a network whose focal pont is the new infant.

Probably one of the first major issues new parents face is the fact that there is a new source of competition in their lives—the baby. Not only do the infant's physical needs have to be met (a more time-consuming aspect of parenting than most people anticipate), but the couple is likely to experience some degree of shift in their patterns of attention and allegiances. This can be disquieting or even threatening. In a couple, each partner usually expects and often can devote ample time and attention to the concerns and needs of the other. Where there are children, however, the attention, the concern, the caring and tending have to be shared, juggled, and spread around.

Not surprisingly, many people begin to wonder after the baby arrives whether their partner really cares about them. The baby seems to effortlessly grab the spotlight. It's no longer just the two of them. Someone else is in the picture, forcing them to compete for the time and attention they used to take for granted. It's not uncommon for partners, both mothers and fathers, finally to ask petulantly "Who's more important to you anyway—me or the baby?"

Children also are, in a sense, a source of competition for each partner. Mothers and fathers soon realize that, with the addition of a child, there is less time for self. Their wily opponent is not really the child, of course, but the *time* the child caring takes, and thus takes away from them.

Parenthood for most people also has a psychological dimension—the ever-present knowledge that one is responsible for the well-being of another person. This is very different from being responsible for changing diapers or daily feedings. It is the constant awareness that someone else is depending on you twenty-four hours a day.

For most parents, this psychological responsibility signals the loss of personal freedom or autonomy. One woman, a former nun who had just had her first baby and was also finishing up her Ph.D. dissertation, talked about her feelings. As much as she loved her child, she said, she also felt angry. She went on to talk about her former life and how she could do as she pleased, arrange her time, separate her attention, and become totally engrossed in her academic work if necessary for long periods of time. All that had changed. She no longer felt free—even when her husband or the baby-sitter was caring for the child.

> I don't just worry about the baby—I worry about the fact that I will always have to worry, to be thinking about someone else. I'm no longer just free to be me. Whatever I am, whatever I do, I will be and do with the knowledge that there is this small person who needs me and is depending on me.

We empathize with her feelings. If there was one rude awakening we experienced as new parents, it was that we could no longer just do as we pleased. Everything had to be planned, scheduled, or considered in the context of children. We couldn't just pick up and walk out the door. And even after we had made whatever arrangements were necessary, we left never feeling totally free.

Psychological responsibility seems to impact on working parents' relationships in yet another way. It often reshapes their pattern of leisure activities together. Parents who work all week and leave children in the care of others seem conflicted about doing so on weekends. Couples who used to spend Saturdays at football games, tennis tournaments, or off skiing suddenly have to come to terms with the fact that pursuing outside activities as a couple means leaving the children. Most are reluctant to do so and may give up or set aside whole parts of themselves and their life together. Now the question becomes: "Can we do it with the kids?" If they have left the children all week, they may feel guilty about doing it on the weekends, too.

In short, children put us into roles that cannot usually be separated in time or space. When you think about the demands of your career versus the demands of your couple relationship, at least you have some chance of attending to one at a time. Career demands occur mainly at the office during work hours; the couple relationship takes priority away from the office. You can separate them to a great extent.

When you have children, however, it becomes difficult if not impossible to separate the spouse and parent roles. You are trying to work on your relationship as a couple and your role as a parent at the same time and in the same place. The two roles are in constant competition, intruding on each other and continually asking that you accommodate one by shifting attention away from the other.

The physical presence of children changes many patterns couples formerly enjoyed. Communication is an important one. It's unrealistic to expect to come home at the end of the day and have uninterrupted periods of time to talk with your spouse. Even when you try to carry on a conversation, it is usually punctuated by remarks, questions, or demands from the rest of the family. As Tim frequently says when we are sitting together trying to talk and the children continue to run in and out, "I get the feeling that no one around here ever gets to finish a sentence!"

Sex is another area where many couples feel children interfere. Not only is fatigue an issue, but free time and privacy are at a premium. Where once they felt free to leave doors open, they now are in a quandary about locking the bedroom door—what if the children should need them? No longer are Saturday mornings a time for lolling around in bed. And forget Sunday afternoon stretched out in front of the fireplace. As many couples complain, sex, like everything else that happens after children, seems to become more and more of a planned activity. Sexual spontaneity is just one of the many freedoms that seems to diminish, if not disappear, with the arrival of children.

Guilty or not guilty?

The price some parents pay for juggling work and parenting is a feeling of guilt. Two kinds of guilt feelings are common. The first centers on anxieties about being a good parent and the effect that one's job involvement may be having on the well-being of the child. The second involves feeling guilty about resenting the child's infringement on one's time, career, or relationship with a spouse.

One of the burdens our society has placed on all parents, but especially on working parents, is the notion that a child's problems or failures are a direct reflection of the parents' incompetence or inadequacy. Parents who both work have less time to devote to parenting. Thus they worry more about the time they do have and how it is spent.

Two-career couples are caught in a real bind— they have no actual model of what good parenting involves in a two-career family. If they look to the traditional family with a full-time homemaker mother, the comparison may leave them feeling that they always come up short.

Dealing with guilt is a matter of coming to terms with your own internal expectations and developing the self-confidence to express and meet these. As we talk to working parents about guilt feelings, it is common to find that much of their guilt is induced by external standards or expectations. Frequently, they have internalized these standards and now expect them of themselves. People who feel less guilty or guilt free about their parenting are those who feel comfortable relying on their own judgment and asserting it.

Working parents who compare themselves to childless couples are also bound to feel troubled about how their parenting roles affect their relationships with other people. Friends who do not have children may not perceive the time conflicts parents face or the emotional demands they must meet. They may, for example, view your interest in your kids or your decision to spend time with them as over-involvement. If you turn down an invitation because of the kids, childless people don't always understand. They expect you to be just as available and intensely interested in doing things as before you became parents. The message you sometimes get is: "Why are your kids standing in the way of our relationship?" Or, "Why are you *letting* your kids get in the way of your life and your career?" What seems to bother working parents most is that their childless friends haven't fully acknowledged the fact that the children are an integral part of their life now.

The second kind of guilt we mentioned involves feeling guilty about our own resentment or anger. If parenthood reduces one's freedom, increases responsibility, and changes relationships with spouse and friends, it's natural to feel some resentment. Why do our lives have to be different? Why do we have to be the accommodators? Then again, we *chose* to become parents. If it was a free choice, why are we having these feelings?

The real guilt seems to arise again out of our expectations. We don't think we are "supposed" to feel resentful or frustrated or stifled. We are supposed to feel proud, happy, and fulfilled. And most parents do feel that way a good part of the time. But when they don't, they feel guilty about their negative feelings. They haven't allowed themselves the luxury, or perhaps just the opportunity, to be *realistic*. Feelings in any relationship are usually a blend of both positive and negative.

Working parents may become especially troubled because they often lack sufficient opportunity to vent these feelings of anger or resentment. They cannot work these feelings through with the child, especially an infant. So the feelings are turned inward. When we internalize our anger and carry it around, it is eventually transformed into depression, anxiety, or guilt. We don't want to feel angry, but we do. Rather than accept the anger as natural or normal, we feel guilty for having such "awful" thoughts in the first place.

Many companies are recognizing that learning to accept and cope with the conflicts of parenting is important for their workers. The New England Life Insurance Company, for example, offered to subsidize a college course at Wheelock College on how to be a better parent. Their rationale for doing so was simple: the company hoped the course would boost their employees' confidence at home and thus increase their concentration in the office. As two-career families increase, employers are recognizing that the parents' ability to manage their families will influence how well they function at work.

Although children do affect couple relationships in a variety of significant and often negative ways, the fact remains that many two-career couples do want and choose to have children. They are willing to make the adjustment from couple to family. The major question for many, however, is: "When?"

The Right Time

Young couples are often divided on the question of time: Should they get their careers established first and then start a family? Or should they get the family underway and then concentrate on their careers (or on her career)? The advantage of establishing careers first is that both are more likely to get off to a successful start. Then, when children do come, the partners are better prepared to cope with a family: they are more mature; they are in more senior positions with more flexibility, autonomy, and influence in their work organizations; they have more money to buy services (such as housekeeping and child care); and, after waiting several years, they can be fairly certain that they sincerely want a family and are willing to make the necessary sacrifices.

Maternity or paternity leaves are becoming far more commonplace. Since the courts have ruled that pregnancy is a "temporary disability," companies, even those without official policies regarding pregnancy and childbirth leaves, are forced to grant time off for pregnancy and childbirth. Some other organizations, such as Braniff Airlines, make it very easy for employees to take unpaid leaves of absence. Further, some couples arrange for one partner to take time off after the woman's recovery period to be with the child in its early months.

Young and very junior (low-ranking) employees often have trouble getting lengthy unpaid leaves of absence for infant care. They simply don't have the corporate clout to negotiate time off. Older couples, however, with five or ten years of experience tend to have an easier time working out leaves, as they have reached more senior levels, have more leverage, and have shown through good performance how valuable they are to the organization.

One couple we know had their first child in their thirties. He was a successful commercial real-estate broker and she was an established architect. Their combined income was well into six figures. With the arrival of the baby, the wife had no trouble negotiating as much leave time as she wanted (even though the firm had no maternity-leave policy) and her boss aranged for her to do a lot of work at home. She was even able to bring her child to work; she had a private office and when she was doing design work alone (i.e., when clients were not in), she was able to set up a playpen in one corner. As she says, there was no way she could have had such a protean career when she was a struggling junior draftsman.

The husband was also able to do much of his work at home. Their apartment was large enough to accommodate a live-in housekeeper and they had a weekend house in New England, where the child had plenty of room to play. They had both become quite established in their careers and were ready to invest a lot of themselves in a family. The child was seen as a very welcome demand on their time and energy, in no way competitive with their careers.

The most obvious cost of having children later is
that family responsibilities remain heavy at a point in the parents' lives
when many of their friends are enjoying the pleasures of having grown
children. Their friends' children are off to college while their own are
still in elementary school. Couples who choose to have children while
young are ensuring themselves greater freedom early in middle age, as
well as the chance to join with their kids in activities such as sports
and entertainment while both generations are able to participate actively. One couple we know, Mickey and Betty, sent their youngest
child off to college when they were in their early forties. They were
both well established in their work and were ready to have fun together. So, they took off on three-week winter cruises, got into hobbies,
and joined personal-growth groups. Best of all, their love blossomed.
And their two children were two of their best friends.

The major disadvantage of having a family early is
the amount of strain it places on the couple. The demands of their
careers and those of the family peak at the same time, creating high
pressure and role conflict.

Another option is for one party to delay career
pursuits and spend more time getting a family started. Most often it is
the woman who takes time off to be home with the children before they
are in school. One problem with this approach is the inherent inequity:
Why should *she* be the one to sacrifice her career? Another problem is
that she is likely to experience great resentment when the family continues to intrude on her work after she has "put in her time." This is
the option we took, with Fran working part-time for about three years
when the children were first born. Then she started graduate school
full time and has worked full time ever since, although she has made
sacrifices in her own career for Tim's.

Even now, with the children nine and eleven years
old, Fran often has to stay up into the wee small hours to finish a report or some other project. When the family intrudes on her work, as
when the dog wants a walk at 2:00 A.M., her reaction is, "I've already
paid the price once. This is *my* time." It's natural to become more
impatient about sacrificing one's career for the sake of the family
when one has already put in many years doing just that.

While there are clear trade-offs associated with
having children early or later in life, the trend among career couples
seems to be to postpone having a family until both careers are established and they *really* feel ready. Many couples wonder, however, what
the risks will be physically or psychologically. Fortunately, there is
increasing evidence to suggest that parenting later in life need not be a
problem—for parents or kids.

While the medical risks to both mother and child increase after the mother is thirty-five, many of these risks are not sufficiently serious to prevent women from becoming pregnant. Furthermore, medical advances in early birth-defect detection, prenatal care, pregnancy management, and delivery techniques are increasingly making the birth of a child later in life something women need not fear.

On the psychological side, the characteristics and attitudes older parents bring to the parent-child relationship can be a benefit rather than a drawback. For one thing, older parents usually feel more secure about themselves and their careers. Thus, they are less likely to resent how their child is affecting or interfering with their work. Older parents also are more likely to have a well-established identity of their own. They can invest in the development of a child for the child's sake rather than as a means of nurturing their own sense of self. While this may mean that the parent is less intensely involved with the child, the child is likely to develop a healthy sense of independence. Older, more established couples generally expect a child to fit into their life-style rather than evolving a life-style that centers around the child.

While there are no hard and fast rules for timing the decision to become a family, it seems clear to us that waiting has its advantages. Apart from career and financial stability, waiting allows a couple to establish a secure relationship. Perhaps most important, it gives them time to develop and grow as individuals before getting into the business of growing offspring.

Learning to Share the Parent Role

Raising kids is not all mothering. It's nurturing, among other things, a role that both men and women engage in. In the two-career family, one of the most important determinants of how successfully couples manage seems to be their ability to share child-raising tasks and responsibilities.

In our interviews and research, we have found that the key to sharing seems to hinge on the extent to which both partners are able to internalize what has been termed the role of the "psychological parent." In other words, both parents need to feel *personal* responsibility for the welfare of the children. Neither sees himself or herself as simply an adjunct to the other. Both partners must feel a primary sense of involvement in what happens and what gets done. Together, not separately, they provide the emotional support structure for their children.

"Do you have any idea what your father and I go through with each other to keep a nuclear family for you?"

All too often, one parent—the mother—assumes the role of primary or psychological parent. "Mothering" and "fathering" take on distinct and separate characteristics, frequently in line with traditional role tasks and activities. Many experts have argued that the reason this occurs is that fathers are frequently excluded from the pregnancy and birth process itself. As one man described it:

> Once you know your wife is pregnant, you have many months to get used to the idea that you are going to *become* a parent, but you don't have any part of *being* a parent. Your wife goes off to the obstetrician's. *She* feels the baby moving inside, and *she* gives birth, while you wait down the hall somewhere. Then suddenly you meet this newborn and you are supposed to feel this overwhelming bond. My God, the kid is a stranger to you. Your wife's been having an affair with him for nine months.

Men who have the opportunity to become involved in the parent role right from the beginning of a pregnancy do report an earlier, if not greater, sense of responsibility and bonding. Sharing in the visits to the doctor's office, taking childbirth classes together, and participating in childbirth are several ways in which both parents can bond to the parent role before the baby arrives home from the hospital.

Learning to share parenting, like sharing housework, involves trusting the other person and giving up our sense of superiority and territoriality. Many women report that their husbands don't share enough in child-care responsibilities. Yet when they are questioned more closely, it becomes clear that these women either don't expect or don't believe that their husbands would be able to provide the same quality of care and attention that they do. In other words, many women either want to or feel they have to be the primary parent. Unless the woman is willing to relinquish her own sense of primacy in the parent-child relationship, it's difficult for the man to get into the act—even when he really wants to.

It's still unclear whether working parents tend to do more role sharing in the area of child care than in the area of house care. Studies on role sharing in each situation are difficult to compare, because of differences in the occupational levels of the sample groups, their previous parental role models, their reasons for working, and individual attitudes toward masculinity and femininity as reflected in their role behavior at home.

One finding that does emerge from interviews with couples who do share child-care roles at home is that such sharing tends to open up and increase their communication. When both partners feel responsible for child care, there are many more interactions and exchanges over decisions, ground rules, developing a shared philosophy, filling each other in, and scheduling what is ahead.

Child-Care Arrangements

One day before Sue H. Bohle, a vice-president of J. Walter Thompson Co. in Los Angeles, was due to return to her job following the birth of her first child, her housekeeper quit. The only last-minute option for child care on one day's notice was a pregnant, foreign-born teenager who spoke no English. Bohle's response?

Leaving my son that morning was just about the hardest thing I've ever done. But I knew if I let this situation stop me, all sorts of things would stop me. It would just be the beginning of the end.[4]

Although we are not all vice-presidents, this sort of daily drama is played out in numerous two-career homes every day. What viable child-care arrangements are available to working couples? What are their effects on children? And how do parents go about selecting a particular type?

A Census Bureau survey of all families in the United States (not just two-career families) in 1974 and 1975 indicated that 33 million of the 41 million children aged three to thirteen are cared for by one of their parents when they are not in school. Of the 8 million children who do not have daytime parental care (because their parents work, for example), 2.1 million (over 25 percent) are cared for at home by a relative. Another 1.8 million (almost one-quarter) take care of themselves until one of the parents returns home from work (the "latch-key" phenomenon). Only 2 percent of the children of working parents are in day-care centers, less than in any other type of day-care arrangement.

According to a study by T.W. Rodes, care by a relative seems to be the most frequent solution to the problem of daytime child care.[5] The advantage here is obviously that the child is in a caring, family situation, one with which the parents are likely to feel comfortable. If you are fortunate enough to have a relative who is able to provide child care, you will probably not look much further for help. If you do not have relatives nearby, you will need to consider other options. Care by nonrelatives in one's own home or in another home is the next most common means of child care, the option selected by about 40 percent of working couples.

It appears, then, that most working parents use some sort of home environment (their own or a sitter's) for child care rather than an institutional setting, such as a day-care center, nursery school, Headstart, or before- and after-school programs. These more formal institutional arrangements make up only about 10 percent of the child-care alternatives used by working parents. Clearly, day care is not the panacea for employed parents that people thought it might be five or ten years ago.

Sometimes the employer will help out as well. Some companies, such as Whirlpool, Avco Printing, Chesapeake & Potomac Telephone Co., Ohio Bell, KLH, and Control Data, provide subsidized child-care facilities for the use of their employees. Such programs may be supported by a consortium of local companies (for example, Control Data pooled resources with two other Minneapolis firms). Usually the company pays for part of the expense and the employee pays the remainder (perhaps $15 to $20 per week per child). Sometimes a government agency will also subsidize part of the cost, especially for low-income employees.

At one time, it appeared that company-supported day care would become a widespread solution to the problems of working mothers. An article in *Administrative Management* in 1972 confidently predicted:

> With more and more women joining the work force, it is almost inevitable that the idea of employee day-care centers for employees' children will

become an issue administrative managers will be confronted with along with other fringe benefits such as more extensive health-insurance coverage and the four-day week.[6]

The four-day week has done all right, but, as our earlier statistics on the low use of institutional care suggest, the prediction about more widespread corporate day care has simply not been borne out. As a rule, companies have found that providing day care is not worth the cost and they are not particularly enthusiastic about being in the child-care business. Firms often find that employees can locate better and cheaper care if the company gives its child-care subsidy directly to the employees and lets them make their own arrangements.

There are other ways companies can help out, however. The Connecticut Savings Bank in New Haven provides a shortened workday for mothers, with hours matching a child's school day. Part-time employees take over their jobs in the summer. As Paul H. Johnson, C.S.B.'s president, put it, "I felt there was an enormous waste of talent among trained women who couldn't fully use their training because they had small children. I felt companies had to be more imaginative and less demanding." Johnson sees this program as a success after three years of operation, even for the third of the bank's mothers who are in management positions.[7]

Flexible work schedules arranged either by the company or by cooperation between the two parents are a godsend for working couples. Flextime, which allows employees to begin work early or end the day late, as long as they work eight hours, has become widespread. Women who wish to continue breast feeding after returning to work are especially in need of flexible work schedules, perhaps a system that permits them to leave and return to work during the day.

Organizations can also add to a couple's flexibility by providing a certain number of days off each year for "personal business." In some cases, these personal days may simply replace sick days. (If the company does not have a formal policy of personal days, as many "sick days" may be taken for a child's illness as for the employee's.)

Less formally, many bosses simply bend the routines for valued employees. The United Banks of Colorado, Inc., for example, held its annual economic forecast seminars a month early, in November, because economist Kathleen M. Cooper was expecting her baby in December.[8]

Partners may need to modify their schedules so that one can start late (and finish late) and thus see the children off to school, while the other starts early and finishes early to be home after school. We know of one pair of teachers who made this sort of arrangement. She teaches elementary school and has to leave early. He teaches at a university and can schedule his own class hours. So, he does all of his teaching between 10:00 and 2:00, so that he can feed the kids breakfast and get them off to school and later be there to welcome them home. Then, when she gets home around 4:30, she takes over the home tasks while he works a few more hours in the den.

In addition to different established work hours, working couples need greater overall flexibility to adjust schedules unexpectedly as family needs arise. If a child becomes sick or gets hurt at school, a parent may have to get home quickly or take a day off to provide care. If a baby-sitter or housekeeper fails to show up, one parent may have to stay home. (Fran has called baby-sitters "the glue in our lives—they hold everything together.") There is also a "couple domino effect" at work here: the person who comes into another couple's home to provide child care may also have children who are being cared for in some other way (family, day care, etc.). If the child-care person has an emergency and cannot come to work, this then becomes an emergency for her employer. Thus, some couples experience the stresses from two careers from both sides: as dual-career employees *and* as employers.

Vacations can present another troublesome scheduling problem. It is hard enough for one person to schedule a vacation to coincide with both the family's vacation activities and the company's work cycle. Being able to arrange *two* vacations at the same time is even harder. And, if there are children, fitting the two parents' vacations in with school vacations can be almost impossible!

We have gone through several years of finding the spring vacations of our two separate universities and the children's elementary school hopelessly out of phase. (Summer vacations are less of a problem. But with more people traveling in spring and winter, vacation conflicts will probably become more troublesome.) Even when we were finally both working at the same university, our two separate schools within the university (the school of management and the evening division) had different spring vacations!

We usually ended up with some sort of compromise, such as being away for half of the kids' vacation and half of one of ours. We would try to make our vacations a bit more flexible by trading some teaching days with colleagues or, if that was not possible, by rescheduling one or two classes.

We realized that vacations are one area in which academics have *less* flexibility than people in industry. The university sets down its vacation schedule literally *years* in advance, and that's that. We professors are not required to do many things at a predetermined time and place, but one thing that is essential is meeting classes as scheduled.

We also realized that the kids' teachers were quite flexible and helpful if we had no choice but to be gone during the school session. With more working couples, the school has learned to deal with vacations better than parents have. They were happy to provide work assignments in advance. But often their attitude was, "Let them catch up when they return. They won't miss too much, and they'll have many more new learning experiences during their week in (California, Jamaica, Hawaii, or wherever) than they would in school." And, in fact, once we overcame our guilt about taking the kids out of school for trips with us, we realized that they never had any problems with missed school activities.

Work-related travel is another area where scheduling can be difficult, especially if both working partners have to travel at the same time. In such cases, overnight or live-in child care will be needed. We find that a university is an ideal place to find students, often couples, who are delighted to live in a "real house" and earn some extra money ($25 per day is the going rate in our area now). Often a graduate-student couple will have children of their own, which means built-in playmates for your kids. We find having a family in the house is a more normal and satisfactory situation for our kids than a single sitter.

Young couples without children often like to baby-sit for a few days because it gives them a chance to "try out" being parents, sort of a family test run. (It has always seemed ironic to us how we usually take on one of life's major and most *permanent* responsibilities, being a parent, with no prior experience.)

Another type of paid assistance is live-in help. Depending on the labor market in a particular area, it is sometimes possible to hire a person for child care and light housekeeping, usually for five or six days a week, in return for room and board and pay of $20–$100 and up per week. This entails having an extra bedroom available, preferably with its own bathroom, in an area of the home that provides the helper and the family a measure of privacy. What this generally means, of course, is that only fairly affluent families with large homes can afford live-in help.

Another way to obtain live-in help is through local adoption agencies, which often seek good homes for unwed mothers while they await the birth of their babies. This arrangement usually costs less, but less work is provided. However, it can be a satisfying way of helping a person in need and it has the advantage of not being permanent. Such an arrangement is an ideal way to try out live-in help. If it works well for you, you can either repeat the temporary arrangement or hire someone permanently.

We had two types of live-in help while we lived in Toronto. One summer, two French-speaking high-school girls from Quebec lived in on two different occasions. (They had come to Ontario to live with families for the summer as a way of learning English.) We also had two Jamaican women living in at different times. They were in their twenties, and these were longer-term arrangements.

None of these arrangements worked well for us. The high-school girls, anxious to improve their English, would want to speak with us after dinner, just when we wanted to be alone and chat over coffee. Plus, being teenagers, they were essentially one more child to care for, with their own sets of problems. The older women we hired simply did not provide enough stimulation for the children, although they were extremely warm and loving. We would come home at the end of the day to find our year-and-a-half-old son and the sitter watching TV, their major daily activity. We also realized that we needed to monitor the kids' well-being more closely than anticipated. This became clear when we discovered a bad rash on Chip that the sitter had known about for days but hadn't mentioned.

The major drawback to us of the live-in arrangement is that, aside from the reduction in privacy, the person who is supposedly there to help you often ends up increasing your problems and responsibilities significantly. She or he is simply one more human being in your life, one more obligation for you to manage. And the last thing a working parent needs is more responsibility.

What Is the Best Kind of Child Care?

What kind of child care is best for your child? Fortunately, no one type seems universally preferable. (We say "fortunately" because not all types are available in all areas to all couples.) According to many child psychologists, such as Dr. Jerome Kagan of Harvard University, child care by conscientious, caring adults outside the home need not impair the child's development in any way. The *type* of care does not matter greatly, but the *quality* of whatever type you use is critical.[9] The caretaker must be stable, responsive, and consistent.[10] The other critical factor in the success of a child-care arrangement is how satisfied you feel with your job and how comfortable you are with the care arrangement. (You could be paying as much as 25 percent of your take-home pay for it, so you'd better be comfortable with it.)

How does a parent go about finding stable, responsive care with which he or she feels comfortable? It sounds impossible! Dr. Stevanne Auerback, co-author with Linda Freedman of *Choosing Child Care: A Guide for Parents*, offers some extremely helpful guidelines in the article reprinted here.

ALL ABOUT DAY CARE

FINDING THE RIGHT BABY-SITTER

If a woman is to work in your home, caring for your child, five days a week, you must have full confidence in her ability to look after your son or daughter more or less as you would yourself. Your babysitter must genuinely care for your child; she must be able to discipline him or her consistently; she must feed and clothe the youngster properly, and be able to recognize when something is troubling your child—physically or emotionally.

In choosing a sitter, it's wise to rely on your instincts—if you don't like the person, your son or daughter probably won't either. Be sure to check the sitter's references and experience, interview her at length, and observe how she and your child get on together.

The following checklist suggests questions to cover in interviewing a sitter. You may also have other points you wish to raise.

INTERVIEWING A SITTER

Explain your situation briefly, and ask about the sitter's background in a general way.

What is the sitter's experience? Ask her to write down the names and phone numbers of at least two references. Then ask specific questions like:

- Why did you change jobs?
- How do you think children should be disciplined?
- What do you expect in regard to the child's eating and toileting?
- Do you drive?
- Have you had a health checkup recently?
- Do you feel confident you can handle my child if an emergency arises?
- Will you be calm and interested in my child, and not overly critical?

Next, make agreements about work schedule and salary, and obtain a medical release form so your child can receive hospital care in case of an emergency, if you are unavailable.

Specify your limitations about such things as: drinking; smoking; use of telephone; food; television.

Show your prospective sitter around the house and, if you have not already done so, introduce her to your child. This meeting is essential to see how they relate to each other.

FINDING THE RIGHT DAY-CARE HOME

To locate child-care services, call The Department of Social Services in your area (this may be called the Office of Children's Services); your State Bureau of Child Health and Welfare; or look in the classified section (under Nursery Schools) of your phone book.

There are two kinds of family day-care homes—small and large. A small home cares for six or fewer children, from infants through children six years of age. A larger home can care for up to twelve children and requires that two adults be present. In general, licensing regulations of these homes are aimed at safeguarding the child's health and safety, but do not always specify the educational or social aspects of the program.

A family day-care home is less expensive than having a babysitter in your house, and provides your child with other children to play with. It will also probably be less expensive than a center, but will offer less in the way of equipment and activities.

The fact that a day-care home is licensed is no guarantee that the social, emotional, and educational climate will meet your own standards. Spend some time in the home, observing the children and their interaction; the chances are that if you are comfortable your children will be too.

FINDING THE RIGHT DAY-CARE CENTER

At the moment there are very few day-care centers which accept infants. Centers are now primarily for pre-school children, although some also offer after-school programs. You will want to choose a center whose hours meet your needs, and one which is easily accessible to your home.

Day-care centers provide for outdoor activities either on their own premises or in a nearby park. They often offer breakfast, as well as lunch and snacks. Activity time and rest time are usually well balanced; staff is usually well trained.

DAY-CARE HOME AND CENTER CHECKLISTS

1. Name of director_____
   Phone _____
   Name and address of home or center_____
   _____

2. Name of person who will provide the care _____
   _____
   Type of experience the person has had _____
   _____

3. Is the place licensed?

4. Are the adults able to handle emergencies that might come up?
   Is there a first aid kit?
   What arrangements are made when a child becomes ill?

5. What records are kept on the children and their development?
   Will you be expected to be part of the program?

6.   Your own questions _____

_____

THE PHYSICAL
FACILITY CHECKLIST

Look over the space for safety features, well-planned and adequate space, the condition of play equipment inside and out and over-all attractiveness.

1.   Does the space seem safe? (Are lights and sockets covered or out of reach?)

2.   Is there enough space, and is it planned to avoid crowding?

3.   Is the equipment varied, sturdy, and easy for a child to use?

4.   Is the place attractive and comfortable? (Are there plants, pets and areas for special activities?)

5.   Can the children get inside and outside safely and easily?

6.   Are the bathroom facilities clean and easy for a child to use?

7.   Are meals nutritious, well balanced and attractive?

8.   Do the children have a comfortable and quiet place for naps?

9.   Does the place have provisions for an ill child?

THE EMOTIONAL
CLIMATE CHECKLIST

The second part of your observation is to become aware of how the children relate to each other, how the staff relates to the children and to each other, and how comfortable you are about visiting. How will your child fit in?

1.   Do the children seem to like and trust the adults?

2.   Are the children happy and relaxed?

3.   Does the staff communicate easily with each child?

4.   Does the discipline reflect your philosophy?

5.   Are the children allowed to pursue their own interests according to their abilities?

6.   Are problems well handled?

7.   Does the director or teacher answer questions openly?

8.   Do you feel comfortable with the staff and the place?

If you can answer "yes" to a majority of the questions on the checklists for the home or center you are considering, the chances are it will provide fun and learning for your child—and peace of mind for you.

_____

Stevanne Auerbach, *Choosing Child Care: A Guide for Parents* (San Francisco: Parents and Child Care Resources). Reprinted by permission.

To Parent or Not—That Is the Issue

We began this chapter by looking at the realities of parenting, so perhaps a good place to end is to ask the question: Who should (or should not) have children? No one can make the decision for you, but the following considerations can help you sort out the many issues involved.

Becoming parents may not be right for you now:

- If you are experiencing a lot of stress, either in your relationship or in your careers.
- If career comes first for both of you and neither of you is ready to make compromises.
- If one or both of you have unfulfilled career aspirations that could not be fulfilled if you had a baby.
- If you think (or hope) that having a baby will improve your relationship, solve a problem, or be a way of bringing you closer together.
- If there is a likelihood of having to separate because of your careers.
- If one of you feels ambivalent or there is clear disagreement between you about whether you really want a baby.
- If you put yourselves first and want, or expect, to keep it that way.
- If you are low on flexibility, have a high need for order, and don't like dealing with uncertainty.
- If you have difficulty making compromises.

CHAPTER SEVEN

LOVING VERSUS WORKING

When working and loving clash, loving often loses. For the two-career couple, work tends to drive out unscheduled, "nonessential" activities, such as socializing, leisure, and romance. In this chapter, we examine the interpersonal impacts of the two-career relationship. We begin by looking at two issues central to the couple relationship: romance and competition. Then, we expand our scope to include relationships with other people: affairs and friendships.

Romance

Every decade dreams new dreams and throws out the ones that went before. The fifties promised commitment while freedom went in chains. And then the sixties came along promising freedom and personal growth, but commitment got lost en route. It is only now in the seventies that we are starting to wonder if there can be freedom without commitment, if there can be personal growth without love, and only now in the seventies that we are starting to ask how we can go about getting them all.[1]

One of the dangers of a successful, involving career is that it is very self-oriented, very narcissistic. Not only is the person caught up in a psychological success cycle, he or she is also caught up in *self*. When people are caught up in success, their self-esteem keeps pace with (or outstrips) their growing career involvement.

This certainly *feels* fantastic—but there often is little room left in the person's life for anyone else. When one is grooving so strongly on personal growth and freedom, it becomes increasingly difficult to make space for a partner.

The alone-at-home spouse—even one with his or her own career—has become a common phenomenon in recent years. He or she may be married to the lawyer who works until midnight six days a week or the magazine editor who moves into her office one week each month to meet a publication deadline. Increasingly, people are becoming so involved in and dependent on their jobs that their time and energy at home dwindle to nothing.

When both spouses work, they may seem better disposed or adjusted to long hours at the office and business-related entertaining—at least initially. Sooner or later, however, the time they do manage to spend alone together (and it gradually diminishes) may begin to sour. In response, the partners turn even more of their energy into office matters, thus further decreasing their time at home—and their chances of recapturing romance in their relationship.

In our research on working couples, we find that many people cannot distinguish between self and career, so that career involvement really does mean self-involvement. For some people, the problem is this inability to divide their lives; they are married to both career and spouse and think that each condones the bigamy. Many of these people are workaholics, a problem we deal with in depth in the next chapter. For others, though, the problem lies in their expectations about love, romance, and passion.

Sociologist Charles Hobart has developed a romanticism scale, which should clarify for you some of the notions you have about love.

The higher your score, the more you tend to romanticize relationships. You think male-female relationships should be romantic. A pragmatist you are not! While many people tend to think that women are more romantic in their views than are men, Hobart's research found that men, in fact, are the more romantic sex.

For career couples, one of the big issues seems to be: What can we realistically expect—and accept—as romantic? "Romance" often takes on new dimensions for working partners. As with most couples, the idealized "hearts and flowers" variety of romance is short-lived. Further, romance necessarily loses much of its spontaneity as life becomes increasingly hectic. One woman we interviewed echoed the sentiments of many couples:

Romanticism Scale[2]

		Agree	Disagree
* 1.	Lovers ought to expect a certain amount of disillusionment after marriage.	_____	_____
* 2.	True love should be suppressed in cases where its existence conflicts with the prevailing standards of morality.	_____	_____
3.	To be truly in love is to be in love forever.	_____	_____
* 4.	The sweetly feminine "clinging vine" girl cannot compare with the capable and sympathetic girl as a sweetheart.	_____	_____
5.	As long as they at least love each other, two people should have no trouble getting along together in marriage.	_____	_____
6.	A girl should expect her sweetheart to be chivalrous on all occasions.	_____	_____
7.	A person should marry whomever he loves regardless of social position.	_____	_____
8.	Lovers should freely confess everything of personal significance to each other.	_____	_____
* 9.	Economic security should be carefully considered before selecting a marriage partner.	_____	_____
*10.	Most of us could sincerely love any one of several people equally well.	_____	_____
11.	A lover without jealousy is hardly to be desired.	_____	_____
*12.	One should not marry against the serious advice of one's parents.	_____	_____

What's your romanticism score? If you agreed with items 3, 5, 6, 7, 8, or 11 (the items without an asterisk), give yourself one point per item. If you disagreed with items 1, 2, 4, 9, 10, or 12 (the items with an asterisk), give yourself one point per item. Record your total score here _____.

When you are juggling two jobs, a home, kids, and other commitments, there just isn't a whole lot of spontaneity in your marriage. You have to find ways to do things that consciously get you back in touch with your sexuality and with the romantic side of your relationship.

Working couples, it seems, must consciously build romance into their lives. While this may sound cold and calculating, it is simply a reflection of the fact that time together, especially time alone together, is one of the dual-career couple's scarcest resources.

Couples who recognize this are likely to schedule in time for romance or devise ways to keep their passion alive.

This is, of course, easier said than done. Many couples report that coping with pressures and stress drains them of energy and leaves them feeling fatigued and disinterested in sex. Francess Dincin, a sex therapist and a group leader at Northwestern University Medical School's Human Sexuality Program, offers some insights.

> People get burdened with the idea that sex always has to be spontaneous and romantic to be good, but it doesn't. I have suggested that some people have a regular appointment for sex just as people have regular appointments for other things they love, like tennis. People need to pay attention to their relationships, to take time for each other just as they did when they were getting to know each other. That is one of the pitfalls. People don't think they have to keep getting to know each other.[3]

Dincin suggests that doing *new* things together is a great way to revive the romance in a relationship. As she told us, "Beginnings are always exciting. They are like experiencing new love all over again, and we feel more alive."

The new activity may be completely new or simply a break from the old routine. For some couples, it may mean new sexual exploration. For others, it may mean taking up a new hobby, a new sport, or even dressing differently. In short, it means getting involved together in something that feels totally frivolous, forbidden, or fun. As one woman told us, "It's hard to be romantic at home. I need to get away." She and her husband find that dinner out alone helps them to recapture feelings of romance. Other couples plan weekend trips together at regular intervals during the year. Their get-away may simply be a weekend at a luxurious hotel in the city or a two-day camping trip.

For many years, we have gone out for breakfast without the kids at least once a week. We jokingly call it "our affair." But what it represents is something slightly illicit. Aren't people supposed to be at the office or at home taking care of the kids at that hour? Another couple we know makes it a point to have a "date" each week. And they treat it as just that—their time to court each other.

The important factor is not where or even what you do together. It's how you perceive it. Opening a bottle of wine late at night and curling up by the fire can be just as much of a romantic break for one couple as a trip to Mexico can be for another. As one woman explained, "Anything that makes you feel special together is romantic."

Sex and two careers

Many people wonder whether two-career couples have particular sexual problems unique to working partners. So far there hasn't been much research on this subject. Although a number of articles have suggested that male sexual dysfunctions have increased since the advent of the women's movement, there are no hard data to support the theory that a successful working woman will *necessarily* cause her husband or lover to experience feelings of sexual inadequacy. Even if these feelings do exist, there is no evidence that the result will always be impotence.

While some men do feel threatened by their partner's success or competence and carry their insecurity into the bedroom, many others find a successful woman a "turn-on." Rather than interpreting her success as their own failure, many men view having a successful career partner as an affirmation of their own strength. It is exciting for them to realize that they are capable of attracting and satisfying a woman who is herself exciting and capable—a woman who doesn't have to depend on them or love them for her fulfillment.

Perhaps the only generalization we can make is that both men and women may experience anxieties about how their career will affect their relationship with a partner. If these are not discussed and resolved, they can have an adverse impact on sexual behavior.

Three factors seem to determine whether working couples experience sexual problems as a result of changes brought about by their careers. The first is the ego strength or security of the partners. A secure partner is less likely to view the other's achievements as a negative reflection on his or her own esteem, self-worth, or control.

The second factor is trust. Partners who trust each other are less likely to feel threatened by the other's career success. They are also less susceptible to fears about potential affairs or loss of love.

The third and most important factor, however, is communication. Partners who are able to discuss their feelings openly and offer one another reassurance are simply less likely to act out their fears in other ways.

Sexual problems in a relationship are usually not *the* problem. More often they are a symptom of something else that is bothering one or both partners. The real problem may be that unex-

"By God, Willkie, you're right! Our affair was made possible by a grant from the Ford Foundation."

Reprinted by permission of G.P. Putnam's Son's from *Terribly Nice People* by William Hamilton, copyright © 1975 by William Hamilton.

pressed feelings are being acted out in the bedroom. Sadly, when sex is used as a weapon, both partners are wounded.

Many couples have learned by experience what research has verified: passionate love does not last forever, perhaps six to thirty months, according to sociologists Elaine and Bill Walster. Happily, though, the relationship may ripen into what the Walsters call "companionate love," when the lover becomes a best friend and the personal bond becomes tender attachment, a feeling of lives intertwined:

> By the time passion flickers out, it has been replaced by companionate love—shared understandings, emotions, and habits. Passionate love is a fragile flower; it wilts in time. Companionate love is a sturdy evergreen: it thrives with contact.[4]

Equity and love

One of the factors that strengthens a relationship is a feeling of *equity* for both parties—the feeling that each partner is benefiting from the relationship as much as he or she is contributing to it. The Walsters explain their equity theory of love as follows:

> 1. People are biologically "set" to seek out pleasure and avoid pain. This biological trait is essential to human survival.

2. Society consists of a collection of selfish people. If society is to survive, its members must learn to compromise. They must accept the notion that you have to give a little to get a little, and that the more you give, the more you can expect to get.

3. People feel most comfortable when they're getting exactly what they feel they deserve in a relationship. *Everyone* in an inequitable relationship feels uneasy. While it's not surprising that deprived partners (who are, after all, getting less than they deserve) should feel resentful and angry about their inequitable treatment, it's perhaps not so obvious why their *over*benefited mates (who are getting more than they deserve) feel uneasy too. But they do. They feel guilty and fearful of losing their favored position.

4. Men and woman who discover that they're in an inequitable relationship attempt to eliminate their mutual distress by restoring equity. They generally go about this in one of three ways:

- They try to restore *actual* equity to their relationship.
- They try to restore *psychological* equity to their relationship. (They try to convince themselves and others that their obviously inequitable relationship really is "perfectly fair.")
- They also simply decide to end their relationship.[5]

What different dimensions are important in evaluating what people give and receive in a relationship? Consider the following:

- *Physical attractiveness.* People tend to date and marry people who are just about as attractive as they are. If a person becomes attached to a person who is less attractive, the other person will probably possess some other compensating quality, such as a sparkling personality or a quick mind.
- *Mental health.* Emotionally healthy people tend to attract each other, as do disturbed people.
- *Physical health.* The same.
- *Family background.* People tend to end up with partners from the same race and religion, with similar socioeconomic background and comparable education.
- *Family solidity.* People whose parents were happily married tend to be drawn to each other, while people from broken homes are also likely to match up.
- *Popularity.* Again, likes attract, and people are drawn to others who have the same level of popularity as they do.[6]

Although people do tend to mate with partners possessing similar attributes, equity can also be achieved by substi-

tuting one attractive feature for another. For example, an older executive may trade his money and comfortable life-style for a younger
woman's attractiveness and energy. The Walsters provide research
support for this balancing and counterbalancing that takes place in
selecting mates. They conclude that "although we can *never* get
exactly what we want, we can get the few things we want most."[7]

To help partners assess their relationship, the
Walsters have developed a short equity scale. You and your partner
might want to evaluate your own relationship by responding to the
question below:

> Considering what you put into a relationship compared to what you get
> out of it . . . and what your partner puts in compared to what he or she
> gets out of it, how does your marriage "stack up?"
>
> − 3 My partner is getting a much better deal.
> − 2 My partner is getting a somewhat better deal.
> − 1 My partner is getting a slightly better deal.
> 0 We are both getting an equal deal.
> + 1 I am getting a slightly better deal.
> + 2 I am getting a somewhat better deal.
> + 3 I am getting a much better deal.[8]

The Walsters found that couples with equitable
relationships were happier and more content than were couples with
inequitable pairings. People who got less than they gave were the least
content and often expressed anger about the imbalance. Interestingly,
people who felt they got far more than they deserved were also
unhappy—they felt guilty about their excess of rewards. The Walsters
point out that being *too good* to one's partner is not really doing them
any favor. When a couple becomes aware of inequity, they attempt to
gain balance through restoring either actual equity (changing the way
one partner behaves toward the other) or psychological equity (adjusting the psychological weighting of various factors in the equation, re-
assuring themselves that things are not so unfair after all).

Competition and Jealousy

What about competition? Isn't it only natural for
working partners to compare the success of their two careers? Doesn't
the less successful one feel jealous of the more successful?

Our impression is that competition is most likely to
be a problem if the partners are in the same career stage or in the
same field. Under these conditions, the two careers are sufficiently

similar to be easily compared. Frequently, friends and colleagues do the comparing and, either implicitly or explicitly, communicate to the couple their assessment of the partners' relative success. Thus, even if the partners do not feel competitive initially, the appraisals they receive from others may generate a feeling of competition.

Given current sex-role stereotypes and norms, competition is less likely if it is the male who has achieved greater recognition and success. The woman may experience jealousy, however, if she has had to make career sacrifices for the sake of her husband's career. In a sense, she has lost in two ways: not only was her spouse's career more successful to begin with, but each relocation (for him) or each nonrelocation (for her) may further increase the gap between his career and hers. She is, in effect, deprived of the chance to catch up.

Her jealousy may be compounded by feelings of ambivalence. After all, in addition to her role as a careerist in her own right, she also holds the role of wife and is likely to identify with her husband's success and enjoy the rewards (status, money, travel) that it brings. Thus, his success is a double-edged sword, and her consequent ambivalence may lead to feelings of guilt about her very legitimate feelings of jealousy. Without knowing exactly why, she is left with a jumble of conflicting emotions and the vague feeling that somehow she is to blame.

What about the young, upwardly mobile couple, say one without children, where the wife is at least as successful as the husband? Here the stage is set for possibly fierce competition. Whether competition occurs depends a great deal on the attitudes and personalities of the two people. For example, one couple in their twenties both work for the same welfare agency, where he is a caseworker and she is the assistant director of the agency, a position two levels higher. Both acknowledge that she is the more successful of the two. However, he is not highly involved in his work and has a wide range of outside interests. He is also, as she describes him, an extremely relaxed, secure person, not at all threatened by her attainments. He plays a nurturant, supportive role in the relationship, acting as a sounding board for her feelings and problems at the end of the day. He also helps her relax by organizing their leisure-time activities, something she acknowledges as very important to the sanity of both. He is very unconflicted about the low centrality of work in his life. If he could afford to retire tommorrow, he would. (In fact, we suspect that he sees his wife's future success as instrumental in obtaining a very early retirement.) Thus, if the male's self-esteem is high and his work involvement low, competition may be minimal or nonexistent.

It is not unusual to find successful, ambitious women married to men who are far less involved in career pursuits. There may be a causal mechanism at work here: early in the relationship, as the man senses the woman's superiority, he may withdraw simply to avoid a contest in which he would lose. (As one male professional put it, "I wouldn't dare compete with my wife; she'd destroy me!") There could also be a selection factor operating in the initial choice of mate. One type of man likely to be attracted or attractive to a strong, successful woman is the self-assured man who regards career success as largely irrelevant (that is, a man with low-career involvement).

Competition between partners is unquestionably a stressful experience, one that couples try to avoid if they can. One medical-school couple in which the wife was the academic star put it this way: "We don't compete or compare ourselves with each other; we wouldn't survive if we did."

They consciously chose different specialties to minimize competition. They also both feel that success as a medical student is quite unrelated to how successful they will be as doctors, which seems to be a way of minimizing the importance of her superior performance to date.

As this couple talked, however, one could see that there were some tender areas related to the wife's superior academic performance. As he says:

> Other people view us in a competitive way. They say they would be competitive with their spouse if they were in our situation. When others view me as inferior, it bothers me. Some professors have done this. How do we deal with it? We talk about it. We feel we are noncompetitive and can separate work from our marriage. Each of us has separate abilities. We have mutual respect for each other and our abilities and weaknesses.

Two other partners in medical school together are similarly disparate academically: she is doing better. Their problem, though, was not grade competition but conflict over how to spend time. She liked to study most of the time and he liked to pursue other leisure interests. So they compromised. He spent more time studying (with her) than he normally would and she cut back on study time a bit to do other activities with her husband.

Sometimes the less successful husband makes career sacrifices to facilitate his wife's career. Take the case of Sue, a feature writer for a big midwestern city newspaper, and Hank, now a freelance photographer. Hank had dropped out of school twice and had several newspaper jobs before he enlisted in the navy, where he was promised an assignment as a photographer. After the navy, Hank held various jobs. In 1975, both husband and wife decided to look for new positions. Whoever got a good job first would accept and the other would follow. Sue got the newspaper job, a very good one, first, and Hank hs been freelancing for the last two years. She is basically supporting them now. She feels she is on an upward career path and he is very content with no career goals, preferring to explore something new every couple of years.

Sue owes much of her success to Hank and fears that she is holding him back. In fact, Hank appears to be quite happy where he is right now, but the shared perception that he has consciously chosen to make a career sacrifice for her makes it easier for both to accept her greater success. Thus, he wins in two ways: it is mutually acknowledged that he could do better if they moved, so her success poses no embarrassment or threat; and, as an added bonus, Hank gets credit for making career sacrifices for Sue.

When both people are upwardly mobile, highly career involved, and competitive, the long-term prospects for the marriage are not good—especially if the wife is more successful. Dave and Kay were both in their thirties and rising rapidly in their companies. He was an executive in a West Coast firm, heading up the Midwest region. She was moving from a professional specialty into management in a Midwest firm. Both were enrolled in a very demanding part-time graduate program. Kay was making more money than Dave and she was also doing better work in graduate school. They had been through various group personal-growth experiences together and thought they had their normally competitive styles pretty well under control. Then, with a change of administration in her firm, Kay was offered two major promotions, a year apart. She had caught the eye of the company president, who was tremendously impressed with her ability, and she was offered a vice-presidency at their headquarters in the Midwest. When Dave heard about this, they did not talk for three days. He had also been offered a promotion, which would have meant moving back to California. After much agonizing and attempting to find a solution, the competing careers won out over the marriage and they went their separate ways.

Competition can also occur when the partners are at quite different career stages. Consider the man at midcareer whose wife is just beginning to get established. She is growing at a rapid rate and literally tingling with success, while his career is levelling off. He may no longer have any desire to compete in the career arena, or he may feel he can't. The woman, on the other hand, is grooving on competition; she is shooting past all kinds of people—men and women—on her way up the professional ladder. She is very much caught up in a success cycle and her self-esteem is escalating rapidly. His, on the other hand, is becoming a bit shaky.

She comes home at the end of the day full of tales of conquest and fulfillment. He comes home tired and edgy and wants to get away from it all. Her open enthusiasm, of course, just grates on his threatened ego and fuels his depression. But he tries to be supportive and to show excitement over her exploits. And the more support he shows, the more successful she becomes and the more she bubbles at home. And the worse he feels.

A milder form of conflict can occur if, instead of feeling stagnant, he just feels ready to slow down a little and enjoy his leisure time more. If she is very hooked on her work, they may clash over how to spend their leisure moments. Do they go out and have fun together? Or does she do something work related—paperwork, business entertaining, preparing for the next day—while he entertains himself?

What do you do if this sort of mixed-stage competition occurs? The critical element seems to be the state of the man's career. His feelings of restlessness or stagnation must be overcome. If his mate is aware of his needs, she can encourage him to discuss his feelings about his career. Perhaps it's time for a major change. He may already have an inkling of what he'd really like to be doing, but views it as too risky or simply out of reach. With her support, however, he may find the strength or means to do it. Or, together they can identify those people in his organization or elsewhere who could be of help in gettng his life back on track.

If the conflict centers on time spent in leisure activity, he may have to learn how to "play alone" for a while. Intrusions on her work are bound to be resented at this stage, and a little independent activity for each would probably do the relationship no harm. After her initial career euphoria begins to wear off, she'll also reach a point where she wants to play more. If he can be patient and supportive and wait for her career to catch up with his, this form of competition cures itself.

Affairs

As more women return to full-time careers, is it reasonable to expect a dramatic increase in work-related affairs? It is true that working closely together can bring people together emotionally. Successful work toward common goals and frequent contact tend to produce positive feelings between people. Further, men and women usually see each other at their best on the job. Both are full of energy, attractively dressed, and eager to build good working relationships.

Contrast this with the way you feel dragging home from the 6:30 train after a hectic twelve-hour-day of being nice to people in situations where you'd give anything to scream. Your partner—and perhaps the kids—may be in the same mood. Given this contrast, it would not be too surprising if those warm feelings about that sweet person at work began to grow over time.

Unfortunately, this is a sensitive and difficult area to study systematically. To our knowledge, the Bureau of Labor Statistics and similar organizations have not been collecting monthly data on the incidence of office romances (although their data seem to cover just about every other kind of activity!). Although social scientists are predicting an increase in work-related romances, no hard data are yet available.[9] The *Wall Street Journal* has suggested that the strains of two careers (including office romances) have contributed to the doubling of the divorce rate over the last ten years. The *Journal* also has quoted marriage counselors who say they are aware of more on-the-job affairs.[10] But, as yet, these assertions remain simply that.

With more women in the work force, there is certainly more opportunity to become romantically involved with someone at work. But whether the two-career couple is more vulnerable to affairs is a debatable issue. People who seek affairs will have time whether they work or not. Working may just mean getting involved with a colleague rather than with a neighbor. Again, the determining factor is the strength of the relationship and what it provides for the partners.

On the positive side, there are several factors operating in two-career relationships that may, in fact, deter extramarital involvements. First, coping with two careers, a home, and perhaps a family, although stressful, can serve to bond partners strongly by way of shared experiences and problems. Their interdependence may cause them to feel closer to one another and to become more aware, more sensitive to, and more responsive to meeting the other's needs.

A second factor is simply lack of time and energy. Many couples are so busy coping with the demands of both work and family that there just isn't enough space in their life to pursue an affair. As one person commented after a moment of thought, "I don't know where I could fit an affair into my life."

Third, many people in two-career marriages are highly career involved in professional or managerial roles, upwardly mobile, and *visible*. They are well aware that an affair at the office might jeopardize their professional position and future prospects. Even if they are tempted to become romantically involved, there is simply too much risk involved and too much to lose.

On the negative side, a relationship that is threatened by the impact of the second career can lead a partner to seek satisfaction, security, or esteem outside the marriage. If one partner's career is a source of competition or jealousy, an insecure partner may look elsewhere for support. An affair can be a great ego trip. If your partner's career is a threat to your own ego, an affair may provide just what you are looking for—comfort rather than competiton.

For both men and women, working may also lead to a greater awareness of their own sexuality and attractiveness. People at the office may be more responsive and attentive to them than are their own partners. Again, if the relationship at home is not providing adequate opportunity to experience and enjoy one's sexuality, then an affair may be very tempting.

In short, couples who actively cultivate satisfaction and sexuality in their own relationship will be less likely to need or seek it elsewhere. Those who take their relationship for granted may be unconsciously drifting into a state of romantic dissatisfaction and disenchantment. In doing so, they may be setting themselves up as likely candidates for a fling or even a full-blown affair.

One fascinating study of office affairs was conducted by Robert Quinn at the Albany and LaGuardia airports (where people feel relatively anonymous).[11] Respondents were asked to complete short questionnaires describing affairs they had observed between two members of the same organization. The researcher reports that people were often very eager to go into even more detail after they had completed the questionnaires!

What factors lead up to an affair at work? Proximity—i.e., simply being together—is probably the most important determinant. Geographical proximity (working near each other) was a factor in 63 percent of the romances described in the study. One respondent told of a boss and a secretary who shared the same office. They worked together for a year without any unusual occurrences, and then the woman started having various personal problems. She spent long periods of time getting advice from her boss, their relationship became more personal, and, after several months, the romance blossomed. Being together in work activities, such as business trips or training programs, was a factor in 77 percent of all romances described. In 94 percent of the cases, the females were characterized as average or above average in physical attractiveness. In 74 percent of the cases, the male held a higher-level position than did the woman. (Forty-eight percent of the women were secretaries.)

Three types of office romances seem to occur. The *fling* provides ego gratification to both parties: high excitement tempered with the belief that the affair is only temporary. People who engage in flings are generally looking for adventure, esteem, and sexual experience. *True love* is based on sincere mutual affection. It usually involves two unmarried people and tends to result in marriage, although a very small number of affairs between attached people are built on true love as well. The *utilitarian relationship* is exactly that— the parties have different, though complementary, motives. The male is usually seeking ego gratification (excitement, esteem, adventure, sex), while the female sees the romance as way to enhance her job or career rewards. Either partner may be after power, money, security, easier work, or a faster way to the top.

How do other people find out about the romance? Although the participants try to keep it a secret, this is always difficult to do. Quinn explains:

> Among the most common activities that alert members of the organization [to an affair] are being observed together away from work, longer or more frequent chats, long lunches together, long discussions behind closed doors, and joint business trips. Less subtle, but surprisingly common tip-offs involve the physical expression of affection. In about a third of the cases, participants are seen embracing in closets, kissing in supply rooms, or fondling in the parking lot.[12]

What are the effects of an office romance? In about one-third of the cases, the male's competence appears to decrease (e.g., he loses the respect of department members). The most frequent change is that the male shows favoritism to the female (72 percent of the cases). Similar changes were seen in the females. A plus factor was that, in about one-quarter of the cases, both parties became easier to get along with!

How did co-workers usually respond to the affair? The majority (around 60 percent) tolerated it and about 20 percent approved (except for the female's subordinates, who were less likely to approve). What actions did people take? The most frequent action was advising the participants about the relationship (over 50 percent of their colleagues did so). Other actions were complaining to a superior or trying to undermine or sabotage one or both of the participants.

The overall impact of the affairs was remarkably mild. Mostly, they just generated a great deal of gossip (70 percent). They caused gripes and hostilities about one-third of the time and they distorted communication in about one-quarter of the cases.

What action did superiors take? In the majority of cases, they did nothing (around 60 percent of the time). Punitive action was taken less than 10 percent of the time. When this did occur, the female was twice as likely to be fired as the male. There was some tendency on the part of superiors to discuss the situation openly with the male (33 percent), but not with the female. The general feeling was that the situation would take care of itself.

Affairs are romantic. They offer instant gratification. Building romance back into a stale relationship takes work and conscious, if not self-conscious, effort. An affair can be a quick way to feel good, loved, sexual, attractive, important, and even powerful.

But affairs are, by definition, temporary. A sustained marital relationship can be permanent. Seeking romance through affairs rather than building it into a permanent relationship is like taking pills rather than curing a disease. It may be harder and take longer to put romance and sexuality back into your marriage, but the satisfaction it can bring is well worth the effort.

Not surprisingly, the very things that make an affair so romantic are the same things couples need to work on to maintain romance in a marriage. They need to care, they need to concentrate on each other, they need to enjoy new experiences together, they need to escape from their routines, and, most important, they need to make each other feel special and sexual as human beings.

Friendships

Two-career couples readily admit that their hectic life-style leaves little time for casual socializing. As more time goes into coping with work and managing home and family, less time is available for relationships with friends. Most people report that it's hard enough to find time to be alone with their spouse, let alone keep up with friends. As one thirty-year-old woman, an elementary-school teacher with a young child, put it, "Being a working mother and having a house and husband, there's just not much time to have friends. So I've had to give up the friend role. We try to make up for it in the summer by getting back in touch with people during our vacation." When asked to list and rank her roles, she ranked the "friend" role number six of eight, coming after (in order) parent, spouse, self, work career, and daughter. This is not an unusual ranking: two-thirds of the two-career couples we have interviewed ranked the friend role four, five, or six.

Although social activity may taper off gradually, the effects can be profound. We were discussing how we felt about the community in which we now live, a place we've been for three-and-a-half years (about average for us, like many other mobile couples). We both admitted that we didn't really feel strongly rooted here. In fact, it was difficult to believe that three years had elapsed. The problem? We just don't have as many close friends as we have had in other places, and we attribute this to the fact that never before were we pursuing careers simultaneously. We had more time for entertaining, for accepting social invitations, and for taking weekend trips to visit good friends. We also had more time to keep in touch by letter and telephone. It's hard to remember the last time we sat down and wrote a letter to out-of-town friends. In the rush of our daily lives, we simply let those less pressing matters slide.

Most of our relationships now center on work: colleagues in the office, clients, students, publishers, and so on. These are all gratifying relationships, but they don't replace having close friends in our neighborhood and community. We don't have time to entertain much and we have to turn down many invitations. As a result, we get fewer invitations. And we don't have time to become active in community organizations (church, politics, cub scouts, etc.), which eliminates another source of good relationships. The result? We look even more to our work roles for satisfaction—in this case, social satisfaction. It's not a good feeling. In fact, it's very disturbing to one day realize that, if you moved away in the middle of the night, your neighbors might not even notice.

William Fox, who interviewed several dual-career couples for a class project, describes how a couple's social network gradually diminishes when the wife goes back to work:

- Her social contacts (developed through the PTA, church activities, clubs, organizations, and so on) are reduced.
- Gradually, both partners are no longer invited out, because they have declined too many invitations in the past.
- Their domestic life settles down and, after a time, they realize they're out of the swing of things.
- Troubled by this, they discuss how to revive their social life.
- They begin by extending invitations, and gradually reestablish a network of friends. (This pertains only to couples who so choose; many are happy without an outside social life.)[13]

The realization that one has lost touch with friends may come only after years of coping with a growing family. Once the children are older, the couple may become acutely aware that "something's missing" in their life. The lack of close relationships is one factor that frequently contributes to lack of fulfillment in two-career relationships.

How about you? If you were to move to a different part of the country, is there anyone you would miss deeply? Who would be upset to see you go? If you moved away and then were back in this area on business, would you stay in someone's home or in a hotel? If a serious personal problem arose tomorrow, whom would you turn to for help? Who in your community has sought out your help recently? Whom do you call just to chat? Do you go fishing, shopping, golfing, or to the movies with one or more friends, with or without spouses?

If your answers to these questions leave you feeling unhappy, you should make time to reach out to friends and develop closer relationships. Once you take the initiative and start calling people, they will respond, and you can reclaim a whole dimension of your life.

In Conclusion

The conflicts two-career couples experience are not limited to clashes with the rest of the world. The relationship itself is at risk. Romance can wither or competition can erupt. An affair might spring up to replace flagging passion. Or, the couple may become so involved in their careers that once-close friends are left by the wayside.

Two qualities seem especially important in working through these problems. The first is strong mutual commitment to the two careers and the relationship. If the partners are firm in their desire to make their life together work, they eventually will. If the commitment is not there, the problems may win out—and perhaps this is for the best.

The other factor is flexibility—the ability to give and take, to compromise, and, as one couple said, "to each give 60 percent to the relationship." If each party stubbornly insists, "I'm right, you're wrong, and there's no middle ground," they will soon fulfill their own prophecy: there will, in fact, be no middle ground. We tend to forget sometimes that a two-career relationship is made up of five elements: two careers, two independent people, and one relationship. In our enthusiasm for developing the first four, let's not crowd out the fifth.

CHAPTER EIGHT

ARE YOU MARRIED TO YOUR JOB?

More and more people are seeking careers that offer them flexibility, autonomy, growth, a feeling of achievement, and, most important, personal satisfaction. As we shall see, a satisfied worker is usually a better spouse.

In this chapter, we look at what makes a job satisfying and how that satisfaction can very easily grow into overinvolvement. When it does, the consequences can be relatively minor—perhaps too much travel or business-related entertaining—or major and potentially destructive—as when success turns into workaholism. We'll also be looking at an increasingly troublesome phenomenon: the conflict that can occur when spouses work in the same industry but for competing companies.

A Red, White, and Blue Job

Recently, there has been renewed interest in quality of work life and ways of improving work, such as job enrichment. Organizations are focusing in on the factors that make a job satisfying. Increasingly, they are learning that satisfaction with work is inextricably linked with satisfaction at home and in one's personal life.

Two opposite theories have been advanced about the relationship between work and family or personal life. One theory, the compensatory view, suggests that the less satisfied you are in your

167

work, the more you will try to achieve satisfaction off the job. Or by the same token, if your work is highly satisfying, you won't have the energy or the interest to participate much in off-the-job activities. The opposing theory, the spillover view, suggests that both work satisfaction and work frustration spill over into off-the-job activities. Thus, you will feel the same about nonwork activities as you do about work.

Although not much research has been done on the relationship between work and nonwork fulfillment, most evidence to date supports the spillover theory. In other words, a satisfying career will probably enhance marriage and family life, and vice versa. Therefore, fulfilled workers make fulfilling lovers. And turned-on lovers get more excitement from their work. Just having a job is not enough. What counts is having a satisfying job, a good job. Huey Long understood and aptly expressed the difference: "There shall be a real job, not a little old sowbelly black-eyed pea job, but a real spending money, beefsteak and gray Chevrolet Ford in the garage, new suit, Thomas Jefferson, Jesus Christ, red, white, and blue job for every man [and woman]."[1]

What makes for a real "red, white, and blue job?" A series of research studies by Drs. Edward Lawler, Richard Hackman, and Greg Oldham identified the following characteristics as factors that give work meaning:

1. *Skill variety.* The extent to which a job requires a variety of different activities in carrying out the work, which involve the use of a number of different skills and talents of the person. . . .

2. *Task identity.* The degree to which the job requires completion of a "whole" and identifiable piece of work—that is, doing a job from beginning to end with a visible outcome. . . .

3. *Task significance.* The degree to which the job has a substantial impact on the lives or work of other people—whether in the immediate organization or in the external environment. . . .

4. *Autonomy.* The degree to which the job provides substantial freedom, independence, and discretion of the individual in scheduling the work and in determining the procedures to be used in carrying it out. . . .

5. *Feedback.* The degree to which carrying out the work activities required by the job results in the individual's obtaining direct and clear information about the effectiveness of his or her performance.[2]

Think for a minute about your job and your partner's in terms of these five important characteristics. Rate each job on each dimension, using a 1 (low) to 7 (high) scale. Enter the score for each job on the graph provided and connect the points for each job. This will give you a profile of that job.

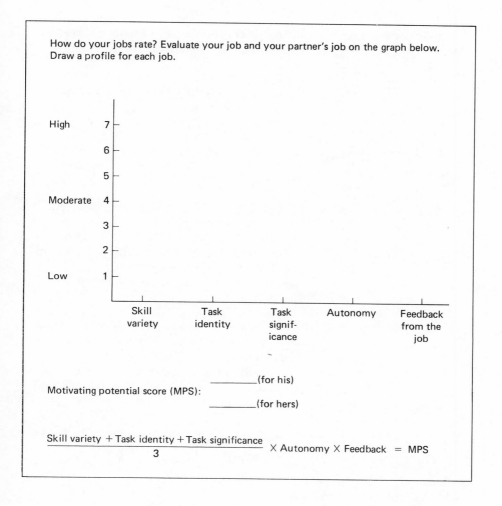

How do your jobs rate? Evaluate your job and your partner's job on the graph below. Draw a profile for each job.

Motivating potential score (MPS):   _____ (for his)
_____ (for hers)

$$\frac{\text{Skill variety} + \text{Task identity} + \text{Task significance}}{3} \times \text{Autonomy} \times \text{Feedback} = \text{MPS}$$

A formula for computing the "motivating potential score" (MPS) for each job is provided at the bottom of the graph. Compute the score for each of your jobs. Scores can range from 1 to 343, and an average job tends to score around 125. If either of your jobs is greatly above 125, you have an unusually attractive job. If you rate much below 125, your job may not have much potential for providing you with satisfaction. For example, Tim rates his job (college professor) as follows:

Skill variety = 5   Different courses, new students, variety of
                           research projects, consulting, etc.

Task identity = 3   No real "product" or end-result service.
                           Some visible product in published research,
                           completion of a course, or a graduating
                           student.

Task significance = 4   Education is socially valued, but no one
                           would suffer much if professors stopped
                           teaching.

Autonomy = 7   The real bonus from college teaching. All
                           that is really prescribed is when and where
                           you meet your classes. End results (e.g.,
                           publication) are prescribed, but how, where,
                           and when you work on them is totally at your
                           own discretion. There is virtually total
                           freedom.

Job feedback = 6   Each course is evaluated by students, each
                           book is reviewed, colleagues are continually
                           commenting on your work in meetings and in
                           their publications, and most academics have
                           a fairly accurate view of how they are seen
                           by their colleagues.

The score for Tim's job is thus $\dfrac{5 + 3 + 4}{3} \times 7 \times 6 = 168$,

which is higher than average. This fits with Tim's high level of job
satisfaction. He feels he has a pretty "good deal" in this job, especially
with the freedom it provides.

How do your jobs look? If one or both of your
scores are too low, you may be feeling some job frustration, which
could be affecting your relationship adversely. On the other hand, if
your score is too high, you may be feeling excessive job pressure,
which could also cause problems at home. We know that moderately
high levels of motivation and pressure from a job are stimulating, energizing, and satisfying. However, if the job demands and motivation are
too high, the result may be feelings of disorganization and stress and a
reduction in performance.

The same holds true for specific job character-
istics. If skill variety is too high, you may feel that you are always
"fighting fires." With so many different tasks demanding attention, you
never get a sense of completing any one (which may show up as low
task identity). Similarly, if the significance of your task is too high, the
pressure may become intolerable. Imagine *always* feeling like it's the
bottom of the ninth inning in the last game of the World Series, with
two men out and two men on base, your team down one run, and it's
your turn at bat. The feeling that everything is riding on you can be
exciting, but only for a while. Not surprisingly, people in high-task-sig-
nificance occupations (like air-traffic controllers) often "burn out" in
their late thirties.

By the same token, too much autonomy and un-
clear job objectives are likely to produce stressful ambiguity. And if
you get too much feedback, or if it is usually negative, or if rewards
and punishments are too closely tied to your immediate performance,
the feedback itself may become a stress producer, something to be
dreaded and feared.

So, take a look at any marked peak in the profiles
of your job and your spouse's. Perhaps this aspect of either job is
causing problems for both of you.

The job dimension that we have found most critical
for dual-career couples is autonomy, the essential element in a protean
career. Coping effectively with two careers requires a degree of freedom on the job, especially if you have children. Kids definitely restrict
your freedom at home. Sooner or later, something has to give, and job
autonomy is another way of saying the job has some "give" to it. If it is
flexible, you can make adjustments in the work sphere to respond to
family needs.

What kinds of jobs are especially difficult for two-
career couples? First on the list are jobs with excessive travel, such as
consulting, sales, real estate, certain training and development jobs,
college recruiting, and public-accounting jobs—jobs that require you to
be on the move when the client or business demands it. Jobs that
require your physical presence in a particular place for a standard
eight-hour day, such as production, banking, accounting, and engi-
neering, may also restrict your freedom. The more flexible jobs are
those in which you are responsible for certain results but are given
leeway in accomplishing them: life-insurance sales, investment, management, journalism, research, and so forth.

Let's assume your job looks pretty satisfying right now. Where does that leave you? Aren't you in relatively good shape, since job satisfaction is an important career goal for most people?

Job satisfaction is a goal for most, but it does have certain consequences. On the positive side, of course, are greater happiness in life and improved relations with spouse and family. But there is a darker side. Job satisfaction resulting from job success can also reinforce a "success syndrome." As we discussed earlier, achieving challenging job goals increases your self-esteem, which makes you more ego involved in your work. The more involved you are, the higher you set your next work goals, and the harder you work for future success. It is a self-reinforcing, escalating cycle.

As long as only a moderate portion of your ego gets caught up in work success, the level of involvement you feel can be very beneficial to both your performance and your future satisfaction. However, success carries hazards as well—promotions to less satisfying jobs, too much traveling, workaholism, and possible conflicts with your spouse. Let's start by looking more closely at job involvement.

Getting Involved

A little job involvement goes a long way. A certain level is essential to effective performance and personal fulfillment, but it can become addictive, and overinvolvement can destroy a marriage. Many people have discovered painfully that the goal they sought so diligently (career success) later betrayed them. Success was not all it was cracked up to be and being married to the job killed their marriage.

The most widely used definition of job involvement comes from the work of Thomas Lodahl and Mathilde Kejner, psychologists at Cornell University:

> Job involvement is the degree to which a person is identified psychologically with his or her work, i.e., the importance of work to the person's total self-image. Therefore, job involvement is a measure of how central the job situation is to a person's sense of identity, in relation to other facets of his or her life. . . .[3]

If we were to depict life roles and their relative importance to our identity, a person *highly involved* in work might look like this:

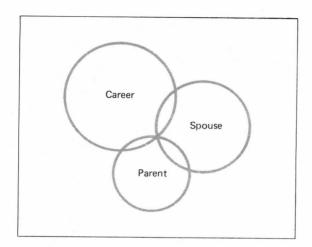

On the other hand, a less job-involved person might look like this:

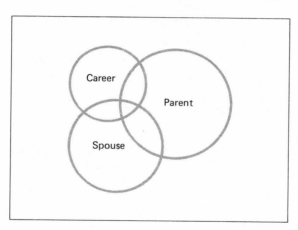

To help you assess your own degree of involvement in work compared to your involvement with your spouse or partner, try filling out the Involvement Analysis questionnaire presented on the next page. After you've answered the questions, compute your career-involvement score (the sum of questions 1–5) and your spouse-involvement score (the sum of questions 6–10). The following guide may be helpful in evaluating your scores:

20–25: Highly involved   10–14: Slightly involved
15–19: Moderately involved   5–9: Uninvolved

Involvement Analysis[4]

Indicate how much you agree or disagree with the statements below. Circle the number representing the correct response.

	Strongly Agree	Agree	Neither Agree nor Disagree	Disagree	Strongly Disagree
1. The most important things that happen to me involve my career.	5	4	3	2	1
2. I live, eat, and breathe my career.	5	4	3	2	1
3. I am very much involved in my career.	5	4	3	2	1
4. Most things in life are more important than my career.	1	2	3	4	5
5. The major satisfaction in my life comes from my career.	5	4	3	2	1

Career involvement: Add scores of questions 1–5 and enter here. _____

6. The major satisfaction in my life comes from my relationship with my spouse or partner.	5	4	3	2	1
7. The most important things that happen to me involve my relationship with my spouse or partner.	5	4	3	2	1
8. I live, eat, and breathe my relationship with my spouse or partner.	5	4	3	2	1
9. I am very much involved personally in my relationship with my spouse or partner.	5	4	3	2	1
10. Most things in life are more important than my relationship with my spouse or partner.	1	2	3	4	5

Spouse or partner involvement: Add scores of questions 6–10 and enter here. ____

If your score was 24 or 25 on career involvement, you may be in danger of being a workaholic (more on that later). If you scored 24 or 25 on spouse involvement, you must be a newlywed!

Another issue to think about is how your career-involvement score compares with your spouse- or partner-involvement score. Is one higher than the other? (We would consider a discrepancy of 4 or 5 points to be a sizable difference in your two involvements.) If there is a difference in involvement, is it consistent with the relative overall importance you attach to the two roles? Often one role may be far more important to us than the other, but we may get more involved in the less important one.

For example, you may feel that what really counts in life is your relationship with your spouse. And yet, when you look at how you spend your time, you may discover that you have let yourself become more involved in work and career than in your relationship.

This situation has been nicely avoided by Perry and Jane, two fourth-year medical students in Chicago. It's hard to think of any activity with more potential for overinvolvement than medical school, with the demands of studies, clinical work, and so on. And as more women enter medical schools (as well as other professional programs), it is becoming increasingly common to find couples going through programs together.

Perry and Jane decided early on (they've been married three years) that their marriage would always come first. They knew the demands of their careers would be intense. Work, in fact, would be such a strong threat to the relationship that they decided there would be no room for any other major role, such as parent. Perry had a vasectomy at a very young age (he's twenty-five now). As Perry says, "This is a radical move compared to other young couples we know." Very family oriented, Perry sees himself expressing this quality by "delivering thousands of babies." They are actively planning their careers and intend to take advantage of the great need for doctors by living all over the world and experiencing many different cultures. Thus, they see their work as a vehicle to permit the kind of life-style they seek. Perry and Jane rate themselves as "moderately involved" in work and "very involved" in their relationship. In their case, despite the temptations and demands of the medical profession, they work to live.

A quite different picture is presented by George, a supervising caseworker in the state public-aid department, and Jean, an assistant director of social work in the same department. She is highly involved in her job, as well as highly motivated and upwardly mobile: she expects to be department director someday. George, on the other hand, is not motivated by upward mobility and, on a scale of involvement ranging from 1 to 5, he rates himself as "minus one-half."

He describes himself as very easygoing and is content in the public-aid job, a position with a certain freedom and few hassles. When we asked him about his career plan, he laughed: "I'd *like* to retire at age thirty. But that's not economically feasible. So I chose the next best thing and became a bureaucrat!" George is very much aware that his wife is more successful than he, but he is extremely satisfied with what he is doing.

Jean, on the other hand, has been moving rapidly up the hierarchy and rates herself a 4 (very involved) on a 1–5 scale of career involvement. Both George and Jean rate themselves at 3 (moderately involved) on a 1–5 scale of marital involvement. What seems even more important than the marriage to each of them is the freedom to pursue their own interests—i.e., Jean's career and George's hobbies and recreation. Both are extremely satisfied with their family. Jean adds that their happiness is largely dependent on two factors: the absence of children and George's easygoing personality. He is definitely not threatened by her attainments and acts as a very supportive helper when she has important problems or decisions to resolve. As she says, "I can be independent yet know I have a secure base to work from."

Your involvement potential

Some job conditions produce higher levels of involvement than others, and people in those positions very frequently get caught up in a success cycle. Involvement breeds greater involvement. We also know that some people just tend naturally to be highly involved in *whatever* work they are doing. In other words, to some extent, work involvement seems to be a personality characteristic.

Who is the involvement-prone person? The best personal predictor of involvement is the conventional work ethic, which stresses the moral character of hard work and one's personal responsibility to the job. A person who holds these values will probably be highly involved in almost any job. Attitudes toward work are generally developed early in life through childhood socialization experiences.

Job-involved people also tend to have what psychologists call an "internal locus of control." This means they believe that the important rewards in life are under their control. People with an external locus of control (the belief that important rewards are controlled by outside forces, such as other people, institutions, fate, or chance) are less involved in their work. Apparently, we are reluctant to become too involved in something over which we feel little control.

A Quiz about Work Involvement[5]

Following are some popular beliefs about involvement, some of which may be just myths. Which are fact and which are folklore?

- *The higher up a person is in an organization, the more job involved he or she is. True or false?*

  This does not appear to be true. In a variety of research studies, degrees of job involvement did not significantly increase from one job level to the next or from blue collar to white collar to managers.

- *Male workers are more job involved than are women. True or false?*

  You might think that, due to sex-role socialization, men might be more job involved than women (i.e., men are raised traditionally to be the breadwinners). However, despite such beliefs, available evidence shows that men are no more (or less) involved in their work than are women.

- *Married people are more involved in their work than are unmarried people. True or false?*

  No, this is a myth. Despite the general belief that married people may be more "settled down" than single people, marriage seems to have no effect on job involvement.

- *Job-involved workers are better performers. True or false?*

  To begin with, it's hard to say exactly what the term "better performers" means. In the research studies we have seen, performance was measured in a variety of ways, including supervisory ratings, self-reports, percentage salary increases, and productivity. In most of these studies, there were no direct relationships between job involvement and job performance. However, if you break "performance" down into the quality of work (e.g., accuracy, reject rate, error rate) and the quantity (number of widgets produced), work quality would probably be related to involvement as a reflection of self-esteem in the case of the job-involved employee.

- *You can make people more involved in their work by paying them more. True or false?*

  It's not that simple. The major causes of involvement are intrinsic qualities of the person and intrinsic characteristics of the work environment. Satisfaction with pay exhibits only a very slight positive correlation with job involvement. It's clear that pay alone will not "turn on" a person to the job.

Does education make a difference? Here the results are mixed. The more important factor may be the kind of job the person has: more highly educated people may have more rewarding jobs, which generate greater involvement.

A very consistent correlate of work involvement is age. Older employees tend to be more work involved than younger ones. Again, this could be due to generational differences rather than actual age: older employees may hold stronger work-ethic values, which accounts for their greater involvement.

Let's put all these ideas together to come up with a profile of the job-involved person. Most likely, he or she:

- believes in the conventional work ethic
- is an older person
- has an internal locus of control
- has a stimulating, challenging job
- participates in decisions affecting his or her job
- is satisfied with the job
- has a history of success.

Hazards of Involvement

The first question all professional people should ask themselves is how they define success. People who define success by internal standards (enjoyment, satisfaction) derive happiness from all of their roles—worker, spouse, friend, parent. For them, problems of overinvolvement are easier to manage, for their job satisfaction is dependent on their own standards alone.

If a person's career involvement is essentially a narcissistic drive, however, he or she will value the external signs of success (admiration of others, salary, title, and so forth) without much regard for internal satisfaction. He or she is also likely to be pretty miserable—the traps of workaholism, excessive work demands (such as travel and business entertaining), and unsatisfying promotions are very real and may eliminate the possibility of ever obtaining true career satisfaction or true success.

Workaholism

Let's take the involvement issue one step further. Say you or your partner scored 25 on the involvement test presented earlier. Is there cause for alarm? We think so. One of you is a workaholic.

What exactly is a workaholic? To us, a hard-core workaholic is someone whose work life has taken over such a major portion of his or her identity as to interfere with bodily health, personal happiness, interpersonal relationships, and organizational effectiveness.

Workaholism has also been linked to a particular personality type, the "Type A" person, a hard-driving, impatient, and results-oriented individual. According to Myer Friedman and Ray Rosenman, who have done much of the medical work in this area, the Type A person is characterized by:

- excessive drive
- aggressiveness
- frequent deadline pressures
- pressure for vocational productivity
- an enhanced sense of time urgency.

The converse pattern, Type B, shows a lack of these qualities and:

- is more relaxed and easygoing
- seldom becomes impatient
- takes time to enjoy avocational pursuits
- works steadily but is not driven by a feeling of lack of time
- is not preoccupied with social and occupational achievement.[6]

Type A behavior and workaholism have been shown to be related to coronary disease, shortened life span, severe depression, and impotence.

To assess whether you may be a workaholic, complete the Workaholism Checklist on page 180. If you answer "yes" to all (or all but one or two) of these questions, you may be a workaholic. If so, it might be helpful to evaluate your motives for spending so much of your time working. At the very least, you should be aware of the harmful consequences of overinvolvement in work.

The story of Amanda Trepla, a state senator's "irreplaceable person," illustrates how workaholism can develop. Here's how Amanda tells it:

> My head throbbed as I sat in the library drafting a committee report, but I had fifteen more reports to finish before early the following morning. For the past week I had managed only four hours of sleep a night, half a sandwich a day, and no physical exercise.

Workaholism Checklist[7]

Some degree of job involvement usually is considered good, but it can reach a negative extreme. In order to evaluate whether you are a potential workaholic, ask yourself the following questions:

___ Yes   ___ No   Do you work longer hours than does the average person in your job?

___ Yes   ___ No   Do you consistently take work home with you at night and on weekends?

___ Yes   ___ No   Do you shun vacation time? If forced to take time off, do you become irritable?

___ Yes   ___ No   Do you appear to be a "loner," with your main friends being your business colleagues?

___ Yes   ___ No   Do you have no outside involvements (e.g., community work, hobbies) which are not job related?

___ Yes   ___ No   Is your outside reading limited to work-related books and periodicals?

___ Yes   ___ No   Do you feel time passes too quickly for what you want to accomplish?

___ Yes   ___ No   Do you compete to win in everything you do, even games with your family?

___ Yes   ___ No   Do you often become impatient?

___ Yes   ___ No   If you were to quit your job tomorrow, would it take several people to figure out how to do your job?

It was 7:00 P.M. I had at least eight hours of work ahead of me. I locked the door and went back to my desk. I didn't sit at the typewriter. Instead I stretched out on the floor, where I cried and cried.

How did I get myself into this mess? I had been so thrilled the year before when I was offered a job in the state House of Representatives. I hadn't worked in sixteen years, since the birth of my oldest daughter. I also had a fourteen-year-old daughter and seven- and nine-year-old sons.

My family was very supportive about my working. My husband took over the laundry and grocery shopping. Our daughters cooked dinner and took care of their younger brothers after school. I was lucky that I didn't have the domestic problems many women face when they take a job.

My problems were different. They were of my own making. I was too good! That's right. I did the job too well.

During my first legislative session, the representative gave me more and more responsibility. I completed each task as quickly and as accurately as I could. My boss was generous with his praise, and this made me work even harder.

After that first session, my boss decided to run for the state Senate. I campaigned hard for him, as did hundreds of others, for he was a popular man. He won. I moved with him from the House to the Senate. The move brought a larger staff and more work.

I don't know why I pushed myself so unmercifully. I have no one but myself to blame. True, the senator asked me to do a great deal of work, but he was terribly busy himself and he didn't realize what was happening to me. He took time to eat and sleep. I am sure he thought I was doing the same.

I spent more and more time in the office. I no longer went out for lunch. In fact, I stopped eating lunch; it took too much time. When I finally got home at night, I was too tired to eat. I would fall into bed, only taking time to set the alarm so I could get to work by 7:30 A.M.

So, there I was, crying on the floor. For the last week I hadn't seen my younger children. They were asleep when I got home and I left the house before they woke up. My husband got a quick kiss at night before I fell asleep, exhausted.

Never had I felt so guilty. I was neither a wife nor a mother. I was only a research assistant, and not even a very good one, for I was making countless mistakes. Finally I finished the reports and got home at 3 A.M. Something had to be done.

I later discussed my overworking with my family. Surprisingly, the younger children had not been as disturbed by the experience as had the older two. The older ones were upset because they felt I was being unfair to their younger brothers.

As long as I worked for the senator, I couldn't be home when the boys returned from school. I promised, however, that I would try to be home by 6:00 each evening and that I would spend more time with all the children on weekends. A short time later my husband was transferred, and we moved to a new state.

I definitely want to work again. As soon as we get settled, I'll look for another job. But I also want to save some time and energy for my husband, children, and home. And, even more important, I want to be fair to myself. This time I hope I've learned my limitations. I hope I'll have the courage to say, "No, I can't do any more today." I'll do my best, but I hope I won't try to do better than my best.[8]

Leisure phobia

One side effect of workaholism, which makes it even harder to cure, is a malady that New York psychologist Dr. Salvatore Didato calls "leisure phobia." In this condition, when people have free time, they have trouble enjoying it. They feel guilty because they aren't "doing something"—of course, "doing something" can only mean "doing work." Psychoanalyst Karen Horney labels this feeling "the tyranny of the *should*."[9]

As Dr. Didato says, "In its miniform, this behavior has been called the 'Sunday neurosis.' It attacks on weekends, when people have time on their hands. It makes some people restless and almost panicky, but when Monday morning rolls around, they feel pacified again."[10]

To help diagnose whether you are suffering from leisure phobia, respond to the following statements with a "yes" or "no."

1. It bothers me to waste time.
2. I get more fun out of my job than I do in my free-time activities.
3. I am an impatient person.
4. I really don't need as much leisure time as the average person seems to need.
5. I enjoy working and playing rapidly.
6. I usually get bored sooner than most others on a long train or plane trip.
7. When I play, I try harder to win than the average person.
8. I usually thrive on activities that keep me on the go and require my full attention.
9. I consider myself an assertive person.
10. I usually have difficulty finding satisfying things to do in my spare time.[11]

This test is based on clinical observations of people who seem to be workaholics. Although it is not a standardized test, your score can be instructive. Give yourself one point for each "yes" answer. A score of seven or less suggests that you are able to enjoy leisure. If your score is eight or more, however, leisure phobia may be a problem for you.

How do you know when it's time to back off, time to enjoy more leisure activities? Sometimes the decision is taken out of our hands: our bodies force us to slow down. Physical symptoms such as chest pains, inability to sleep, headaches, or even blackouts may be early warnings of overwork. Sometimes it takes a heart attack or stroke to convey the message. Many of our friends have drastically altered their life-style and work style after an early coronary attack.

It is easier to separate yourself from work if you have something specific to substitute for it. Planning for leisure is just as important as planning your work and career. Recently, a TV news show ran a story on "leisure counselors," individuals who help people identify the leisure activity that would best fit their interests—at the rate of $40 per hour. Unless you program in leisure activities—signing up for an evening course, buying season theater tickets, joining a tennis club—you'll probably never get around to taking part in these activities. Make a commitment to leisure. An acquaintance of ours plays squash religiously every day during his lunch hour. His attitude is, "Nothing is more important to my life than my body and my health. Everything else depends on that."

Children can also be helpful allies in shaking workaholism. As they get old enough to take up tennis or skiing or sailing or camping, make these activities a family affair. Such activities can bring you all closer together, and they're good for your body as well.

"The way I had it planned, about now we'd be splitting our time between a big apartment and a Corbu house in the south of France."

A recent poll in *Psychology Today* revealed that the main form of leisure and getting away from work pressures is physical exercise, in particular jogging.[12] It delights us to see our Type A friends take up jogging in an attempt to become Type B's. It seems to make sense—that is, until you hear the comments at cocktail parties: "How fast can you do a mile?" "How many miles each day do you run?" "Have you tried these new [expensive, trendy brand] jogging shoes?" "How big was the largest dog that ever attacked you?" And the real killer: "After I run at 5:00 P.M., I'm all set for another three hours of work."

In short, running and other forms of getting away from Type A behavior often become simply new arenas for overwork. And, to further subvert the intended purpose, they become ways of replenishing one's energy to make *more* Type A behavior possible. So, when you plan leisure activities to get you away from work, make sure you really do get away.

Dr. Didato suggests one way to ensure an escape from work. Identify characteristic aspects of your job and then choose a vacation that provides just the opposite experiences. For example, if you work alone in a quiet office, say as an accountant or researcher, maybe you would enjoy a cruise or a resort with a lot of friendly people to satisfy your need for excitement and social life. Or, if you have a very fast-paced, people-oriented job, say as a consultant or sales person, a good change of pace might be an isolated vacation in the woods, mountains, or at the seashore. Identifying clear objectives and expectations for your trip can be very useful. Paradoxical as it may seem, a plan of action for your vacation can make it more relaxing and satisfying. And talking to friends who have been where you're going can provide useful tips and help you know what to expect. Dr. Didato quotes an old Chinese proverb to make his point: "To be for one day entirely at leisure is to be for one day immortal." When was the last time you had your day?

Maybe you're not a workaholic. Maybe you do know how to take time off. Still, there are other pitfalls of the success cycle to beware of, some so subtle you may be seduced into thinking they're rewards for all your good work. For the protean careerist, however, and especially for the two-career protean person, these "rewards" can often turn out to be real drawbacks.

Promotion pitfalls

One of the great ironies of work life is that one of the rewards for success is promotion to a different kind of work,

usually managerial or administrative positions that give you less autonomy and less opportunity to do the work you were promoted for. Thus,
you are "rewarded" by being pulled out of the work you love and put
into a position where you are held accountable for the work of other
people. You are given recognition and rewards (pay, more promotions)
if your subordinates are successful, but it's not the same as achieving
those successes yourself.

Moving from a professional job (e.g., engineer, consultant, analyst) to a management position means adjusting to the constraints of a nine-to-five routine. You have to attend more meetings
than before. You are part of a management team rather than an independent professional. You may be expected to keep your hand in some
professional work while doing your management job, so your work load
increases. It takes far longer to get things done, because you now have
to work through other people. And you quickly realize that, even
though you are in the "superior" position, you are quite dependent on
your subordinates for getting tasks accomplished. Your main accomplishments now are largely administrative (e.g., starting up a new program) rather than professional (e.g., completing a big investment trans-
action), so you may value your achievements less. In other words, a
supposed promotion could result in a job with a lower motivating-poten-
tial score for you. And the overall result could be job dissatisfaction or
extreme unhappiness.

Therefore, when "good things" like promotions are
offered to you, check them out in depth. Look beyond the higher status
and salary. Think of how that job would affect the rest of your life. If
the promotion would reduce your freedom, make sure your spouse's job
or the family has enough flexibility to handle it.

Our hunch is that upward mobility may be a bit
lower among dual-career couples than among single-career couples for
this reason. Working couples are likely to be less willing to take geographical transfers or to accept the reduced freedom inherent in a
higher-level position. It may be only the two-career couples without
children who can afford to pursue this kind of advancement, given the
investments of time and energy required.

For example, when Fran left her job as a professor
at Wisconsin-Parkside to become an associate dean at Northwestern,
we really didn't think much about the change in job content. We were
too excited about the prospect of finally being at the same university
(after about four years of waiting). It was also a very tempting upward
move for Fran both in terms of promotion (from assistant professor
to associate dean) and in terms of the relative status of the two universities.

Like many couples, we didn't stop to think that she
was also moving from being a *professor* (a job she loved) to being an
administrator. She very quickly realized that being an administrator
meant being the first in and the last out of the office every day. Plus,
there was some teaching involved two evenings a week. And her job
consisted of staffing courses, setting up programs, and reorganizing the
office, but the dean had final say about these matters. So Fran's autonomy was very low, infinitely lower than it had been as a professor.
Variety was okay, task identity was zero (nothing was ever "finished,"
there was always more paper to be processed), significance (to her)
was low, and feedback was moderate. The end result was a sharp drop
in the motivating potential of her job.

If we had thought more carefully about the actual
content of this "promotion," we would have realized before she made
the move that this was not a good job for her. But we were seduced by
extrinsic factors, such as status. And we paid the price of not looking
before she leaped.

The perks: travel and entertaining

Like promotions, business travel is generally considered one of the glamorous aspects of a successful career. However,
as many two-career couples can attest, travel can take its toll on a
relationship. Often, travel cuts into "personal" time, generally either
mornings or evenings, but sometimes weekends as well. To meet one's
own office responsibilities while away, extra work must be done in
advance of a trip. On the road, the schedule can be gruelling: early
planes to catch, clients to meet, late nights of "talking shop." You eat
too much and drink too much, you don't sleep well in a hot, dry hotel
room with the too-firm bed, you rush to the airport only to get the last
seat on the return plane (smoking section, between two 300 pounders),
and you arrive home exhausted. Your kids can't wait to tell you about
their A's in spelling and about their friend's broken arm. But instead of
being able to devote time to them, you have to immediately start writing follow-up letters, your trip report, and your expense report.

The next day isn't any improvement. When you
arrive back at the office, a mountain of mail and phone messages await
you. And the appointments you had to reschedule because of your trip
begin at 10:00 A.M. In short, travel does not relieve you of any routine
office responsibilities—it only postpones them. It also generates more
work, cuts into family time, and robs you of much of the energy you
need to cope. When you add the stress of travel on to the already
excessive stress of a two-careers relationship, you may lose whatever

modicum of family tranquility you've been able to establish. No wonder, then, that dual-career couples try to avoid jobs with excessive travel demands—management consulting, sales in large territories, public accounting, international banking, college recruiting, and the like.

Business entertaining, once dependent on the presence of a dutiful wife willing to serve as hostess and keeper of the family calendar, has of necessity undergone change. Before the rapid increase in two-career families, organizations often got two workers for the price of one: a working husband and a hostess wife. The "two-person career" phenomenon was not limited to executives and professionals; college deans and presidents, ministers, and politicians also fell into this category.

A few years ago at Michigan State University, Dr. Clifford Wharton, university president, was the subject of some criticism because his salary was very high, higher even than the governor's. Dr. Wharton's explanation nicely illustrates our point: he stated that his salary was, in effect, for two people, since his wife was in charge of the fund drive for a new performing-arts building and was highly involved in many other university projects.

It has been quite a few years since we have seen a university administrator's spouse entertain faculty and students. Contemporary college social activities are more likely to be once-a-year, large-scale affairs, with the local caterer in charge. (In fact, many former wife-hostesses have organized their own catering services, making a nice income doing what they used to do for free.)

Business entertaining has moved the same way. Rather than having parties at home, executives are more likely to host a gathering at the local club. Instead of having associates to dinner, the executive will make reservations at that nice French restaurant downtown.

The decrease in business entertaining is quite compatible with another recent trend: two-career couples, jealous of their time with the family, are less inclined to spend their evenings or weekends attending company-related social activities. The "job" is now defined more specifically to include only obligations incurred during normal working hours.

Conflicts of Interest

As more couples choose to pursue a two-career life-style, professional conflicts of interest are bound to increase. People tend to be attracted to partners who work in similar profes-

sional fields. But what happens when a banker marries another
banker, or a public-interest lawyer marries a corporate counsel?

> Judith Rich gave Ronald B. Millman a briefcase for his birthday. She put
> her initials inside, she says, because "that's the only way I'll ever get
> inside his work." Rich is senior vice-president and creative director for
> the public-relations firm of Daniel J. Edelman, Inc. in Chicago and Mill-
> man's steady date for the past three years. Millman is Rich's opposite
> number at Harshe-Rotman & Druck, Inc., a rival public-relations firm. "I
> haven't used the briefcase yet," Millman says, "because I haven't found
> where she bugged it."[13]

Amusing as this situation may sound, it can gener-
ate real problems for a couple. In a *Wall Street Journal* article, author
Joann Lublin describes a pair of Harvard Business School students who
planned careers in investment banking in New York. When the firms
they were interviewing frowned at the idea of husband and wife working for competitors, they were forced to decide whose career was more
important. In the end, the wife took a commercial banking job—at a
lower salary. Lublin also describes a Chicago executive who claims his
pending divorce was the result of a professional conflict of interest.
His wife was an employment recruiter whose firm was used by his
corporation; when he told his legal counsel about his wife's job, his
corporation stopped doing business with her company.[14]

Before Joann Lublin wrote her article on conflicts
of interest, she had a relevant experience of her own, as reported in a
separate *Wall Street Journal* article:

> The Chicago-based *Wall Street Journal* reporter who wrote the accom-
> panying article has firsthand experience with a potential conflict-of-inter-
> est situation.
>
> Last February, her husband became a Chicago correspondent for *Business
> Week* magazine. The editors at the rival publications weren't happy about
> the arrangement but decided to trust the two reporters' professional
> integrity.
>
> To stay clear of conflicts, he requested a different beat from hers. The
> couple feel it's impossible to bar "shop talk" at home. So they limit work
> discussions to their own experiences and keep the information "off the
> record."
>
> To date, the two journalists have only worked once on the identical news
> story, a story that broke over a weekend. They both needed to reach
> Donald H. Rumsfeld, the former Secretary of Defense who was rumored to
> be G. D. Searle & Co.'s new president.
>
> At a restaurant with friends, he hinted that he had found Mr. Rumsfeld
> and would call him shortly. She badgered her husband for the phone

number, but he refused and they began to argue. One friend, a lawyer, jokingly offered to take the matter to divorce court.

The conflict eventually resolved itself when neither reporter was able to reach Mr. Rumsfeld. The rumor later proved to be true.[15]

How do companies deal with potential conflicts of interest? Few formal policies have been established; generally, situations that do arise are handled on a case-by-case basis. Some organizations simply assume that their employees are indeed professionals and, as such, possess the integrity to avoid sharing sensitive information with a spouse in a competing job. Other companies worry about leaks:

> When Susan T., a patent attorney for Baxter Travenol Laboratories decided to marry a patent lawyer for rival Abbott Laboratories, her boss acted "as if I had just kidnapped the Lindbergh baby," she recalls. "He said that if any Baxter secrets leaked to Abbott, he would assume I had passed them on." Upset by his lack of trust, Susan reluctantly quit the Deerfield, Illinois, hospital-supply concern a few months later. . . .

> Her former boss says he never questioned Susan's integrity but worried about sensitive information slipping out inadvertently at home. "I mean, if you had a choice between two patent attorneys of roughly equal competence, wouldn't you choose the one that didn't have the problem?" he asks.[16]

Conflicts of interest in the political arena often make headlines. Senator Robert Dole's wife, Elizabeth, had to quit her government job when her husband ran for vice-president in 1976, and the wife of Senator Jacob Javitts reluctantly gave up her $67,000-a-year job doing public relations for Iran because it hurt his image as a supporter of Israel.

Some companies do have formal rules to deal with the matter. Public-accounting firms require professional staff members to sign oaths annually specifying that no relatives work for clients. Similarly, the Blue Cross health-insurance plan in Columbus, Georgia, prohibits the hiring or continued employment of anyone whose spouse works for a competitor. This rule was challenged unsuccessfully in court by a female secretary who charged that it constituted sex discrimination.

Some companies try to arrange quiet transfers or to seek resignations when conflicts of interest are discovered. Many executives feel uncomfortable dealing with the situation. The personnel director of Montgomery Ward & Co. explains the difficulty:

> You'd have a difficult time policing who was married to whom and who they worked for. And what do you do if an unmarried person comes to

work here [Montgomery Wards] and then marries someone at Sears? Where do you draw the line?"[17]

How do couples deal with the issue? The most common method seems to be a ban on shop talk at home.

"Our rule is to keep our business and private lives very separate. I just keep my mouth shut about the specifics of my working day," says a senior VP of a Los Angeles bank and the wife of the president of a competing bank.[18]

"We talk, but not about specific clients for either of our firms," says Beue Olson, a consultant with Booz Allen & Hamilton, and wife of Cliff Olson, a consultant for Peat, Marwick, Mitchell & Co. She recently offered to drop him off for a presentation to a client, "but he refused to even tell me where he was going."[19]

Whether they ban shop talk or openly compete professionally, the two-career couple with a conflict of interest has a tough time of it. The solutions ultimately must come from organizations, as they recognize the special problems—and the special assets—of their two-career employees and develop policies to help them.

Red, White, and Blue—or Black-and-Blue?

Locating two satisfying jobs in the same area may be the first major hurdle for two-career couples, but it's certainly not the last. As we have seen, even though your two jobs may be terribly exciting, your relationship could eventually take a beating from the demands and overinvolvement they can create. Two red, white, and blue jobs can produce a black-and-blue marriage.

Like most of the issues we have discussed thus far, the solution involves getting in control, becoming more protean. First, you have to assess whether you are in danger of workaholism. If so, consciously making time for leisure and recreation activities can eventually diminish leisure phobia and lead to a more balanced involvement in career and recreation. The beginning is the critical point. Once you make the first move—joining a tennis club or taking a trip with friends —you may be on your way to kicking the work habit.

If you've got workaholism under control, you probably still should think about your work patterns to determine if the seductive perks—promotions, travel, and entertaining—are manipulating you. In the next chapter, we look at two of the biggest problems two-career people face: transfers and relocations. Here, too, we need a strong commitment to the protean style and to our partner's right to the same.

CHAPTER NINE

IT'S YOUR MOVE: COPING WITH TRANSFERS

In a recent cartoon, a confused-looking man confided to his drinking partner: "My company sent me to New York. My wife's firm transferred her to Denver. I don't know what happened to the kids." This befuddled individual is a victim (in the humorous extreme) of one of the major problems facing professional couples—coping with mobility and the prospect of relocation.

Common dilemma: you're both happy and successful working in San Francisco and her boss says she's up for a promotion—if she'll move to Peoria. Or he gets caught in a merger crunch and can only find a new position 600 miles from where his wife runs a flourishing clothing store and his children are finally doing well in school. When you're a dual-career couple, the trauma and chaos of changing cities is magnified; with two careers to consider, what may be beneficial to one may well be disastrous to the other.

In this chapter we discuss how couples manage the problems of moving around (or not) and talk about the issues of sacrificing either one partner's career or aspects of their relationship. We also try to show how couples have to resolve these problems through their life-style choices and what organizations can and should be doing to help.

The Dilemma

The dilemma is, quite simply, whether to move or not. You may want to make a job change that involves a move or a new job opportunity with a company in another city may be offered to you. Or the choice may be less in your control: you may be transferred by your organization or you may have to move—you've lost your job and the opportunities lie elsewhere.

Whatever the conditions, you're faced with a difficult decision, one that you cannot make alone. Your spouse and family need to be consulted if you are to accurately assess the alternatives open to you. What starts out as a seemingly straightforward choice between two options quickly evolves into a more complex problem. If I do move, can my spouse (and family) move with me? If not, should I still move? If yes, what about our marriage? If not, what about my career?

There are four basic options open to the person faced with a potential move: to turn the offer down; to accept it and relocate the whole family; to accept it and to relocate only yourself, seeing your spouse and perhaps children when it can be arranged; or to come up with a creative alternative, an arrangement satisfactory to your employer, your spouse (and his or her employer), and the children.

Let's look at the consequences of each alternative in terms of typical couples. In order to make a sound decision, you need a better sense of the real choices and trade-offs involved.

Deciding to Say "No"

Companies generally use relocation as a way of providing career development for employees, especially younger professional employees. When the person's spouse does not have a career, he or she is not as strongly rooted in an area and a geographical move is easier. When the spouse is settled in, with a satisfying job and good future career potential, it is far more difficult to relocate the employee without taking the spouse into account.

Working spouses are a major factor in employees' rejection of transfers and relocation, along with their desire to remain in an area that offers the quality of life they seek. The personnel executives we interviewed expressed the opinion that career growth might be a bit slower for people with career spouses because of their reluctance to move. This feeling was echoed in our interviews with couples. Many people mentioned specific promotions that they had turned down because a move was involved—and the spouse couldn't move.

One government administrator, for example, is "200 percent bored" in her present regional job in the Midwest and has been offered a better job in Washington. As long as her husband cannot relocate there, however, she will stay put.

More and more, people are choosing *not* to relocate. After evaluating the choices, they decide that the risk of losing one or both partners' identity professionally and as a partner/parent is too great to be offset by the benefits the job offers. Other factors, usually related to the quality of life at work and at home, also come into play.

A year after we moved to Chicago, a major university approached both of us about moving together. When the offers finally arrived, we decided not to accept them. We had just moved a year before and were still trying to sell a summer home in Michigan. While the move would definitely improve the career opportunities for one of us, it was probably not as good as staying put for the other. Meanwhile, the children were five houses down the street from an excellent public school. Moving them would also mean intracity busing in the new location. When we added up the costs and benefits, the total was clear. While one of us stood to gain, jobwise, the other did not. Moreover, the entire family would pay a quality-of-life price. When we added in the psychological-adjustment costs of another geographic move within twelve months, we decided it wasn't worth it.

Other couples are prepared to move, but weigh different factors. Geographic location and job conditions are often important. Even the restaurants available in a city can influence a decision. One couple we know was concerned about skating schools. Their son, involved in his own career as a skater, needed to be near a top-notch ice arena and coach.

Cultural differences can also be a factor. People who have grown up in New York may view a move to a small midwestern city as cultural deprivation. Another factor in saying "no" is the job itself. Is it really better? Will you have another opportunity if you refuse this one?

In some companies, turning down a move is taboo. As one person put it, however, "If they are willing to write me off that quickly, then it's not the kind of company I want to stay with anyway." Saying "no" may or may not have career costs attached to it. It is, in the final analysis, an act of independence. It requires taking charge of your own life and values—creating a protean style—rather than letting the company dictate them.

But then again . . .

Refusing an attractive offer is a difficult step to take. It is also pretty permanent. Three months after you've turned a corporation down, you usually can't go back and tell them you've changed your mind (although it certainly has been done). So, it's important that you're as certain as you can be when you make that decision.

We've prepared an "expectancy table" to help you consider all the possible consequences associated with a "yes" or a "no" decision. For each consequence, we assign a probability that it will actually happen. In other words, we try to guess the likelihood that a given choice will result in certain outcomes. We also assign a value to each outcome and multiply the probability by this value. After we have done this for each alternative, we compare the total expectancy values for the different alternatives or choices. Since there are usually "pluses" and "minuses" associated with each choice, we can compare how they add up. It is simply a way of systematically weighing the different costs and benefits associated with relocation. Let's look more closely at how it actually works.

First, we identify all of the possible outcomes or factors that are important considerations in our decision. When we have these listed, we are in a position to assess the alternatives or choices in terms of the probability that a particular choice will, in fact, result in or lead to a particular outcome. The probability can range from 0 to + 1.

When doing this, you should list as many considerations as possible. These should reflect all the issues that are important in your careers, your personal lives, and your family relationships. In addition to listing possible outcomes, it is also necessary to assign weights or values to each possible outcome. These may range from a high value of + 5 to a low value of − 5.

For example, three of your considerations may be: the job, the location, and schools for your children. While all three may be important to you, the possible outcomes associated with various choices on these three dimensions may be different and have different values for you. The job and schools, for example, may carry more positive value under one choice than the location does. Thus, your expectancy table should include the value you attach to the potential outcomes for *that* alternative or choice. The basic format looks like this:

Choice 1: If I accept the transfer . . .

Outcome	Value	× Probability =	Expectancy
We will live in an urban area.	− 3	1.0	− 3.0
I will have a better job.	+ 5	1.0	+ 5.0
Poor neighborhood schools.	− 4	0.5	− 2.0
Spouse will have job.	+ 5	0.2	+ 1.0
Total:			+ 1.0

While you aren't sure about the chances of your spouse getting a job, they look pretty low. Now let's look at the expectancy table for another choice—turning down the transfer.

Choice 2: If I turn down the transfer . . .

Outcome	Value	× Probability =	Expectancy
We will live in a suburban area.	+ 3	1.0	+ 3.0
I will have a better job eventually.	+ 5	0.4	+ 2.0
Good schools for the kids.	+ 4	0.9	+ 3.6
Spouse will have guaranteed job.	+ 5	1.0	+ 5.0
Total:			+ 13.6

When you compare the two choices in terms of possible outcomes, the second alternative (turning down the transfer) has a much higher total expectancy of resulting in positively valued outcomes. But what are the trade-offs? Clearly, accepting the transfer will result in a better job for you (which you value). To achieve this right now, however, means living with several negative outcomes. There is certainty that you will live in a negatively valued area, a fifty-fifty chance that schools for the kids will be poor (also a negatively valued outcome), and very little chance that your spouse will have a guaranteed job (also important to you). So, to gain a better job for yourself, your spouse and family will have to make some sacrifices.

The second alternative means that you forego the certainty of a better job now, with some probability of getting one eventually. At the same time, you increase the expectancy that you will have good schools, a good location, and a job for your spouse.

As you have probably realized by now, preparing an expectancy table is a bit of a guessing game. It is like betting, in a sense. One never knows for sure what the real probabilities are. It does raise an important question: Can you *do* anything to increase the probability that a positively valued outcome will result or to decrease the probability that a negatively valued choice will result? In other words, once you have an initial expectancy table, can you manipulate the likelihood of certain outcomes? The answer is yes—or at least you can try.

Look again, for example, at the two sample tables. Now ask yourself: What can I do (or what would I have to do) to increase the positive total expectancy associated with choice 1—the transfer? This is clearly the choice *you* want because it guarantees you the best job. To make it worthwhile for everyone else, however, you would have to manipulate location, schools, and your spouse's chances of getting a job. Is it possible to live in the suburbs, commute, and find a good school? Are private schools a possibility? Now try the expectancy table again, this time listing these different outcomes. What values do you attach to them and how do they work out?

Choice 1 (revised): If I accept the transfer . . .

Outcome	Value	× Probability	= Expectancy
We can live in the suburbs.	+ 3	1.0	+ 3.0
I will have to commute.	− 2 (?)	1.0	− 2.0 (need info.)
I will have a better job.	+ 5	1.0	+ 5.0
Good schools for the kids.	+ 4	0.9	+ 3.6
Spouse will have a job.	+ 5	0.2	+ 1.0 (need info.)
Total:			+ 10.6

Clearly, the positive expectancy of this choice is now approaching the expectancy associated with staying where you are. And, there are really two unknowns. The probability you assign to your spouse having a job is questionable. If you could be sure that he or she would find a job, then the positively valued outcomes associated with the move would clearly indicate that it is a good choice. Of course, to have the better job, you will have to commute if your family is going to continue to live in a surburban area. You are not sure how you value that (probably negatively).

At this point, it is usually helpful to get more information. The probability of getting a job for your spouse may be greater than you think. Commuting may be better or worse than you think. If there is a suburb with good train service into the city, it could turn out to be a plus factor—time to read and relax each day. If you have to battle traffic for two hours a day, it may be too high a price to pay for the job.

While the expectancy table doesn't make a decision for you, it is a good way to sort out all the issues associated with a decision and to assess how important they are to you as a couple. It also helps you to zero in on those variable factors that you may be able to do something about. Often we accept certain outcomes as givens, when, in fact, they are things we *can* change. As our example shows, location and schools may be more flexible dimensions of a move than you initially assume. Similarly, your spouse's job may be something you can explore (and secure) before committing yourself.

Increasingly, employers are coming to terms with the special problems of the two-career couple. Companies are realizing that they have to help if they want to recruit or develop good people. Not long ago, while sitting in the J. Walter Thompson agency in Chicago, one of us overheard a conversation about job hunting for the wife of a new recruit. When asked about it, the person admitted that the way the agency people were able to recruit the man was by going out of their way to help his wife get a job. For the couple, this means that expectancies can often be increased by open negotiations with employers.

The gut factor

So far we have been discussing very simple examples of factors to consider when evaluating the possibility of a move. For most couples, the actual list would be much longer and more complex. It would invariably include many intangibles—issues that go beyond such objective considerations as job, salary, location, and so forth. For most people, the emotional aspects of moving are as important, if not more important, than the job.

We call this emotional dimension of decision making the "gut factor," the almost visceral feeling one has about a choice. It is a personal, subjective, and emotional reaction to a decision. Something about the decision "feels" right or wrong, good or bad—no matter what the objective facts are. Here is how one couple expressed their gut feeling about living in Chicago:

> Objectively we know this is a good place to live. There is a lot of action and the business connections are probably as good as anywhere. It's a convenient city. We can get to the airport with no traffic in less than forty minutes and make a direct connection to almost anywhere in the country. We live in a lovely large home in one of the best suburbs in the city— maybe in the country. The schools are excellent and the kids can walk everywhere. There are fine restaurants and more "culture" than we can

take advantage of. The lake is only a few blocks away. By anyone's standard, we "have it made."

The voice went on, picking up energy and force.

But subjectively, deep down inside, it feels *flat*. It's pleasant. It's cordial. But it lacks something. There is . . . an excitement or a vitality that is missing. The only way people seem to capture that is by getting on a plane and going somewhere *else*. Sometimes we think it is the lack of an ocean, or the mountains, or the intellectual stimulation that almost hangs in the air in the East. I don't know what it is. Maybe it's just the Midwest. Everything is *nice*. Nice! That's it. Nothing is exciting. It's just so *middle*. I guess what I'm saying is that at some gut level it just doesn't feel very good.

Feelings are an important part of making the right decision. No amount of rational information can compensate for the intuitive feelings that we all have about choices in our lives. Couples (or partners) who make decisions *only* on the basis of rational considerations often regret them later.

The Chicago couple quoted above based their decisions to move on purely rational grounds. Looking back, they said that each decision had been a "good" decision—the best one at the time. But none of their decisions had taken into account the gut factor. As they contemplated leaving Chicago, they expressed a strong need to go back to the East, the ocean, and a subculture that satisfied their emotional needs.

Beware the seductive plushes

One of the dangers inherent in deciding to relocate is a phenomenon that Roy Lewicki of Duke University calls "organizational seduction."[1] This is a process by which companies attract people and develop local commitment, often at the personal and professional expense of the individual. How do organizations do it?

One way is by offering or using "plushes." "PLUSH" is an acronym coined by Professor Lewicki to stand for "PLentiful, Unlimited, Supply of Hygienes." "Hygienes" are attractive features of the work context, the extra goodies that companies include in an offer or employ as a tactic to court a prospective employee. A company may fly both you and your partner into town, wine and dine you, and show you all the best places to live. You may meet with top people in the firm and see nothing but executive offices and miles of wall-to-wall carpeting. If you get hooked on the plushes, you may ac-

cept the job without getting a very realistic preview of what day-to-day
life in the firm or the community would be like for you. The beautiful
homes and the country club may be very real, but not for people in
your income bracket. Once inside the company, you may never again,
or only rarely, see the executive suite.

What you need most at this point is a realistic
job—and move—preview. This means discussing the "bad news" along
with the good. For example, in recruiting telephone operators, some
telephone companies tell recruits about the routine work and close
supervision (unpleasant features) as well as about the good pay and
benefits, opportunities to provide customer service, and the pleasant
work group. Research by Professor John Wanous of Michigan State
University has shown that companies that do provide a realistic preview for their recruits have a lower turnover rate and higher employee
satisfaction.[2] If your prospective employer doesn't provide enough
information about what day-to-day life would be like, then you need to
do some independent research. Talk with people in the company on an
informal basis, if you can. Take a few extra days and go exploring—
alone. Get the yellow pages and see if the services you are used to are
available. Visit different communities, stores, and so on to try to get a
feel for what life is really like.

Putting it all together

By now it should be obvious that the decision to
relocate is a very complex process. The prospective job is only one factor in your decision, and often not the most important one. The needs of
you and your family, the need for role continuity, the local subculture,
day-to-day life-styles, and, especially, your feelings, are all crucial
considerations.

To develop your own expectancy tables, we would
suggest that you try to list *all* possible outcomes that might result for
each alternative. To do this, begin by thinking about your present life,
personally and professionally. What factors are important and positively valued? What factors are negatively valued? Which would you
change, and how or in what ways would you change them? Relocation
may offer an opportunity to make these changes.

Think about the different aspects of your life.
While people vary in terms of the dimensions they think are important,
certain considerations are typical. The following list suggests some factors to consider in deciding to relocate or not. Some dimensions may be
very relevant to your life, while others are not pertinent at all.

Work factors (both for you and your partner)

Your professional identity
Professional/career/business contacts
Job security
Salary
The organization
The nature of the job/work itself
Colleagues
The work environment and facilities
Future career opportunities

Life-style and family factors

Geographic location
Living areas accessible to work
Types of housing available
Neighborhoods (you can afford)
Transportation
Schools
Shopping
Cultural facilities
Recreational facilities
Local social norms, attitudes, and subculture
Cost of living/unusual expenses
Sports
Local government/politics
Community organizations
Baby-sitters/day-care facilities
Household and other help
Restaurants
Churches, synagogues, etc.
Other special facilities or needs
Social relationships/people/friends
Family/relatives
Media/communications

Personal and individual factors

Unique personal losses or gains involved in the choice
Giving up old friends
The energy required to make the move
Emotional costs of readjusting to job changes
Emotional costs of readjusting to new social relationships
Emotional costs of integrating self into new neighborhood

Emotional costs of integrating self into new schools
Emotional costs of changes in family relationships
Anxiety about proving self in new job or environment
Excitement of new opportunities in new location

The gut factor

What are your subjective feelings about the choices?
What emotions do the choices elicit in you?
If you had to make the decision *right now,* what would you decide?

Getting in touch with your values

As you contemplate your list and prepare your own expectancy table, you may be unsure about what values to attach to the various outcomes associated with your choices. How important are certain dimensions of your jobs or your life-styles? Sometimes we tend to overrate or underestimate the value of certain aspects of our lives, perhaps because the seductive plushes of the move cause us to lose our perspective. A fancy office can never compensate, in the long run, for dissatisfaction with your community.

When we left Connecticut to move to Toronto, we suddenly found ourselves faced with what Alvin Toffler has termed "future shock." We bought a beautiful new home in a new subdivision and found ourselves *hating* it. We were miserable for a whole year, until we realized why. We had both spent all of our lives living in older homes surrounded by trees. They were like old familiar clothes—they had always been a part of our existence. The new environment was naked, barren, and cold. When we realized what was troubling us, we decided to move into an older, established neighborhood with tree-lined streets. The old homes and trees made all the difference. We were once again surrounded by the comfortable and familiar.

Many aspects of our environment are so familiar that we take them for granted. Your environment is like wallpaper: you become so used to seeing it that you no longer discern the pattern. But if the wallpaper is suddenly stripped away, the loss can have a devastating impact.

Coping with the decision

When you have analyzed the move carefully and made a decision that you believe is based on thoughtful, honest reasons, you still must deal with the consequences of that decision. In the next sections, we look at what happens when people agree to a transfer and move either their families or just themselves.

Any decision, whether positive or negative, generally has two immediate effects of which you should be aware. One is post-decision dissonance, a feeling that prompts us to try to reduce any feelings of conflict we may still have about the decision. During this time we rationalize our decision—to ourselves and to others. If we've accepted a job, we're likely to go around telling everyone how fantastic it is; if we've turned down a job, we do the opposite. The more conflict we experience in making the decision, the more we feel a need to justify it. This is a very normal way of dealing with the impending changes that relocation decisions bring.

The second effect to be expected is stress. Obviously, the likelihood of stress is greatest in changing jobs or relocating. But even the decision to turn down a job can be extremely stressful. The person who refuses an offer because of partner or family may be realizing fully for the first time that he or she cannot act independently or that the relationship is now different. The very process of deciding may have introduced change—a coming to terms with values and priorities that have disrupted the status quo.

Most people who make a decision expect a certain amount of stress and recognize that they will have to adjust. What many people do not prepare for is *how* to cope. Many familiar coping mechanisms—like old friends to talk to—will be missing from the new environment. Most people who decide to relocate, whether alone or together, tend to overlook and underprepare for the stress and adaptation they will face.

Accepting the Job and Moving the Family

Until recently, we never even considered the possibility of *not* moving together. We are a family—a unit—and that has always been the most important factor in our minds. Staying together as a family came first. Everything else had to be worked out around that.

After relocating with her husband several times, one working woman knew only too well what "everything else" entails. As she wearily explains:

> We always seemed to be just getting settled when the next opportunity—
> a move—would undo it for us. In our first major relocation I had to give
> up all the local business ties that were important in my work. I swore I'd
> never become dependent on local ties again. But no matter how profes-
> sional you are in your work, you still come to depend on local factors.
> There is the transportation, the day-care centers, cleaning help, baby-

sitters, etc. Every time we've moved for my husband, I've had to find a new job for myself *and* reestablish the whole support structure that enables me to pursue my career. We've stayed together as a family, but my husband and I recognize that the cost has been an enormous amount of energy and the loss of personal relationships and permanent roots.

Are you prepared to handle a major move? Let's say that, based on the results of your expectancy table, your gut reaction, and mutual agreement on a move, you decide to accept that offer 600 miles away. The most serious problem facing you will be a loss of identity. Each time a person moves, he or she has to rebuild a sense of belonging—in the immediate work environment, in the community, in the schools, and so on. This takes time—time to prove yourself, time to build new relationships, time to learn your way around and get connected, and time to be accepted and reinforced as a worthwhile member of the organization. For most people, the interim is a lonely and depressing period.

"Do you realize what the promotion means—it means at last we can afford a divorce!"

Reprinted by permission of G.P. Putnam's Sons from *Husbands, Wives and Live-Togethers* by William Hamilton, copyright © 1976 by William Hamilton.

In our own experience, the minimum period of
adjustment is usually a year. This means enough time to come full circle, to repeat a cycle and begin to do things for the second time. At this
point, just knowing what to expect and feeling a bit like an insider
again seems to mark the end of the transition.

Most people find the key to making this transition
in their work role. Having a new work role creates an "instant identity" and provides a sense of continuity in the midst of change. For the
person who is used to working, relocation without a job prospect can
be both professionally and psychologically damaging.

> The first time we moved, it was for my wife. I arrived without a job. I
> knew that I would get one eventually, but I didn't expect the period
> between jobs to hit me like it did. Each day my wife would leave the house
> and I would spend the day realizing I didn't *belong* anywhere. Writing
> letters was what got to me the most. I had no stationery—no organization-
> al letterhead—and no title. Suddenly, I felt like I didn't exist anymore.
> The routine I had always been used to was gone. My identity seemed to
> disappear with it. My energy level went down, my interest in things
> waned, and I didn't even care how I looked anymore. Suddenly I felt an
> affinity for my father and what happened to him when he retired. I vowed
> never to move again without a firm job offer at the other end.

For the two-career couple, the critical issue in the
"we all relocate together" choice is whether *both* spouses (and children) can preserve continuity in their professional work roles and identities. Certainly other factors, such as career prospects, salary, and job
conditions, are important, but the central issue seems to be role continuity. Can we relocate and maintain the professional identities we
have established? Will my personal identity as a family member be sufficient to withstand the loss of a professional role, or sustain me until I
can rebuild a new one? If not, then relocating together may not, in fact,
be the way to preserve your marriage and family.

Two factors seem to affect partners' attitudes
about making career sacrifices. The first is whether the sacrificing
partner's career is "established" or not. A second is whether the need
to relocate is forced or voluntary.

> In our first move we had little choice. My husband was out of a job, so I
> didn't have much to say about things. I accepted it as inevitable and
> directed all of my anger at his employer. I was at a turning point, too,
> planning to go back to school. It was possible to do that elsewhere. My
> career wasn't really anchored, which made it easier to accept the move.

In this example, the wife's acceptance of career trade-offs was made easier by the fact that external circumstances were to blame. She could direct her anger toward a third party—the employer. For her, this facilitated the adjustment. She also had a new role—becoming a student—to occupy her. Thus, her psychological adjustment was aided by circumstances.

When one partner forces the other to move, however, the partner who stands to lose has no one else to blame. Often anger and hostility are carried over a period of years (and moves), eventually surfacing as a crisis later in life.

When Connie followed Ralph, it was eight months prior to finishing her bachelor's degree. He refused to stay on in the area for her and she felt she couldn't stay alone with their two young children. After the move, she returned to school again, but this time to a certificate program. Later, after putting everything aside to complete it, she took a job that would allow her to work and still carry the responsibility for the home and children. Ralph changed jobs and began to travel extensively. Connie couldn't handle everything and again quit what she was doing for the sake of her husband and children. As a consequence, she suffered severe emotional stress.

Two years later, Connie admitted that she had come to terms with her situation by giving up her career aspirations. Her husband, she added, would have to accept responsibility for that. She was tired of trying to cope for both of them. She now accepted her role as wife and mother, but expected her husband to carry the total financial responsibility for the family as well as the responsibility for her aborted career.

Connie and Ralph have stayed together, but only because she has accepted that she must put her marriage and family ahead of her career. Couples who accept relocating together at the expense of a job or career seem to do so because they feel it is an "either/or" situation. Either we stay together or our careers come first. Children seem to make a big difference in whether couples perceive their situation in these either/or terms. Separating a family for the sake of a job has a higher cost attached to it than separating a childless couple.

What can partners who choose to relocate without two jobs expect? One major consequence appears to be depression and resentment on the part of the sacrificing partner. Often, however, this does not surface at first. The new location may seem to offer many exciting possibilities and the unemployed partner may be confident that "something will turn up." Thus, he or she is not prepared to face the total loss of identity and connectedness that may result if a satisfactory job doesn't quickly materialize.

Couples faced with a relocation decision should seriously consider whether the benefits that one partner stands to gain can *really* offset the loss to the other partner and the psychological strains this will impose on the family and their relationship. While couples vary, the following conditions generally mean that relocating without a job for the uprooted partner will prove traumatic:

- The partner is highly work involved.
- The partner has an established career role and support network.
- The partner's self-concept is defined primarily by his/her work role.
- The partner does not have other life roles that are established and important to him/her.
- The partner has never experienced a job loss or been unemployed.

Because of the potential trauma, many couples are opting either to stay put or to commute. Some find that it is easier to live apart than to give up a career.

Saying "Yes" and Living Apart

When offered an attractive job in a new locale, many people choose to move their work life without altering their family base or location. The costs of disrupting a partner's or family members' careers are viewed as too high a price to pay for living together seven days a week. Many of these families also find that living in one location isn't the basis for their relationship or identity as a family.

> The basis of our relationship is companionship, not location. It's established on what we share and care about, not where or when we do it. The common ground is emotional—we feel and see ourselves as a couple. That's different from being a couple just because you happen to live together in a house in the suburbs. Sometimes we do more communicating in a week over the phone long distance than a lot of couples who sit next to each other every night glued to the T.V. Maybe that's because we don't sit in the same place at night—so we make the most of the time we do have together whether it's on weekends or over the phone.

The choice of relocating alone seems to be particularly attractive (or at least feasible) if one partner has an established career with little chance of relocating; if both partners had highly mobile careers *before* getting married; or if one partner's career involves a great deal of travel and time away from the family anyway.

Most couples who choose a commuting life-style are people who recognize and respect the professional rights of their partners. They readily admit that each of their careers is more important than being together. This does *not* mean that their careers are more important than their relationship. For most, the relationship is simply not dependent on living together seven days a week.

Couples contemplating the live-apart alternative need to ask themselves: Can we sustain our identity and relationship as a family without living together all the time? Will the opportunity to continue and develop in our professional roles threaten or strengthen our marriage/family life?

Agnes Ferris, reporting on a study of ten working couples, found that the typical commuting pattern generally enhances work involvement and accomplishment.[3] Thus, for the highly career-oriented individual, choosing to live apart has advantages that fit with career priorities.

In the commuting life-style, there is usually a segregation of work and home roles for the commuting partner. He or she is able to be totally immersed in work when away from home. As a result, role competition is effectively eliminated. Rather than experiencing conflict between work and home demands, the person is able to concentrate fully on one role at a time. People who used to bring office work home nights or on weekends report that they are able to accomplish much more simply by concentrating solely on work during a specified number of days each week. As a result, they can then devote themselves totally to partner and family when together. In a high-pressure job, this can be a benefit for all concerned.

A degree of job flexibility helps to make a commuting schedule possible. If the commuting partner is able to schedule days off, work at home occasionally, and leave early or arrive late to accommodate travel schedules, some of the hassles of commuting can be greatly alleviated.

The typical commuter schedule seems to be a weekends-together arrangement, which Ferris reports is more satisfactory than when couples can only be together on a monthly or occasional basis. This seems particularly important when children are involved. A major problem for live-apart families is establishing good, reliable child-care and home-help arrangements.

Typically, couples who commute are those who can afford the additional help as well as absorb the expenses involved in extra travel, phone bills, and rent. *Business Week* reports that commuting couples may spend up to $10,000 a year on travel alone.[4] Phone calls add an additional financial burden, but seem to be the only way couples can share their day-to-day experiences. (When you live apart, it's helpful to work for an employer who has a toll-free phone line.) It seems clear that much of the income generated by two working partners has to go to support the commuting life-style. Thus, working apart is not an attractive economic alternative—the choice to pursue it is usually motivated by personal and career-growth reasons.

Even when couples are willing and able to assume the financial burden of living apart, there are other potential costs associated with this life-style. One of these is the emotional cost of being separated. Many experts feel that a relationship can grow only if the partners share experiences. Many partners fear that living apart will cause them to grow apart. Whether this becomes a problem seems to depend on how couples use their time together.

Conscious planning to maximize the benefits of being together is crucial. An important part of this is scheduling time to "catch up with each other." Commuting presents the problem of regularly having to reestablish contact on Friday evenings, only to say good-bye again on Sunday nights. Travel can add to the usual pressures and partners often report the need simply to unwind together. When people have only a few days at a time to share their thoughts, feelings, and experiences, communication is necessarily intensified.

What this may mean is that time together is reserved solely for couple or family activities; outside social contacts are limited. Most live-apart couples agree that they are jealous of their time together and cautious about how they spend it. Families with children are especially anxious to spend time at home. Family unity takes priority over socializing with others.

Loneliness is another cost of working apart. "Once you sit and realize how alone you are, and you realize the person you miss is 300 miles away," a commuting husband said, "the loneliness is very real." This man and his wife lived in separate cities for the first two years of their marriage. They saved almost no money in that time (despite a combined income of over $40,000), because, as he explained, a marriage "held together by bus or taxi, Allegheny or TWA, and . . . limousines" is very expensive. On the positive side, though, he agrees with the basic premise all commuting couples must accept: "You don't need proximity to grow with another person."[5]

What about infidelity? Parents and in-laws often automatically assume that separate residences mean a trial separation and new love interests. And the partners themselves may be somewhat anxious about this possibility. To make a long-distance relationship work, trust is essential. David and Diane lived apart for sixteen months to accommodate her career, believing that "if your marriage isn't a strong one, it isn't going to work." Their agreement was that they didn't want to know what the other person did as long as it never got in the way of their relationship. The temptation, Diane says, is always there, and to a certain degree it depends on availability. The success of a commuting marriage also "depends on how much you want to try, and sometimes long distance makes you try harder."

Researchers and couples seem to agree with Diane and David that the biggest factor involved in making a commuter life-style work is the strength of the relationship. Not only do both partners have to be commited to the commuter arrangement (and willing to do whatever is necessary to make it work), but they must have a deep sense of basic trust in one another.

Commuting is a viable option and would probably not be as traumatic as giving up a career if you have the following conditions going for you:

- You both have a strong, implicit commitment to your marriage or relationship.
- You trust each other.
- You have the salaries to support travel and other expenses.
- You have and are willing to expend the energy necessary to commute.
- You can work out the travel logistics and plan to be together on a regular basis.
- You can organize your life and home or child-care help to allow you to commute.
- You are both willing to do whatever is necessary to sustain this life-style.

As difficult as it may be for some people to imagine why anyone would choose a commuting life-style, we find ourselves empathizing with couples who do so and encouraging people to consider options that will preserve career continuity for *both* partners.

Creating Your Own Style

The three basic alternatives we've just explored, although certainly the most common, by no means exhaust the options for couples contemplating relocation. Some two-career couples combine elements of all three approaches; others come up with something totally new.

One man, when approached about a transfer to company headquarters, said neither yes nor no. Instead, he bargained with the company: he would be willing to move, but only after a year, when his wife finished her schooling. The company agreed.

For other couples, the situation may be reversed. One woman, offered a promotion (and move), agreed to accept it if the company would help her husband find a new job in the city where they would be going. The company did.

Living apart on a temporary basis is another possibility. This provides time for one partner to try out the new location or for the other to find a new job before giving up the present one. Still other couples choose to create new career opportunities where they are rather than move. When a professor of oriental philosophy was not promoted, he decided to open up his own business—a Chinese catering service and cooking school—rather than look for a position elsewhere. A move would have required his wife to give up her job.

Other couples have tried yet another strategy. Knowing that the chances of continually finding two jobs together will be difficult, they have decided to seek a "job-sharing" position: two people for the price of one. For example, they may share a university teaching job, each taking half of the class load. Each is able to maintain a career identity and, between them, they have time to raise their family and pursue outside interests.

Coming up with creative alternatives *is* possible. It usually involves at least one of two tactics—bargaining with your employer or organization or finding independent career options. If you choose to bargain with your employer about the logistics of the move, it might be useful to know some of the ways responsive organizations are currently helping the two-career couple. Procter & Gamble, for example, has a policy of hiring a placement firm, if needed, to help an employee's spouse find employment in the new location. This is a very tangible form of corporate support for both careers. By hiring an outside firm to assist the spouse, Procter & Gamble's staff need not become involved in the spouse's career. Apparently, the company feels that the placement fee is a small price to pay for relocating a valuable employee.

A major insurance firm has instituted a policy of temporary transfer if the move is being made for developmental purposes. The company makes a commitment to the employee in advance that she or he will be moved back to the original location after a certain period of time, say two years. The company also makes all necessary arrangements to rent the employee's house and to help the employee find another house to rent in the new location. At the end of the temporary transfer, the employee moves back into his or her own house. This change was implemented in response to the rapid rate of inflation in the real-estate market. People transferred temporarily away from areas like New York, Chicago, and Los Angeles were often unable to afford to move back into their former neighborhoods. Also, since the company has a policy of providing mortgages at very attractive rates to employees, the higher loans the company had to provide after a short transfer were very costly in tied-up capital. So, with clearly agreed temporary transfers, everyone wins:

- The company saves money on employee mortgages.
- If the employees rent their houses furnished, the company incurs far lower moving costs.
- The relocation is far less stressful to the employee and the family because they know it is temporary, they know how long it will last, and they know they will return to their own house.

Some companies have tried to deal with the most basic question: Are so many geographical relocations really necessary? A transfer is very costly for the organization. Costs include management and personnel staff time to arrange for the move; the cost of selling the employee's house and absorbing the loss if he or she can't get market value; hiring the services of a relocation firm; the loss of the employee's full efficiency just before, during, and after the move; and the actual packing and moving expenses. With inflation, these moving expenses are soaring.

A move is obviously costly to the employee as well, both in money (some of the costs of a move, such as home remodeling, are never fully recovered) and in family stress. If you have moved, you know what we mean.

One oil company was having trouble moving research scientists from its research lab in Denver to field locations in Texas, Oklahoma, and on offshore oil rigs. The organization was forced to examine some alternatives, simply because no one would accept a transfer. What they hit on was the idea of temporary assignments in the field. For example, when an offshore rig was having unique technical problems, a scientist was sent there for six months. His family stayed put and the company flew him home every few weeks. Although he missed his family, the knowledge that it was only a six-month separation, with fortnightly trips home, made it all easier. And he really immersed himself in the project when he was on the rig—that's about all there was to do! The managers and workers on the rig learned a great deal about how practical and helpful people from the research lab ("those eggheads") could really be. In short, the company found that this temporary assignment produced as much learning (for both the scientist and the production personnel) as a two-year rotational move.

An insurance-company executive told of a similar arrangement. He was assigned to act as troubleshooter for a particularly sticky problem the company was having in a field location halfway across the country. He was asked to stay until the problem was solved. Although no definite time period was specified, it was clearly a situation that could be resolved in six months, at most. He accepted the assignment cheerfully, since it was an interesting challenge (*and* because a rotational move to this location might be necessary if the problem wasn't fixed). Again, stress and strain for his family were minimized and, as he says, "I was definitely motivated to clear up that situation as fast as possible, so I could come back home." The assignment was completed early and successfully. From the company's perspective, one more gain had been made in relations between head office and the field.

These strategies for helping employees develop expertise or use their unique skills elsewhere without permanently relocating are very encouraging. They suggest that we can probably be far more creative and effective in developing more protean organizations and more protean employees. The company's and the couple's need for more flexible work styles are highly compatible: as life and work become more complex and unpredictable, all parties need more room to maneuver.

A Life-Style Choice

After almost eight years of moving around, we have concluded that the basic issue for couples is whether their careers or their family life will dictate their life-style. Our experience has convinced us that a traditional family life and two *mobile* career paths are virtually impossible. In our case, Fran's career has undergone continuous shifts and changes as a result of coping with relocation decisions while trying to maintain a traditional, nuclear family.

Much of the decision making earlier in our life, we realize, was based on the fact that we were a nuclear family with children before we had two established careers. Had we started out giving equal priority to both careers, we would probably have made very different life-style choices. We certainly would have been forced to consider options we never contemplated. Had our individual careers come first, day-to-day family life might have been sacrificed. Tim might have explored other job opportunities that would have benefited Fran's career. In other words, it would have been possible to maximize our career opportunities had we let the careers dictate our family life-style. But we didn't. We let the family and Tim's career dictate Fran's options or lack of them.

Clearly, young couples who are just starting off together have a greater chance of working out a life-style to accommodate their careers than do couples in transition. If living apart is what you are used to, then it can seem just as natural as living together. Having a full-time housekeeper who cares for the children can be just as satisfactory an arrangement as being responsible for all child care yourselves.

What is difficult is trying to change gears in midstream. Once priorities and life-styles are determined, most couples find it hard, if not impossible, to restructure them. There is a great deal more flexibility early in a relationship, before children are born and before either partner has established a career. As one partner's career takes shape, the couple's flexibility decreases. Ultimately, any career paths requiring mobility may be closed off to the second partner. While young couples can design a life-style around their career goals, established families often find this option closed to them.

PART III

MAKING IT WORK

CHAPTER TEN

SPLITTING UP OR STAYING TOGETHER

The preceding chapters have made one fact very clear: it's tough to be a two-career couple.

Managing two careers and a relationship requires both sacrifice and stamina. It's only natural for couples to question the wisdom of embarking on a course that seems likely to drive them apart rather than bring them closer together.

Whether two-career couples split up or stay together seems to depend more on how they deal with career issues in their relationship than on the stress associated with these issues. Their basic attitude—how committed they are to maintaining their relationship—is another key factor. As family therapist John Moss told us:

> Two careers are one of many, many stresses couples experience. The ones who are affected the most suspect that there is a more basic issue in the relationship that gets hung on that peg. Two careers have pluses and minuses. The real issue is how people deal with these. What kind of commitment do people have and what are they willing to do to maintain continuity in their lives? People who say "to hell" with marriage usually don't have a good marriage to start with or else just put more stock into their careers. . . . They are looking for an excuse, and a spouse's career can be a convenient excuse.[1]

Careers: Cause or Catalyst?

In our research, in our interviews with couples, and in our discussions with divorce counselors, one finding has emerged very clearly: careers do not *cause* people to split up. They may serve as a catalyst, however—one of the many factors that cause latent problems in a relationship to surface. The second career—most often the wife's—may force the two-career couple to face issues that the traditional couple avoid, even to the point of remaining in an unhappy or unhealthy relationship.

In some cases, the success of the woman or her ability to achieve satisfaction and fulfillment outside of the relationship poses a threat to her partner. Rather than seeing her accomplishments as positive additions to their life, the man views these as negative reflections on his ability to carry out the roles of partner and provider.

In other cases, the woman's career serves as an "escape hatch." Her devotion to a career and her commitment of time and energy to it may signal a basic dissatisfaction with her couple relationship.

In still other cases, the sheer demands of their jobs may force partners to question their priorities—or hers. How much time and energy are they willing to put into working on the relationship versus their careers? Let's listen to what some couples had to say on the subject of career and divorce.

When we first called Esther, she said her career had "absolutely nothing to do with my divorce." Later, when we interviewed her, she had second thoughts about that statement.

> My career did have some influence. I tend to be strong, self-directed, with lots of initiative. I think my husband needed to feel superior rather than equal. I don't think he could perceive the relationship in that manner. Even statements he made years after the divorce about his new companion reflected that. He would say, "I can feel superior to her," or "She can't get along without me."

Esther and her husband married young. She admits they "had a lot of growing to do and grew apart."

> I reached a point where I was just fed up and wanted a different type of life. I reached a point where I was ready to deal with the fact that I was ready to let go. That turned out to be the best decision I ever made. It gave me an opportunity to explore and develop my potential without fearing how it would affect my marital relationship.

> When you marry young, you don't have any perspective and you model people around you. I started out modeling my traditional family. But my views changed and my husband could not become accustomed to me in a new role.

Cary also presented a threat to her husband, although he was a successful businessman whose achievements she feels she could never match.

> I tried to be the traditional wife and hold down a job. Now I look back and see that was a bad thing. The more involved I got in the job or community, the more it threatened him. I decided I wanted to go back to school and he fought it: "Don't expect me to contribute at all." He never was supportive. He wanted a life and I was supposed to contribute to it, but not have a life of my own.

> When I won a citizen award it was a real reversal. I gave the speech and he was the spouse sitting in the audience. He just couldn't handle it.

> My God, he's made it. I could never meet his achievements. I don't know what needs wouldn't be met by my working. I think deep down inside was his fear that I would leave if I became independent. And it did happen.

Cary admits that she probably would have stayed in the relationship if she hadn't realized that she could be independent. She initiated the divorce. She described her former husband as "passive aggressive."

> He wouldn't say things—just do things. He couldn't come out and say it was threatening. He couldn't talk about his feelings about having to deal with fulfilling my needs, too.

> I was at a point where I had tried to go to marriage counselors, and when he was confronted with ways he could change, he would just quit. He wouldn't change. So divorce was the only way I could see to meet my needs.

As in Cary's case, Evelyn's success not only threatened her husband but became an issue of open competition.

> Four years ago I received my B.A. and his comment was, "My God, not only are you going to have the same degree, but you're graduating with a higher grade-point average."

> At that point I said, "I've been asked to go on to graduate school." He immediately blew up. "I will not have my wife with a master's degree when I only have a bachelor's." I told him, "If it becomes important to me, I intend to get it and you won't stand in my way."

> I realized that our marriage couldn't go on if that kind of competition was going to go on. My husband couldn't communicate feelings and couldn't express himself. He couldn't really tell me what was bothering him. I would ask him what he was afraid of.

> As long as I was content to be a mop, things were fine. But as soon as that mop had a name and wanted to be somebody and do something for myself, things change.

At one point, Evelyn talked to her husband's boss to see if the turmoil at home was affecting his job.

> His boss told me that he couldn't do long-range planning. Maybe he just couldn't deal with change. I guess it was growth on my part and changes on my part that he couldn't accept.

For Jackie, the emerging opportunities and rewards at work propelled her more and more into her career and less and less into a relationship that she admits wasn't that great even before her career took off.

> Money became an issue. He felt like I was ripping him off. I felt protective of what I was earning and he resented the taxes that were the result of our higher income bracket.
>
> He was very threatened—so insecure. He didn't want to do anything to make the dual thing work. If I had to go out of town he would plan his business trips at the same time to sabotage me with child-care problems. If it was snowing and one of the cars had a problem, he wouldn't even discuss it. He'd just take off in the good car and leave me high and dry.

For Jackie, a career provided the escape hatch out of an unsatisfactory relationship. Her salary gave her the financial security she needed to file for divorce.

Economics does seem to be one reason why dual-career couples are able to split up more easily than one-career couples, regardless of the reason for the divorce. Author Judy Blume discussed her career and how it entered into her divorce decision in a *Chicago Tribune* interview:

> He enjoyed my career as long as it didn't interfere with his life-style. If I could handle it and he didn't have added responsibilities, it was okay. I took a long time to leave that marriage. I think part of it was economics. I would like to think that I would have had the guts to get up and walk out of that marriage without a career, but I'm not sure I would have. When I realized I could support myself, I left.[2]

Ray and Doris were not married, just living together. Still, he believes that two careers did add to the demise of their relationship.

> We both worked long, hard hours and had high-pressure jobs. We were both eager to achieve. Doris commuted three hours a day, got home tired, didn't feel like cooking. She was usually cranky. It strained the relationship. It became so that working at the relationship was just too hard. She wouldn't quit working. We couldn't deal with it, so we separated. Having both a career and a relationship requires full commitment. We couldn't maintain both.

Al openly admits that their inability to work on problems was the reason he and Sharon split up. He describes their situation in retrospect:

> Knowing that one has to face issues means knowing that someone has to compromise. We were both very ambitious. Neither of us was willing to make compromises. We just avoided a lot of things. After a while, if no one will give, divorce becomes the only alternative.

For Rick, the problem was not that his wife had a career, but that she put it ahead of him.

> I could handle Kris working okay, but I couldn't handle being second in her life. She openly admitted that things stacked up in that order. When I realized her job was more important than me, I cut out.

Most partners agree that, although two careers are not the *cause* of divorce, the issues working couples must grapple with put pressure on the relationship and test the partners' tolerance, adaptability, commitment, willingness to solve problems, and ability to communicate feelings. As Marge told us:

> Careers put marriage in a different perspective. The contracts and communication really have to be honest, crisp, and clear. Otherwise it won't work. It's like living in a lab where your relationship is always being tested.

Marge and her husband were in the process of working out their divorce when we interviewed her. They had both been rising young executives. He was a regional vice-president for a company and she had been promoted to executive assistant to the president of a large international corporation. She describes their situation:

> My career had a significant effect in putting pressure on our relationship. I was constantly having to make decisions between my career and Joe. When you get to a certain level in management, you have to work your tail off. In my mind I was going to do that. Both of us were not willing to negotiate that. He felt I wasn't giving him enough time.

The real crisis or decision point for Marge came when her husband had an opportunity to take a position on the West Coast. They knew they would have to make a decision and kept putting it off. She initiated the divorce.

> It crystallized for me when it became apparent that he really wanted to go to California and do his own thing—and it knocked the shit out of me. He went to talk about the new job and I decided, "That's it!" Take care of yourself now. Do what you need to do and don't feel guilty about it.

He came back. The job offer wasn't what he wanted. He wanted me to be supportive and go back to where we had been and I wouldn't do it. It was downhill from there. One night I just told him I was leaving.

We talked a lot about what was going on but weren't all that successful in dealing with all of the issues. I don't think the intensity and depth of concern on both of our parts was ever really expressed—we never really achieved that.

She talked again about her decision to leave:

The real decision is made when you come to a point where you say, "Enough already—it's not going to work any more." It's not what you want and you're not going to put any more into it. You feel a lot of pain. It's a terrible experience.

The relationship was deteriorating for a very long time. The career decisions just brought it to a head. That made me decide to take care of me instead of worrying about both of us. I just got tired of coping, living with guilt, worrying about the relationship, and trying to do the career thing too.

She wound up her interview by admitting that a career cannot be a substitute for a marriage.

What a marriage offers—an interdependent relationship with another person—cannot be met by a career. When you decide in favor of a career someone has to give up a lot in the relationship if it is going to go on. Maybe in a few years I will have more control [over my career] and be able to manage a relationship again.

Where Marriages Break Down

If careers are the catalyst rather than the cause of divorce, what other factors contribute to the failure of a two-career marriage or relationship? Many experts agree that a basic problem for many couples is never taking stock of their needs and expectations, never realistically assessing what they can or cannot expect from a marriage. As we mentioned in our opening chapter, people no longer enter into marriage solely for the sake of physical survival. People are concerned about their emotional and psychological well-being and they bring these concerns and expectations to the marriage. In many cases, however, they have not established or evolved their roles and relationship consistent with these needs.

William Lederer and Don Jackson, authors of *The Mirages of Marriage* state that most people enter into marriage with false assumptions about what it is or what it can do.[3] Marriages break down when people are unable to come to terms with what marriage *is not* and what they will have to do to make it work. The authors make several points that are particularly relevant to the two-career couple.

One of the most basic (and erroneous) assumptions many individuals hold is that problems in marriage are caused by innate differences between men and women. According to Lederer and Jackson, the problems are caused not by differences between the sexes, but by the partners' inability to choose and activate the desirable or necessary roles in their relationship. They may be stuck in traditional male or female roles that are no longer appropriate for their situation.

A second assumption people often make is that children will improve a troubled relationship, will fill the emotional distance that exists between the partners. While children may add something to a relationship, they will not eliminate existing problems or difficulties. They may, in fact, add sufficient stress to cause those problems to surface or to become even more problematic. According to Lyn Delliquadri, author of *Mother Care,* one out of three divorces takes place within a year after the introduction of a child into the family.[4]

A third assumption Lederer and Jackson dispute is the notion that open conflict is a sign of a poor marriage. Couples who believe this may never openly confront differences, communicate feelings honestly, or learn to feel comfortable telling each other where to get off.

When communication breaks down, the partners are unable to give or get constructive feedback, to negotiate bargains, to make arrangements, or to deal with their feelings of hostility, anger, hurt, fear, jealousy, and so forth. If a marriage is to endure, the partners must be able and willing to work on the dynamics of their relationship, especially if changes are called for in the course of pursuing two evolving careers.

Career couples may split up simply because they are not *willing* to work on the relationship. Another source of satisfaction is available to them. As Joseph Federico told us:

> It's easier to succeed at a career than at a relationship. You get all the rewards and you don't have to give the same things of yourself that you do in a relationship. When push comes to shove, it may be easier to go with the career.[5]

In the final analysis, it is a matter of priorities—people have to decide how much work they are willing to put into their relationship versus their careers.

"My love for you could withstand anything—even marriage!"

Reprinted by permission of G.P. Putnam's Sons from *Husbands, Wives and Live-Togethers* by William Hamilton, copyright © 1976 by William Hamilton.

Making It Work

It seems clear that the single most important factor in the success of a relationship is the couple's *willingness* to work at making it work. Two-career couples are probably no different from single-career couples in the kinds of skills they need to accomplish this. Where they differ, perhaps, is in the amount of stress they undergo simply because they are living together under conditions that constantly test the strength and flexibility of their relationship. Thus, they are required to use their problem-solving skills ably and more often. This is hard work. For many dual-career couples, the bottom line is whether the relationship is *worth* working on, given the effort it will take and the relative satisfaction it provides compared to one's career.

What makes it worth working on? Couples who stay together usually do so because they recognize that their relationship provides something very special, something they could never achieve alone. What they derive from the relationship is very different from the satisfactions a career can provide. Sandy and Mike have discovered this. He describes their relationship:

> We've had our ups and downs, but throughout it all we've stayed together. I think the reason is that we're really each other's best friend. It's hard to replace a good friend—someone who'll support you, be your ally when you need it. We can do that for each other, but neither one of us has ever found that kind of support at work or outside our relationship.
>
> After a while you develop a faith in one another that's hard to shake. It's more than just trust or love. It's the knowledge that the other person implicitly believes in you. It would be hard to walk away from a relationship that offers that.

Beth and Brian believe that their sense of being a family has made them feel—and stay—together.

> A lot of things have not turned out the way we thought they would. We've had to get past all the idealistic notions we had years ago. What has taken their place, though, has been a sense of unity and togetherness as a family. It isn't easy. We've both made compromises along the way. But I can't imagine that splitting up—going it alone—could ever replace or be as satisfying as what we have together. Some of it may be just a sense of security, but I think it's more than that. I think it's the satisfaction of working together to overcome problems, raise the kids, and build something between the two of us. It's the *sharing* that gives you a sense of being part of something really terrific. Our careers alone could never do that. Maybe we have just invested so much in the relationship and the family over the years that we can't imagine pulling out. Whatever it is, I know it has made us stronger.

What are the characteristics of the two-career couples who survive? They are not unlike the qualities Patricia O'Brien found among the diverse yet intact marriages she studied and describes in her book *Staying Together*.[6]

First, while couples who survive see marriage as a process they are both part of, each is able to feel and maintain an identity separate from it. Neither partner feels (or is made to feel) that he or she is totally defined by the relationship. In other words, the end of the relationship would not destroy the person.

Survivors also have what O'Brien calls "healthy selfishness." They exhibit this in what they say as well as in what they do within the relationship. Healthy selfishness is not a total "me" orientation. It is simply the ability to voice and assert one's own needs and rights.

Another characteristic of intact couples—one that assumes added significance when we look at couples who split—is the ability to tackle problems and crises head-on. They are able to acknowledge and confront difficulties rather than gloss over or ignore them. Further, they demonstrate a genuine willingness to accommodate one another, to take the other person into account.

Couples who make a go of it are also able to deal with their respective roles and role relationships in the marriage. Role confusion is not an insurmountable problem for them. Although, like others, they experience feelings of ambivalence at time, both partners are willing to cope with role changes and are capable of adjusting their life and life-style accordingly. In other words, they are flexible enough to make transitions rather than automatically resist or reject them.

Similarly, they are not thrown off track by issues of power or money. Their method of dealing with power is analogous to two people facing each other on a seesaw—they take turns being the one on top. While one partner reaches the heights, the other acts as a stabilizing anchor. Eventually, by mutual consent, the balance will shift.

As might be expected, O'Brien also found that sex is not the glue that bonds couples together. Sex is part of a good relationship, but it is not an adequate foundation. Partners who stay together show an active interest in one another as individuals. Their relationship is a source of stimulation and satisfaction rather than boredom, so work does not become, by default, the center of their lives.

Finally, and perhaps most important, O'Brien found that intact partners do not depend on each other to become what they want to be. They have established what Reverend Thomas O. Edmunds describes as "a working alliance." According to him, "People have to be willing to be autonomous, but also recognize that they have shared responsibilities and that they can no longer exist with unbalanced dependency needs."[7]

Survival Skills

The desire to survive the pressures of two careers must be backed by solid skills and problem-solving guidelines. When we asked several therapists what couples need to work on to keep their relationships alive, certain factors were cited again and again.

- Partners need to become more realistic.

- They need to be flexible—that is, willing to change themselves and to accept change in a spouse or in the relationship.
- They need to be able to talk directly with each other about emotionally charged issues and feelings.
- They need to allow, encourage, and tolerate conflict.
- They need to be able to function as individuals rather than rely solely on the marriage for their emotional support.
- They need to develop a basic sense of mutual trust, respect, and esteem.
- They must be willing to negotiate and renegotiate their expectations.
- They must be willing to confront and settle differences.
- They must feel a real commitment to the relationship, a willingness to stick with it and do what is necessary to work things out.
- They need a sense of their own identity as separate and distinct from that of their partner. This is essential to negotiation and cooperation.
- They must be tolerant.
- They must recognize that marriage is a process, a constantly changing relationship that requires continued attention and care.

In short, partners need to love each other with the kind of caring, loyalty, and trust that is not dependent on circumstance or shaken by adversity. It is really a matter of being good friends as well as lovers, the kind of friends who can share the best of times and the worst of times together.

CHAPTER ELEVEN

TOWARD THE FUTURE

Will two-career couples of the twenty-first century have it any easier than their present-day counterparts? Will time-saving technological improvements and labor-saving devices make the self-sufficient, carefree couple of our prologue less of a myth and more of a reality? Will organizations learn to accommodate working spouses? What kinds of problems will second- and third-generation two-career couples—children raised in two-career families—face? How will they solve them?

In the short run, we would expect the current trend toward increased self-direction to continue—both in managing relationships and in pursuing careers. As people devote more attention to identifying their personal career needs and expectations, psychological success will gain precedence over status, income, and upward mobility. Although organizations may find their employees harder to "manage" they will also find them highly motivated and very committed to the tasks they do value.

In the more distant future, we will probably see fewer people "backing in" to two-career relationships. Career goals will be discussed *before* rather than after marriage, and the question of whether or when to have children will be assessed realistically and with foresight. Similarly, the middle-aged wife who decides to go back to work or launch a new career will not be acting blindly; she will have observed too many friends ahead of her on this career path not to realize the problems that escalating career involvement may present. In short, people are likely to be exercising more self-direction in their work lives, in their relationships, and in their choice of a life-style that maximizes the overall quality of their lives.

So much for the good news. Increasing career freedom can also be expected to have a backlash effect. Already many women are objecting to the pressure they feel to pursue careers when they really don't want to. In a recent career seminar conducted for a group of executive wives, the conversation quickly turned from career development to a heated discussion of the reasons why these women *don't* want to be employed. Quite simply, they have achieved psychological success in their home and community roles and resent the implication that their accomplishments are inferior to those of women employed outside the home.

A second kind of dual-career backlash can be expected from working couples who, after years of coping with the stresses of two careers, finally decide that the costs are simply too high. A life-style that once seemed exciting and glamorous may now seem demanding, routine, and far less rewarding. While the costs remain substantial, the benefits have diminished considerably. As a result, one or both partners may drop out or cut back on career involvement.

Every social trend eventually sparks an equal and opposite countertrend. The activism of the sixties, for example, gave way to the conservatism of the seventies. In the last ten years, we have seen a massive increase in the number of women entering the work force. This increase is bound to level off at some point. Further, as greater stress is placed on the importance of the family, more women are likely to once again view homemaking as a profession that carries status—a socially acceptable alternative to outside employment.

Paradoxically, a third kind of backlash may accompany this new recognition. Many women first entered the work force for reasons other than financial. However, with the rapid rise in the cost of living, the second income they provide has, in many cases, become a necessity—their families now *need* their income. Thus, just as a woman is deciding that the homemaker role is an appealing one, she may discover that she is trapped. Her work, once viewed as satisfying, may now feel stifling.

Corporate backlash is another real possibility. If a company's attempts to make special accommodations for a valued couple do not work out well, the organization is likely to look less favorably on future couples' requests. Also, if future legislation requires employers to pay the same benefits to part-time workers as to full-time employees, an important incentive for providing more protean (i.e., part-time) jobs will be eliminated. Similarly, changes in tax law could make dual-career management more difficult. If the tax-deductible status of company aids to couples (such as a placement firm's fees to help a spouse relocate, moving subsidies, or couple counseling) is discontinued, organizations may be less willing to help partners find solutions to career conflicts.

The Name of the Game

To survive the pressures to come, two-career couples may need even greater flexibility in their homes, jobs, and personal relationships than ever before. In some instances, this flexibility will take the form of compromise—trade-offs between roles that demand attention and energy. For Paul Newman, husband of actress Joanne Woodward, one trade-off was agreeing to appear in one of her films. As he puts it, she had made plenty of sacrifices for his career and it was now his turn to help her.

> Joanne asked me if I would do the film with her; so I looked at the script and told her that it really was the woman's picture and that there wasn't much of a part for me. Well, she fired back, "You son of a bitch, I've traveled around the world with you, carted the kids off to Israel when you were making *Exodus,* and now when I ask you to make a movie with me, you tell me there's nothing in it for you!" Well, what could I do? I made the movie.[1]

Many two-career couples view their jobs as an actual boon to their marriage, regardless of the trade-offs involved. When both husband and wife are experiencing career pressures, it is far easier to empathize with a partner's situation. One executive recalled his wife's anger when he arrived home an hour late for a special dinner she had spent the day preparing. Now that she is also working, she often has late meetings or unexpected emergencies herself, so she understands the dilemmas a job can create. Furthermore, because she too spends the day at the office, her husband's arrival home is no longer the charged moment it once was; she hasn't been working in the kitchen all day and doesn't need his recognition of her culinary skills to feel capable.

We talked with a television producer recently about this issue. Her husband works for a different station in a technical area of the business. She produces a daily talk show. If a particular day's guest doesn't show up or if it's necessary to tape extra shows because of upcoming holidays or vacations, it is not uncommon for her to have to spend all night or all weekend at the station. Does this create a problem for her husband? Not at all, because he sometimes has to do the same. She concludes:

> Our marriage would never last if I were a full-time housewife, because I simply wouldn't believe all the crazy reasons he has for working these God-awful hours! And if he weren't in the same business I am in, he'd never understand what I go through. We understand each other's pressures. We don't add to the pressure by hassling each other. And because we know each other's work, we know how to say the right thing to provide support when things get tough.

A bank executive pointed out that having a working spouse essentially doubles the business contacts you make. These contacts are especially important in service activities such as banking, consulting, public accounting, investments, commercial real estate, advertising, and so forth. A large part of a person's effectiveness in business is being "hooked in" to various networks in the business community, and an employed spouse doubles the number of opportunities for this connecting process to occur.

Protean Employers

The burden of compromise and flexibility should not lie solely with the two-career couple. It is time for employers to accept the dual-career trend and to engage actively in developing programs and policies to help working partners.

Conflicts of interest are likely to increase as more and more women enter the work force and as working couples move from early career positions into midcareer. Recruiting, scheduling, and transferring professional personnel will become more difficult. Problems regarding travel, benefits, and career paths are also sure to grow.

Although companies admit that problems do exist, most feel that it is up to the employee to work out solutions. When they do react, it is on a case-by-case basis. Few actual programs for dual-career employees have been developed. An orientation program for spouses is the most frequent—and often the only—action taken.

Like it or not, organizations will eventually have to adapt to their employees' increasing desire for self-direction. Some companies may try to resist this trend by selecting more passive or easily socialized individuals—a short-term solution with very high long-term costs (increasing corporate rigidity). The more sensible corporate response, of course, is to develop more flexible management policies and practices, so that the protean employee's potential for growth and creativity is not only tolerated but utilized for increased corporate success. Let's consider some of the specific ways companies can accommodate the employee who is one-half of a two-career couple.[2]

Providing flexible work environments. Flexible working hours and environments are probably the most effective strategies organizations have used to meet working parents' needs. "Flextime" has been implemented by numerous companies and has proved a real boon to working couples. Even if the company has no formal policy of flextime, it may be possible for individual employees to negotiate with their bosses for a revised work schedule. Perhaps the arrangement could be somewhat fewer hours at reduced pay, or just different hours with the same weekly total. The establishment of family-emergency days or "personal days" is another helpful policy. Some companies, such as research and consulting firms, allow employees to work at home when necessary to do "think work," write reports, or engage in other tasks better accomplished away from office distractions.

Flexibility can also be built in to a job by permitting employees to take unpaid leaves of absence. This gives them the opportunity to spend time at home, to schedule more convenient vacations, or simply to rest for a while when the strain of the job becomes too great.

One factor that considerably reduces flexibility for working couples is the shortage of challenging, professional part-time jobs. As we found in a survey of working wives, the best jobs tend to be full-time positions; part-time jobs are more routine and less challenging. Wives who worked full time, although they felt more pressures, expressed far more satsifaction with their jobs than did women in part-time jobs.

Some companies have directly addressed this problem by making two part-time jobs out of what had been one full-time job. Again, the main motive is increased flexibility. Two part-timers can be scheduled to cover times when full-time employees may not want to work, such as on evenings or weekends. The organization benefits from establishing a good pool of talented personnel (often housewives or retired persons who are delighted to have interesting part-time jobs), for it then becomes easier to adjust to fluctuations in staffing needs simply by increasing or decreasing the hours of part-timers.

This increased flexibility for the company fits nicely with the employee's need for flexibility—it is a real "win-win" proposition.

In some cases, if partners both work in the same field, job sharing may be possible. Two pediatricians may divide up clinic hours or two math professors may split a class load. In this way, each has a part-time job, while the organization gets two people for the price of one. Since each person is likely to put in more than half of the job's expected number of hours, the employer benefits from the arrangement. The partners agree to coordinate activities so that continuity is assured.

Revising transfer policies. Companies should always seriously consider whether an employee's advancement can be achieved without geographical transfer. Can field experience be acquired locally through cases, simulations, or the use of videotape or other training devices? Can familiarity with certain facilities, products, and processes be achieved in new ways (perhaps through temporary assignments of, say, two or three months' duration)? Can shorter workweeks and staggered schedules be set up to allow couples to commute more easily? Can more training moves and tracks be developed within limited geographical areas?

In most cases, both training programs and career tracks are based on precedent and are rarely subjected to critical examination. People are developed on the basis of how long it has taken *other* people to move up, and certain jobs are regarded as the necessary prerequisite to more advanced positions. A new, less rigid approach, instituted at Sears, Roebuck, identifies career tracks by way of a skills analysis. What skills does a person need to advance? How long does it take to acquire these? In what range of positions can these skills be developed?

When transfers are necessary, companies can help in several ways to make the move easier. They may assist in locating day-care or child-care arrangements; in selling or buying a home (including absorbing any loss in the sale of a house); in getting advance information about the new community; and in helping the couple become integrated into the community once the move is made.

Special recruiting techniques. One useful recruiting technique is the preselection job preview for couples. By giving *both* partners a realistic picture of the organization, the job, and the typical career advancement track in terms of hours, travel, and so on, the program helps eliminate potentially bad couple/company fits. A second technique is dual recruiting—seeking husband-wife teams at the hiring end. Couple counseling and orientation immediately after selection but before placement is also a wise strategy. Through counseling, the couple identifies potential conflicts and begins to plan coping mechanisms before the job begins.

Many personnel departments are also beginning to try, at least informally, to help the spouse of a relocating employee find a new job in the area. They may circulate the spouse's résumé to friends in the personnel departments of other companies or advise the spouse on potential employers in the vicinity. Few companies actually promise to find the spouse a job, but there is an increased effort to help. As more and more employees make career decisions on the basis of family considerations, the "boundary" of organizational responsibility has been extended to include employees' families.

Assisting couples in career management. The packaged career materials on the market today, although good in many respects, are geared primarily to individual career planning. In our seminars, we have found that couple planning is critical, even if the focus is on one partner's career. This is also true, we find, in the single-career family. Even if one spouse is not currently in the work force, he or she may be planning to go back to school or to reenter the job market. These decisions are by no means independent of the working spouse's career goals. When both partners work, career decisions regarding advancement or relocation become even more complex.

Organizations can help by providing information to assist couples in assessing their opportunities, choices, potential conflicts, and developmental needs. Seminars, workshops, and training materials have been successfully used to educate people in dual-career management techniques. One insurance company in Boston has begun to underwrite employee participation in seminars designed to help individuals manage conflicting job and family demands. A major oil company, after experiencing much difficulty in transferring personnel to Saudi Arabia and keeping them there, instituted orientation sessions for husbands and wives. When couples were asked to decide *together* whether to accept a transfer, there was a great reduction in the number of people who returned before completing their tour of duty.

Other seminars focus on coping strategies and problem solving. One program we developed, for example, helps couples better understand career and life roles and the various techniques for managing role conflict. Another examines typical two-career decisions and problems. By presenting couples with case studies, we encourage them to anticipate some of the problems they will encounter and to plan a strategy for solving these problems. As their skills improve, the dual-career situation becomes less threatening to them as well as less of a problem for their employers.

Providing local support services. Although we do not necessarily advocate company-sponsored day-care centers, company clout can be wielded in many communities to advance the needs of working parents and their children. Lunch programs, after-school centers or sports programs, and facilities to accommodate the children of working parents on school holidays are just some of the ways communities can meet the needs of two-career families.

Training supervisors in career-counseling skills. Probably the best source of counsel—if not for the couple, then at least for the employee—is the skilled supervisor. To better equip supervisors for this role, organizations can provide seminars to alert them to the typical dual-career conflicts; develop their third-party skills in counseling, coaching, and listening; and provide simulations in handling employee problems caused by spouse and family needs.

Revising nepotism policies. In many major firms, nepotism rules are being changed to allow companies to hire spouses. Typically, the policy is that relatives may now be employed by the company, but may not supervise a relative or be involved in his or her salary, performance, or promotion evaluations.

Revising travel policies. Extensive travel can impose severe strains on a two-career family. Some companies, such as United Energy Resources of Houston, will pay for any extra child-care expenses (such as a live-in babysitter) incurred in connection with a business trip. While this does not relieve all of the strain of traveling, it does reduce the financial burden. Other companies, recognizing that business travel, especially to interesting places, can bring a couple closer together rather than separate them, offer to pay the expenses of a spouse who wishes to accompany his or her mate on certain business trips, generally to conventions or conferences.

Providing marital counseling. At many points in the process of goal setting, planning, and problem solving, couples need the assistance of an objective and skilled third party to help them sort out their priorities and resolve conflicts. Again, the employer can provide this help, in the form of either an in-house counselor or an outside resource person. By making professional help readily available and cost-free, the employer encourages employees to seek help before the problem interferes with job performance.

"We think we're going to go the distance."

Conclusion: From "Me" to "We"

Earlier we described how social trends operate in pendulum swings. Another swing we see now is the reaction against the extreme preoccupation with the self that characterized much of the 1970s. With the proliferation of manuals, guides, and courses to promote self-satisfaction, happiness, career success, personal power, sexual expertise, and a host of other individual needs, we have been through a highly narcissistic period in our history.[3] But for many people, success and self-gratification, once attained, may not bring real happiness. People are now feeling a need to commit to something or someone outside themselves, to find a larger purpose and a deeper sense of meaning in their lives.

One form this reaction against narcissism may take is a renewed commitment to relationships: to a spouse, to the family, and to other partners in life. There is already evidence of people's needing to connect with roots, through geneology, history, and religion. Now there is more concern about the present family. People need to move from "me" to "we," and in this shift can obtain both. In giving ourselves to someone else, we discover ourselves. The two-career relationship is an ideal way of attaining both personal identity and attachment to loved ones.

With the support of each other and of their employers, the two-career couple can live a rich, rewarding life. They can enjoy the best of both worlds, able to actively pursue both love and work. Our feeling is that each enhances the other—happiness at work makes you happier at home, and vice versa. The ultimate task for two-career couples can be quite simply expressed: to love one's work while working at loving.

NOTES

Chapter One

1. For a fuller discussion of his ideas on mental health, see Abraham A. Maslow, "A Theory of Metamotivation: The Biological Rooting of Value-Life," *Psychology Today* (July 1968): 38, 39, 56–61.

2. Hannah Papanek, "Men, Women, and Work: Reflections on the Two-Person Career," *American Journal of Sociology*, 78 (1973): 852–872.

3. Daniel Yankelovich, "The New Psychological Contract at Work," *Psychology Today* (May 1978): 47. Reprinted by permission.

4. Patricia Renwick, Edward E. Lawler, and the *Psychology Today* staff, "What Do You Really Want from Your Job?" *Psychology Today* (May 1978): 53–65, 118. © 1978 Ziff-Davis Publishing Co. Reprinted by permission.

5. *Ibid.*, p. 53.

6. Yankelovich, "The New Psychological Contract at Work," pp. 49–50.

7. Charles N. Weaver, "What Women Want in a Job," *The Personnel Administrator* (June 1977): 66–71.

8. "Women and Their Work," *Redbook* (April 1978): 69–76.

9. Myra M. Ferree, "The Confused American Housewife," *Psychology Today* (September 1976): 76, 78, 80.

10. Daniel Yankelovich, "Turbulence in the Working World—Angry Workers, Happy Grads," *Psychology Today* (December 1974): 81.

11. Joseph Federico, Ph.D., The Divorce Adjustment Institute, Evanston, IL; phone interview, November 8, 1978.

Chapter Two

1. Douglas T. Hall, *Careers in Organizations* (Santa Monica, CA: Goodyear, 1976), pp. 81–82.

2. Harry Levinson, "On Being a Middle-Aged Manager," *Harvard Business Review* (July–August 1969): 51–60.

3. Robert F. Morrison, "Career Adaptivity: The Effective Adaptation of Managers to Changing Role Demands," *Journal of Applied Psychology*, 67 (October 1977): 549–558.

4. Daniel Levinson, *The Seasons of a Man's Life* (New York: Knopf, 1978).

5. T. S. Eliot, "Little Gidding," in *Four Quartets* (New York: Harcourt Brace, 1943), Stanza V, lines 26–29. Reprinted by permission of the publisher.

6. Donald E. Super, *The Psychology of Careers* (New York: Harper & Row, 1957), p. 159.

7. L. D. Cain, Jr., "Life Course and Social Structure," in *Handbook of Modern Sociology*, ed. R. Faris (Chicago: Rand McNally, 1964).

8. Helena Z. Lopata, "The Life Cycle of the Housewife," *Sociology and Social Research*, 51 (1966): 5–22.

9. Douglas T. Hall, "Pressures from Work, Self, and Home in the Life Stages of Married Women," *Journal of Vocational Behavior*, 6 (1975): 121–132.

10. This section is based on Francine S. Hall and Douglas T. Hall, "Dual Careers: How Do Couples and Companies Cope with the Problems?" *Organizational Dynamics* (Spring 1978): 60–65. © 1978 by AMACOM, a division of American Management Associations.

Chapter Three

1. Erik H. Erikson, *Identity: Youth and Crisis* (New York: W. W. Norton, 1968), p. 91.

2. Susan A. Darley, "Big Time Careers for the Little Woman: A Dual-Role Dilemma," *Journal of Social Issues*, 32 (1976): 85–99.

3. Mike McGrady, *The Kitchen Sink Papers: My Life as a Househusband* (New York: Doubleday, 1975; reprint ed. Signet, 1976), p. 212.

4. Theodore Nadelson and Leon Eisenberg, "The Successful Professional Woman: On Being Married to One," *American Journal of Psychiatry*, 134 (October 1977): 1072.

5. James D. Thompson, *Organization in Action* (New York: McGraw-Hill, 1967), p. 134.

Chapter Four

1. Robert Kreitner, "Managing the Two Faces of Stress," *Arizona Business* (October 1977): 9–14.

2. Hans Selye, *Stress Without Distress* (New York: Lippincott, 1974; reprint ed. Signet, 1975).

3. Rhona Rapoport and Robert N. Rapoport, "The Dual Career Family: A Variant Pattern and Social Change," *Human Relations*, 22 (1969): 3–29. See also A. C. Bebbington, "The Function of Stress in the Establishment of the Dual Career Family," *Journal of Marriage and the Family*, 35 (August 1973): 530–537.

4. Kreitner, "Managing the Two Faces of Stress," p. 11.

5. Louise Plumb, "Managers React to Stress," *The Canadian Banker and ICB Review* (November/December 1975): 36–39.

6. Herbert Benson, *The Relaxation Response* (New York: William Morrow, 1975).

7. Alan Lakein, *How to Get Control of Your Time and Your Life* (New York: Peter H. Wyden, 1973; reprint ed. Signet, 1974).

8. Eleanor B. Schwartz and R. Alec MacKenzie, "Time Management Strategy for Women," *Management Review* (September 1977): 21.

9. Jane G. Bensahel, "How to Get Home Unpursued by the Five Work Demons," *International Management* (March 1978): 55.

Chapter Five

1. Gabrielle Burton, "I'm Running Away from Home—But I'm Not Allowed to Cross the Street," *Ms.* (February 1973): 72–75, 101.

2. Warren Farrell, *The Liberated Man* (New York: Random House, 1975; reprint ed. Bantam, 1975), Chapter 10.

3. Barbara Grizzuti Harrison, "Confessions of a Housework Dropout," *Working Woman* (January 1977): 73.

Chapter Six

1. Angus Campbell, "The American Way of Mating: Marriage Si, Children Only Maybe," *Psychology Today* (May 1975): 39.

2. "Saving the Family," *Newsweek* (May 15, 1977): 64.

3. "The Volcanic Upheaval Called Baby," *Behavior Today* (November 28, 1977): 4–5. Contact the Cowans, care of Department of Psychology, University of California, Berkeley, CA 94720; the Coies, care of Psychology Department, Duke University, Durham, NC 27706.

4. "When Mothers Are Also Managers," *Business Week* (April 18, 1977): 155.

5. T. W. Rodes, *National Child Care Consumer Study: 1975, Vols. I–II: Basic Tabulation, Current Pattern of Child Care Use in the United States, American Consumer Attitudes and Opinion on Child Care.* Prepared under HEW Contract #105-74-1107, Office of Child Development, Department of HEW, Washington, D.C., 1976.

6. Tom Maxwell, "Corporate Day Care Takes Its First Step," *Administrative Management* (May, 1972): 66.

7. "When Mothers Are Also Managers," p. 156.

8. *Ibid.*, pp. 155–156.

9. See Lois W. Hoffman and F. Ivan Nye, *Working Mothers* (San Francisco: Jossey-Bass, 1975).

10. Mary Rowe, "Choosing Child Care: Many Options," in *Working Couples*, eds. Robert and Rhona Rapoport (New York: Harper & Row, 1978): 89–99.

Chapter Seven

1. Merle Shain, *When Lovers Are Friends* (Toronto: McClelland and Stewart, 1978), p. 19.

2. C. W. Hobart, "The Incidence of Romanticism During Courtship," *Social Forces*, 36 (1958): 364. © The University of North Carolina Press. Reprinted by permission.

3. Francess Dincin; phone interview, December 1978.

4. Elaine Hatfield Walster and William Walster, *A New Look at Love* (Reading, MA: Addison-Wesley, 1978): 125. Reprinted by permission.

5. *Ibid.*, p. 135.

6. E. W. Burgess and P. Wallin, *Engagement and Marriage* (Philadelphia: Lippincott, 1953).

7. Walster and Walster, *A New Look at Love*, p. 134.

8. *Ibid.*, p. 142.

9. David Bradford, Alice G. Sargent, and M. S. Sprague, "The Executive Men and Women: The Issue of Sexuality," in *Bringing Women into Management*, eds. Francine Gordon and Myra Strober (New York: McGraw-Hill, 1975): 35–58. See also Robert E. Quinn, "Coping with Cupid: The Formation, Impact, and Management of Romantic Relationships in Organizations," *Administrative Science Quarterly*, 22 (March 1977): 30–45. © 1977 Cornell University. Reprinted by permission.

10. "Marital Relationships Often Undergo Strain When Wives Get Jobs," *Wall Street Journal* (September 19, 1978): 1, 16.

11. Quinn, "Coping With Cupid: The Formation, Impact, and Management of Romantic Relationships in Organizations," pp. 30–45.

12. *Ibid.*, pp. 37–38.

13. William A. Fox, "Dual Careers," a term paper completed for interpersonal and organizational behavior, Northwestern University Evening Divisions, 1977.

Chapter Eight

1. Quoted in William F. Dowling, "Job Redesign on the Assembly Line: Farewell to Blue-Collar Blues," *Organizational Dynamics* (Autumn 1973): 51–67.

2. J. Richard Hackman, "Designing Work for Individuals and for Groups," in J. R. Hackman, E. E. Lawler, and L. W. Porter, *Perspectives on Behavior in Organizations* (New York: McGraw-Hill, 1977): 242–256.

3. Thomas Lodahl and Mathilde Kejner, "The Definition and Measurement of Job Involvement," *Journal of Applied Psychology,* 49 (1965): 24–33.

4. Adapted from Lodahl and Kejner's Job Involvement Scale.

5. Douglas T. Hall and Samuel Rabinowitz, "Caught Up in Work," *Wharton Magazine,* 2 (Fall 1977): 22, 24. © 1977 The Wharton School of the University of Pennsylvania. Reprinted by permission.

6. Myer Friedman and Ray Rosenman, *Type A Behavior and Your Heart* (New York: Knopf, 1974).

7. Adapted from Hall and Rabinowitz, "Caught Up in Work."

8. Amanda Trepla, "I Used to Work Round the Clock," *McCalls* (August 1978): 82–84, 186. © 1978 the McCall Publishing Co. Reprinted by permission.

9. Salvatore Didato, Ph.D., "Leisure Phobia: Culprit on Weekends, Vacations," *Chicago Tribune* (August 20, 1978, Section 4, p. 1). Reprinted by permission of the author.

10. *Ibid.*

11. *Ibid.*

12. Patricia Renwick, Edward E. Lawler, and The Psychology Today staff, "What You Really Want from Your Job," *Psychology Today* (May, 1978): 53–65, 118.

13. "When Career Couples Have Conflicts of Interest," *Business Week* (December 13, 1976): 86. © 1976 McGraw-Hill, Inc., NY. All rights reserved. Reprinted by special permission.

14. Joann S. Lublin, "Working Couples Find an Increasing Chance of Conflicts in Jobs," *Wall Street Journal* (November 8, 1977): 1.

15. "Here's First-hand Story of a Reporter's Conflict," *Wall Street Journal* (November 8, 1977): 12. © 1977 Dow-Jones, Inc. All rights reserved. Reprinted by permission.

16. Lublin, "Working Couples Find an Increasing Chance of Conflicts in Jobs."

17. "When Career Couples Have Conflicts of Interest," p. 86.

18. *Ibid.*

19. Lublin, "Working Couples Find an Increasing Chance of Conflicts in Jobs," p. 12.

Chapter Nine

1. Roy J. Lewicki, "Organizational Seduction: The Pararationality of Organizational Commitment," Graduate School of Business Administration, Duke University, Durham, NC.

2. John P. Wanouns, "Effects of Realistic Job Preview on Job Acceptance, Job Attitudes, and Job Survival," *Journal of Applied Psychology,* 58 (1973): 327–332.

3. Agnes Ferris, "Commuting," in *Working Couples,* eds. Robert and Rhona Rapoport (New York: Harper & Row, 1978): 100–107.

4. "Commuting: A Solution for Two Career Couples," *Business Week* (April 3, 1978): 68.

5. "Mr. and Mrs. Ryan Sleep Alone—Except on Weekends," *New York Times Sunday News Magazine* (October 2, 1977): 24–42.

Chapter Ten

1. John Moss, Family Therapist, Family Service Center of Wilmette, Glenview, Kenilworth, and Northbrook, IL; phone interview, November 8, 1978.

2. Mary Daniels, "Preteen Readers Find Their Boswell in Blume," *Chicago Tribune* (July 23, 1978), Section 5, p. 3. Reprinted by permission.

3. William J. Lederer and Don D. Jackson, *The Mirages of Marriage* (New York: Norton, 1968).

4. Quoted in Mary Daniels, "The New Mother: A Guide to Her Care, Feeding," *Chicago Tribune* (August 27, 1978), Section 5, p. 3.

5. Joseph Federico, Ph.D., The Divorce Adjustment Institute, Evanston, IL; phone interview, November 1978.

6. Patricia O'Brien, *Staying Together* (New York: Random House, 1977; reprint ed. Pocket Books, 1978).

7. Reverend Thomas O. Edmunds, Executive Director, The Institute for Living, Winnetka, IL; phone interview, November 1978.

Chapter Eleven

1. Quoted in Richard Christiansen, "Paul Newman," *Chicago Tribune* (September 17, 1978), Section 6, p. 3. Reprinted by permission.

2. Adapted from Francine S. Hall and Douglas T. Hall, "Dual Careers: How Do Couples and Companies Cope with the Problems?" *Organizational Dynamics* (Spring 1978): 72–76. © 1978 by AMACOM, a division of American Management Associations.

3. Christopher Lasche, *The Culture of Narcissism* (New York: Norton, 1978).

RESOURCES

Books

Bailyn, Lotte, "Involvement and accommodation in technical careers: An inquiry into the relation to work at mid-career," in J. Van Maanen, ed., *Organizational Careers: Some New Perspectives* (London: Wiley, 1977).

Bernard, Jessie, *The Future of Marriage* (New York: World Publishing, 1972).

Curtis, Jean, *Working Mothers* (New York: Doubleday, 1976).

Fogarty, Michael, Rhona Rapoport and Robert Rapoport, *Sex, Career and Family* (Beverly Hills, CA: Sage Publications, 1971).

Hall, Douglas T., *Careers in Organizations* (Santa Monica, CA: Goodyear, 1976).

Herman, Jeanne B., and James D. Werbel, *The Effects of Job Transfer on Employees and Their Families* (Washington, D.C.: Employee Relocation Council).

Hoffman, Lenore, and Gloria DeSale, eds., *Career and Couples: An Academic Question* (New York: Modern Language Association, 1976).

Hoffman, Lois W., and F. Ivan Nye, *Working Mothers* (San Francisco: Jossey-Bass, 1975).

Holmstrom, Lynda Lytle, *The Two-Career Family* (Cambridge, MA: Schenkman, 1973).

Kanter, Rosabeth Moss, *Work and Family in the United States: A Critical Review and Agenda for Research and Policy* (New York: Russell Sage, 1977).

Levine, Joseph, *Who Will Raise the Children?* (Philadelphia: J. B. Lippincott, 1976).

O'Brien, Patricia, *Staying Together—Marriages That Work* (New York: Pocket Books, 1978).

Rapoport, Rhona, and Robert N. Rapoport, *Dual-Career Families* (Harmondsworth, England: Penguin Books, 1971).

Rapoport, Rhona, and Robert N. Rapoport, *Dual-Careers Reexamined: New Integrations of Work and Family* (New York: Harper & Row, 1976).

Rapoport, Robert N., and Rhona Rapoport, eds., *Working Couples* (New York: Harper & Row, 1978).

Seidenberg, Robert, *Corporate Wives—Corporate Casualties?* (Garden City, NY: Anchor Press/Doubleday, 1975).

Simon, Joseph, *Living Together—Communication in the Unmarried Relationship* (Chicago: Nelson–Hall, 1978).

Skolnick, Arlene, and Jerome Skolnick, eds., *Family in Transition* (Boston: Little Brown, 1977).

Walster, Elaine, and G. William Walster, *A New Look at Love* (Reading, MA: Addison-Wesley, 1978).

Young, Michael, and P. Wilmont, *The Symmetrical Family* (New York: Random House–Pantheon, 1973).

Journal Articles

Aldous, Joan, "Wives' Employment Status and Lower Class Men as Husband–Fathers: Support for the Moynihan Thesis," *Journal of Marriage and the Family* (August 1969): 469–476.

Arnott, Catherine, "Husbands' Attitudes and Wives' Commitment to Employment," *Journal of Marriage and the Family* (November 1972): 673–684.

Bailyn, Lotte, "Notes on the Role of Choice in the Psychology of Professional Women," *Daedalus*, 93 (1964): 700–710.

Bailyn, Lotte, "Career and Family Orientations of Husbands and Wives in Relation to Marital Happiness," *Human Relations*, 23 (1970): 97–113.

Banducci, Raymond, "The Effect of Mother's Employment on the Achievement, Aspirations and Expectations of the Child," *Personnel and Guidance Journal*, 46 (November 1967): 263–267.

Bebbington, A. C., "The Function of Stress in the Establishment of the Dual-Career Family," *Journal of Marriage and the Family* (August 1973): 530–557.

Berger, Michael, *et al.*, "You and Me Against the World: Dual-Career Couples and Joint Job Seeking," *Journal of Research and Development in Education*, 10 (Summer 1977): 30–37.

Booth, Alan, "Wife's Employment and Husband's Stress: A Replication and Refutation," *Journal of Marriage and the Family* (November 1977): 645–650.

Broschart, Kay R., "Family Status and Professional Achievement: A Study of Women Doctorates," *Journal of Marriage and the Family* (February 1978): 71–76.

Bryson, I., J. Bryson, M. Licht, and B. Licht, "The Professional Pair: Husband and Wife Psychologists," *American Psychologist*, 31 (January 1976).

Burke, Ronald J., and Tamara Weir, "Relationship of Wives' Employment Status to Husband, Wife and Pair Satisfaction and Performance," *Journal of Marriage and the Family* (May 1976): 279–287.

Burke, Ronald J., and Tamara Weir, "Some Personality Differences Between Members of One-Career and Two-Career Families," *Journal of Marriage and the Family* (August 1976): 453–459.

Clark, Robert A., F. I. Nye, and Viktor Gecase, "Husbands' Work Involvement and Marital Role Performance," *Journal of Marriage and the Family* (February 1978): 9–21.

Cleland, Virginia S., "Role Bargaining for Working Wives," *American Journal of Nursing,* 70 (June 1970): 1242–1246.

Clutterbuck, David, "The Double Life of the Corporate Bigamist," *International Management* (September 1977): 15–18.

Constable, Robert T., "Mobile Families and the School," *Social Casework* (July 1978): 419–427.

Cummings, Laurie D., "Value Stretch in Definitions of Career Among College Women: Horatia Alger as Feminist Model," *Social Problems* (October 1977): 65–74.

Darian, Jean C., "Factors Influencing the Rising Labor Force Participation Rates of Married Women with Preschool Children," *Social Science Quarterly* (March 1976): 614–630.

Darley, Susan A., "Big-Time Careers for the Little Woman: A Dual-Role Dilemma," *Journal of Social Issues,* 32 (Summer 1976): 85–98.

Duncan, R. Paul, and Carolyn C. Perrucci, "Dual Occupation Families and Migration," *American Sociological Review,* 41 (April 1976): 252–261.

Epstein, Cynthia F., "Law Partners and Marital Partners," *Human Relations,* 24 (1971): 549–564.

Foegen, J. H., "If It Means Moving, Forget It!" *Personnel Journal* (August 1977): 414–416.

Frank, Robert H., "Family Location Constraints and the Geographic Distribution of Female Professionals," *Journal of Political Economy* (February 1978): 117–130.

Gannon, Martin J., and D. Hunt Hendrickson, "Career Orientation and Job Satisfaction Among Working Wives," *Journal of Applied Psychology,* 57 (June 1973): 339–340.

Gerber, Gwendolyn L., "The Effect of Competition on Stereotypes About Sex-Role and Marital Satisfaction," *Journal of Psychology,* 97 (December 1977): 297–308.

Gramm, Wendy L., "Household Utility Maximization and the Working Wife," *American Economic Review,* 65 (March 1975): 90–100.

Hall, Douglas T., "A Model of Coping with Role Conflict: The Role Behavior of College Educated Women," *Administrative Science Quarterly* (December 1972): 471–485.

Hall, Douglas T. and Francine E. Gordon, "Career Choices of Married Women: Effects on Conflict, Role Behavior, and Satisfaction," *Journal of Applied Psychology*, 58 (August 1973): 42–48.

Hall, Douglas T., and Francine S. Hall, "What's New in Career Management?" *Organizational Dynamics* (Summer 1976): 17–33.

Hall, Francine S., and Douglas T. Hall, "Dual-Career Couples—How Do Couples and Companies Cope with the Problems?" *Organizational Dynamics* (Spring 1978): 57–77.

Heckman, Norma A., Rebecca Bryson, and Jeff B. Bryson, "Problems of Professional Couples: A Content Analysis," *Journal of Marriage and the Family* (May 1977): 323–330.

Hunt, Janet G., and Larry L. Hunt, "Dilemmas and Contradictions of Status: The Case of the Dual-Career Family," *Social Problems*, 24 (April 1977): 407–416.

Johnson, Colleen L., and Frank A. Johnson, "Attitudes Toward Parenting in Dual-Career Families," *American Journal of Psychiatry*, 134 (April 1977): 391–395.

Kaly, H., "Attitudes Toward the Dual Role of the Married Professional Woman," *American Psychologist*, 26 (1971): 301–306.

Long, Larry H., "Women's Labor Force Participation and the Residential Mobility of Families," *Social Forces*, 52 (March 1974): 342–348.

Madani, Homai, and Cary L. Cooper, "The Impact of Dual-Career Family Development on Organizational Life," *Management Decision*, 15 (November 6, 1977): 487–493.

Marshall, Judi, and Cary L. Cooper, "The Mobile Manager and His Wife," *Management Decision*, 14 (1976): 179–225.

Matthews, E., and D. V. Tiedeman, "Attitudes Toward Career and Marriage and the Development of Life-Style in Young Women," *Journal of Counseling Psychology*, 11 (1964): 375–385.

Martin, Thomas W., Kenneth J. Berry, and R. B. Jacobsen, "The Impact of Dual-Career Marriages on Female Professional Careers: An Empirical Test of a Parsonian Hypothesis," *Journal of Marriage and the Family* (November 1975): 734–742.

Miller, Dana V., and William W. Philliber, "The Derivation of Status Benefits from Occupational Attainments of Working Wives," *Journal of Marriage and the Family* (February 1978): 63–69.

Mueller, Charles W., and Blair G. Campbell, "Female Occupational Achievement and Marital Status: A Research Note," *Journal of Marriage and the Family* (August 1977): 587–593.

Munro, Brenda, and Gerald R. Adams, "Love American Style: A Test of Role Structure Theory on Changes in Attitudes Toward Love," *Human Relations*, 31 (March 1978): 215–228.

Nadelson, Theodore, and Leon Eisenberg, "The Successful Professional Woman: On Being Married to One," *American Journal of Psychiatry*, 134 (October 1977): 1071–1076.

Oliver, Laurel, "Achievement and Affiliation Motivation in Career-Oriented and Homemaking-Oriented Women," *Journal of Vocational Behavior*, 4 (1974): 275–281.

Orden, Susan R., and Norman M. Bradburn, "Working Wives and Marriage Happiness," *American Journal of Sociology*, 74 (January 1969): 392–407.

Paisios, John, and Miriam Ringo, "A New Dimension in Executive Recruiting," *California Management Review*, 14 (Spring 1972): 20–23.

Papanek, Hannah, "Men, Women, and Work: Reflections on the Two-Person Career," *American Journal of Sociology*, 78 (1973): 852–872.

Peterson, Candida, and J. Peterson, "Issues Concerning Collaborating Careers," *Journal of Vocational Behavior*, 7 (1975): 173–180.

Rapoport, Rhona, and Robert N. Rapoport, "The Dual-Career Family: A Variant Pattern and Social Change," *Human Relations*, 22 (1969): 3–29.

Rapoport, Rhona, and Robert Rapoport, "Men, Women, and Equity," *The Family Coordinator*, 24 (1975): 421–432.

Reagan, Barbara B., "Two Supply Curves for Economists? Implications of Mobility and Career Attachment of Women," *American Economic Review*, 65 (May 1975): 100–107.

Ridley, Carl A., "Exploring the Impact of Work Satisfaction and Involvement on Marital Interaction When Both Partners are Employed," *Journal of Marriage and the Family* (May 1973): 229–237.

Robinson, David, "Working Parents Choose Home-Based Child Care Arrangements," *Behavior Today*, 8 (April 4, 1977): 1.

Rosen, Benson, Thomas H. Jerdee, and Thomas L. Prestwich, "Dual-Career Marital Adjustment: Potential Effects of Discriminatory Managerial Attitudes," *Journal of Marriage and the Family* (August 1975): 565–572.

Strober, Myra H., and Charles B. Weinberg, "Working Wives and Major Family Expenditures," *Journal of Consumer Research*, 14 (December 1977): 141–147.

Sussman, Marvin B., and Betty E. Cogswell, "Family Influences on Job Movement," *Human Relations*, 24 (December 1971): 477–487.

Szinovacz, Maximilian E., "Role Allocation, Family Structure and Female Employment," *Journal of Marriage and the Family* (November 1977): 781–791.

Tallman, Irving, "Working-Class Wives in Suburbia: Fulfillment or Crisis?" *Journal of Marriage and the Family* (February 1969): 65–72.

Waite, Linda J., and Kristin A. Moore, "The Impact of an Early First Baby on Young Women's Educational Attainment," *Social Forces*, 56 (March 1978): 845–865.

Walker, E. Jerry, " 'Til Business Us Do Part?" *Harvard Business Review* (January–February 1976): 94–101.

Welch, Susan, and Alan Booth, "Employment and Health Among Married Women with Children," *Sex Roles*, 3 (August 1977): 385–397.

Wolf, Wendy C., and Rachel Rosenfeld, "Sex Structures of Occupations and Job Mobility," *Social Forces*, 56 (March 1978): 823–844.

Magazine Articles

"America's New Elite," *Time*, August 21, 1978, pp. 56–57.

Bedell, Madelon, "Super Mom," *Ms.*, May 1973, pp. 84, 86, 87, 99, 100.

Byrne, Susan, "Nobody Home: The Erosion of the American Family," *Psychology Today*, May 1977, p. 41.

Campbell, Angus, "The American Way of Mating: Marriage Si, Children Only Maybe," *Psychology Today*, May 1975, p. 37.

Closson, M., "Job Sharing," *Business Week*, October 25, 1976, p. 112e.

"Commuting: A Solution for Two-Career Couples," *Business Week*, April 3, 1978, p. 78.

"Company Couples Flourish," *Business Week*, August 2, 1976, p. 54.

Davidson, Margaret, "When You Both Work," *Parents'*, April 1977, pp. 66–68.

Dix, Carol, "Doing Your Own Thing Versus Being with the Man You Love," *New Woman*, March/April 1978, p. 98.

Edmiston, Susan, "Love, Honor and Earn—The Two-Income Marriage," *Working Woman*, November 1976, pp. 28–32.

Ferree, Myra M., "The Confused American Housewife," *Psychology Today*, September 1976, p. 76.

Francke, Linda B., "Working at Marriage," *Newsweek*, November 24, 1975, p. 74.

Frank, Hal, "Two-Career Families," *MBA*, July/August 1976, p. 38.

Ginzberg, Eli, "Special Report on the Families of Seven Working Mothers," *Parents'*, April 1977, p. 34.

Haskins, Ron, Dale C. Farran, and Joseph Sanders, "Making the Day Care Decision," *Parents'*, April 1978, p. 58.

Hassett, James, "A New Look at Living Together," *Psychology Today*, December 1977, p. 82.

"How You Going to Get 'Em Back in the Kitchen? (You Aren't)," *Forbes*, November 15, 1977, pp. 177–180, 182–184.

Kagan, Jerome, "All About Day Care," *Parents'*, April 1977, p. 40.

Kaye, Dena, "Mixing Marriage and Business," *Mainliner*, December 1976, p. 10.

Klein, Norma, "The Myth of Female Competition," *Working Woman*, January 1977, pp. 36–39.

Koch, Joanne, and Lew Koch, "The Urgent Drive to Make Good Marriages Better," *Psychology Today*, September 1976, p. 33.

Kron, Joan, "The Dual-Career Dilemma," *New York Magazine*, October 1976.

Lake, Bonnie, "Dual-Career Marriages—Can Two Work Better Than One?" *Passages*, November 1977, pp. 20–24.

Lasswell, Marcia, and Norman Lobsenz, "How Working Couples Make Marriage Work," *McCalls*, July 1978, p. 78.

Lasswell, Marcia, and Norman Lobsenz, "Can You Be Sure Love Will Last?" *McCalls*, August 1978, p. 76.

Levine, James A., "Job Sharing: How One Couple Does It," *Working Woman*, December 1976, pp. 57–59.

Linden, Fabian, "The Two- (and Three-) Earner Family," *Across the Board*, May 1977, pp. 49–51.

"Living Apart to Stay Together," *New Woman*, November/December 1976, pp. 41–43.

Mace, David R., "Family Stress or Satisfaction? Which Will it Be When Mothers Are in the Labor Force?" *Parents'*, April 1977, p. 28.

Maxwell, Tom, "Corporate Day Care Takes Its First Step," *Administrative Management*, May 1972, pp. 62–66.

Murphy, Mary, "He Rearranges His Life for Her," *New Woman*, November/December 1976, pp. 30–32.

Nichols, William C., "Pitfalls of the Fifty-Fifty Partnership," *Parents'*, April 1978, p. 14.

"Pluck and Partners—How Mothers Make It as Managers," *Industry Week*, October 1974, pp. 13–14.

Pogrebin, Letty C., "When She Earns More Than He Does," *Ladies' Home Journal*, February 1976, p. 70.

Poloma, Margaret M., and T. Neal Garland, "The Dual-Profession Family: Some Implications for the Future," *National Business Woman*, 52, March 1961, pp. 6–7.

"Pros and Cons of Whether Wives Should Work," *U.S. News and World Report*, November 27, 1978, pp. 82–83.

Randolph, Eleanor, "Conflict of Interest: A Growing Problem for Couples," *Esquire*, February 1978, p. 55.

Renwick, Patricia A., and Edward E. Lawler, "What Do You Really Want from Your Job?" *Psychology Today*, May 1978, p. 53.

Schmidt, Peggy, "Does A Woman's Success Spell Disaster for Her Marriage?" *Glamour*, September 1978, p. 222.

Schoen, Elin, "The New American Marriage," *New York*, October 25, 1976, p. 40.

"Sensitivity Essential for Two-Career Marriage," *APGA Guidepost*, 6, October 1977, pp. 1, 3.

"The Great Male Cop-Out from the Work Ethic," *Business Week*, November 14, 1977, p. 156.

"The Two-Paycheck Life," *Money*, January 1979, pp. 34–64.

"To Love, Honor, and . . . Share," *Ms.*, June 1973, p. 62.

"Transplanting the Executive Family," *Business Week*, November 15, 1976, pp. 159–161, 164, 170.

Turner, C., "Dual-Work Households and Marital Dissolution," *Human Relations*, 24, 1971, pp. 535–548.

Van Horne, Harriet, "Working Parents/Wonderful Kids," *Parents'*, April 1978, p. 55.

"When Corporate Couples Have Conflicts of Interest," *Business Week*, December 13, 1976, p. 86.

"When Mothers Are Also Managers," *Business Week*, April 18, 1977, p. 155.

"Working at Marriage," *Newsweek*, November 24, 1975, pp. 74, 77.

Woodward, Kenneth L., *et al.*, "Saving the Family," *Newsweek*, May 15, 1978, pp. 63–90.

INDEX